PATTERN DATES
FOR
BRITISH ORDNANCE SMALL ARMS
1718 - 1783

by De Witt Bailey, Ph.D.

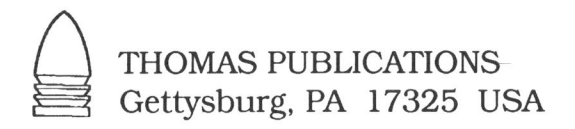

THOMAS PUBLICATIONS
Gettysburg, PA 17325 USA

Copyright © 1997 De Witt Bailey, Ph.D.

Printed and bound in the United States of America

Published by THOMAS PUBLICATIONS
P.O. Box 3031
Gettysburg, Pa. 17325

All rights reserved. No part of this book may be used or reproduced without written permission of the author and the publisher, except in the case of brief quotations embodied in critical essays and reviews.

ISBN-1-57747-016-8

Cover design by Ryan C. Stouch

Cover illustration, "British soldier of the 29th Regiment circa 1770" by Don Troiani. Courtesy of Historical Art Prints, Southbury, CT.

*Dedicated to all those
who have a serious interest in
the history of
British military small arms*

Contents

Acknowledgements vi
Author's Note vii
Glossary viii
Introduction xi
Basis of the New System 1

The Components

Barrels 4
Locks 9
Land and Sea Service Pattern Furniture 23
Stocks 49
Pattern-Date Designations 55
Wallpieces 55
Land Service Muskets 55
    Long 55
    Short 57
    Marine 58
Sea Service Muskets 59
Carbines 59
    Land Service 59
    Sea Service (musketoons, blunderbusses, seven-barrel gun) 61
Rifles 62
Land Service Pistols 62
Sea Service Pistols 63

Complete Arms (Detailed Measurements by Pattern)

Wallpiece 91
Land Service Muskets 92
    Long 92
    Short 95
    Marine or Militia 97
Sea Service Muskets 99
Carbines 102
    Land Service 102
    Sea Service (musketoons, blunderbusses, seven-barrel gun) 108
Rifles 110
Land Service Pistols 112
Sea Service Pistols 114

Acknowledgements

While developing a system involving a large number of examples to be examined, recorded and photographed, it is obvious that the compiler of such a system must be dependent upon, and indebted to, a wide variety of people and sources, public and private, for his information. The present study is no exception.

My first and largest debt is to the three public collections in Great Britain which have made their British military small arms available to me on numerous occasions without stint or hindrance: The Royal Armouries in the Tower of London, The National Army Museum, and the Scottish United Services Museum in Edinburgh Castle. Graeme Rimer, Mark Murray-Flutter and Martin Pegler of the Armouries; Michael Baldwin, Keith Miller and Martin Hinchcliffe at the National Army Museum; and Stephen Wood in Edinburgh have each rendered me their time, interest, and full cooperation in working with their examples.

In America I am happy to gratefully acknowledge the assistance, cooperation and valuable editorial advice of Jay Gaynor at Colonial Williamsburg, whose organization possesses the largest and finest collection of early 18th Century British muskets of which I am presently aware. Also for the assistance and cooperation of Robert W. Fisch at the West Point Museum and of Nicholas Westbrook, Bruce Moseley and Christopher Fox at Fort Ticonderoga, and to Dona McDermott of the Valley Forge National Historical Park for access to their excellent collection.

The private sector has also been of immense and essential assistance. I would particularly like to thank Joan and Herman O. Benninghoff, II, Robert D. Cheel, Jr., Charles L. Hill, Jr., Clark R. Hoffman, Ross MacInnis, Clinton M. Miller, J. Craig Nannos, Joseph R. Salter, Don Troiani, and Fred Wilkinson for making available detailed information on various pieces in their collections which were otherwise not available for examination from other sources. Kit Ravenshear's long experience in, and skill at, 18th Century gunmaking history and techniques was invaluable in evaluating the detailed technical data. Although space denies me the opportunity to list every serious collector who took the time to complete one of my long and detailed data-forms, nevertheless I am, and all those who will use this system are, tremendously grateful to them for their invaluable contributions.

I would also like to express my particular gratitude to Michael Baldwin and David Harding for their meticulous proof-reading, and for the constructive suggestions which sprang from it.

Not only has my wife Sarah done all the things writers always thank their wives for at this point, she has also put many hours of hard work and valuable thought into the creation, correction and editing of this work, for which, in addition to her encouragement and support, I will always be more grateful than I can say.

Author's Note

The introduction of a system based on dates for identifying British military firearms of the Eighteenth Century will no doubt come as a great surprise to many students and collectors. I can assure them that the realization that it would be appropriate to do so came as an equally big surprise to me. After more than twenty-seven years of examining the records and then working up the material I had gathered, I realized that the use of dates to distinguish one pattern from another would be historically appropriate to indicate the progression of arms manufacture.

This conclusion has been significantly supported by a detailed analysis of the construction of several examples of each of the common patterns identified in the records. This analysis clearly shows that the weapons were manufactured "to the Pattern" and that very close tolerances and standards of inspection were enforced on each of the major components, including their final assembly.

Board of Ordnance records made constant use of the terms "New Pattern" and "Old Pattern" in relation to their production over the decades. When production figures are examined in great detail it becomes plain that the substitution of dates for "New" and "Old" would have been fully understood by those ordering and producing the arms. Once a "new pattern" went into production "old patterns" rarely overlapped or remained in production. The exceptions are few and are clear in the records. Old arms were broken up and/or sold at public auctions twice-yearly and the old brasswork was returned to the founders to be recast into "new pattern" pieces. The continuation of several basic forms of stock or furniture over the decades makes it possible to define a "new pattern" in terms of specific new features in a design produced after a certain date.

The new Pattern-date Designation System will assist students and collectors to identify examples with a precision previously absent, gaining incidental information about the piece by knowing exactly what it is. The effective operation of the new system will require much greater attention to detail than has previously been given to the examination of British military firearms; this will result in greater knowledge for the examiner, and the ability to pass on that information to others with a minimum of confusion.

This is a preliminary study intended to cover only the classification and basic identification of those British military small arms carried by British forces serving in North America during the French and Indian War of 1755-60, Pontiac's Rebellion of 1763-4 and the American War of 1775-83. The next work, entitled "British Military Small Arms in North America 1737-1783" will be comprehensive in nature, discussing not only the arms but their numbers, marksmanship training, use, maintenance, ammunition and accessories as carried by the various British and provincial units in America during the period. A final work, "British Military Small Arms 1689-1815" will include all weapons made during this period for and by the Board of Ordnance, manufacturing and distribution details, information on contracts and contractors, and a fully developed Pattern-date Designation System covering the period indicated.

Many readers may be puzzled by the apparently random dates with which this study opens and concludes. Between 1722 and 1730 there was almost no production of small arms by the Board of Ordnance, and the last series of arms produced between 1718 and 1722 (the Pattern 1718 series) was produced under a compromise system combining features of the older method and some features of the new. At the time of writing no examples of the Pattern 1718 series have been identified, with the exception of the two pistols. The Ordnance records clearly indicate, however, that all of this series used flat "plain" (i.e. without either pan-or tumbler-bridles) locks and iron furniture on both Land and Sea Service arms, the sole exception being Land Service carbines. The Pattern 1730 series are the first arms entirely manufactured under the "Ordnance System" of centralized design and control. There was sustained production of small arms from 1730 until the end of the American War in 1783, with a significant reduction only during the early 1750s. The period from 1783 until 1792 was largely one of experimentation with various arms. Only small groups of specific arms were produced as required by a system which represents a partial abandonment of the Ordnance System, which had begun to break down from the middle years of the American War. So the dates 1730 and 1783 represent the appearance of newly organized and sustained production, and the termination and re-organization of that production, with gaps in production on either side of the respective dates.

—De Witt Bailey

Glossary

Because this work is written as a tool for the use of beginners as well as experienced collectors and students in this field, and because of the confusion between English and American usage, and due to the use of many Eighteenth Century terms in the late Twentieth Century, the list of terms which follows is given. It is hoped that some of the confusion may be eliminated and the definition of various terms clarified for readers at all levels.

Terms in CAPITALS within a definition are defined elsewhere in the list.

Apron. The raised areas in the stock around the barrel tang and at the front and rear of the lock and SIDEPIECE FLAT.

Assembly marks. Internal markings relating one component to another, usually in the form of file cuts rendered as Roman numerals. They are found on both wood and metal parts. Ideally they should all be the same on one particular arm.

Baluster-Moulding. The reinforcing ornamental moulding at the breech of the barrel where it joins the breechplug tang. Description derived from its profile.

Banana lockplate. Shape of lockplate curving noticeably downwards at the tail, in use on Ordnance small arms until 1756. The drop on a musket lock amounts to one-quarter inch below the front lower edge of the lockplate.

Belt-Hook. Modern term for what the Ordnance called a Rib. A thin flat strip of iron fastened to the left side of Sea Service pistols so that they could be carried on a belt or in the waistband of the breeches.

Blunderbuss. As interpreted by the Ordnance these were Sea Service arms with a full-length stock, relatively thin-walled barrel having a gradual flare towards the muzzle, and fitted with conventional Sea Service brass furniture. The records suggest manufacture by the Small Gun Office workforce in the Tower rather than by contractors.

Bridle. A supporting piece fitted either over the tumbler inside a gunlock, or on the outside of the lock as a forward extension of the priming pan to support the steel-axis screw.

Cock. The S-shaped piece with jaws holding a flint on a flint lock and having the same axis as the tumbler. The term "hammer" replaced it during the late percussion period.

Cock-Screw. The vertical screw holding and used to tighten the top-jaw around a flint in the jaws of the cock. Often called the "top-jaw screw."

Collar. A narrow raised band or ring around the edge of a ramrod pipe, serving as a reinforcement against wear.

Comb (of the butt). The upper surface of the butt of the stock between the wrist or grip of the stock and the HEEL of the butt.

Comb (of the cock). The vertical support at the top rear of the cock used to support the top jaw. Until the 1770s most Land Service locks have a comb which, when seen from the rear, is a long oval, or leaf-shaped; when seen from the side it is very thin. The other major type of comb used during the period covered by this study is a pillar, rectangular in section with its thin edge to front and rear; on this form the top-jaw was notched and moved up and down the comb. This type was used on Sea Service locks throughout the period, and on Land Service locks from 1777.

Composite-Pipe. Term used to describe a long trumpet forepipe used on carbines for mounted troops. It appears to be made up from two separate pipes, a flared-mouth tapered pipe at the front, with collars behind the flare and at the base and a barrel-shaped and collared pipe brazed to its rear, giving a "double-collared" effect in the middle of the pipe. The design was obviously built up in this manner but the pipes as used are in fact cast as one piece.

Double-Bridle (lock). A lock fitted with both the internal tumbler bridle and an external bridle between the front edge of the pan and the steel pivot-screw, to support the screw.

Faceted (Bevelled) **Pan.** The underside of the pan is filed with three flat faces or facets, instead of being rounded. Typical on most flat-surfaced lockplates until the P/1777 locks. Sometimes referred to as a "bevelled pan."

Feather-Spring. Eighteenth Century term for the spring against which the steel (frizzen) acted. The Ordnance term was "hammer-spring" since the steel (frizzen) was then normally called the "hammer."

Fence. The vertical upward extension at the rear of the priming pan to prevent the pan-flash reaching the face of the shooter. Used on all Land Service locks, but not normally on Sea Service locks. On civilian locks it was considered a feature of "quality" locks.

Finial. Ornamental termination of any component. Used in this work to describe the terminations of furniture and barrel TANGS and the lower termination of the FEATHER-SPRING.

Furniture *(Mounts).* As used in this work, the brass stock fittings used to protect and/or strengthen various areas of the stock, and taken to include (from muzzle to butt): the nose-band (-cap), ramrod pipes, trigger guard, trigger plate, sidepiece, thumbpiece and buttplate. Also including where appropriate iron fittings such as sling-swivels, sling-bar, and belt-hook.

Heel. The upper end of the buttplate at the top or comb of the butt, where the tang meets the buttplate at an approximate right-angle. On the STEEL, the forward extension of the pan cover which comes to rest on the upper surface of the feather-spring when the steel is thrown back, or "open."

Iron Rammer. See RAMMER and STEEL RAMMER.

King's Proof. A mark composed of a Crown over GR over a Broad Arrow facing downward. Struck during the period covered by this work on the top of the barrel about three inches ahead of the barrel tang. The term as used in this work also includes the View Mark, struck below the above mark and composed of a Crown over crossed sceptres.

Lock Flat. The right side of a pair of parallel flat surfaces on the stock into which the lock cavity is cut and the lock mounted.

Loop *(Lug, Tenon).* The small iron studs dovetailed and brazed on the underside of the barrel through which the barrel fastening pins and the upper sling-swivel screw pass. The loop for the sling-swivel screw is much larger and heavier than those for the barrel-pins.

Musketoon. Sea Service longarms with a full-length stock and Sea Service brass furniture, fitted with a heavy-walled brass or iron barrel with a so-called "cannon-mouth" configuration of rings at the muzzle and a very slight flare in the bore just at the muzzle. These were made in small batches by the contractor force.

Noseband. Ordnance term for a sheet-brass reinforce fitted to the front of the fore-end of the stock to prevent splitting. Normally used for reinforcing fore-ends originally finished plain.

Nosecap *(fore-end cap).* Ordnance term for a cast-brass cap fitted to the front of the fore-end on small arms. Commonly found on longarms intended for use with a bayonet and steel rammer.

Pins. Iron wire used to secure the barrel, furniture and trigger to Ordnance small arms. The brass furniture was cast with integral tenons through which the pins passed. Pin was often used in the 18th century gun-trade as a synonym for screw, e.g. "breech-pin" for barrel-tang screw.

Plain *(lock).* A lock without either an internal tumbler-bridle or an external pan-bridle. Sea Service locks were plain locks throughout the period of this study.

Pratt Pipe. A ramrod pipe designed by gunmaker/Ordnance contractor John Pratt in the spring of 1777, to be used as a second pipe, below the long trumpet forepipe, to help keep the rammer in its channel when returning it after loading. It is collared in the usual way, but is *straight-tapered* between the collars. It is not flared at the mouth, but evenly tapered throughout its length. (Plate 33)

Private Tower Proof. A proof test carried out at the King's Proof House in the Tower of London from c. 1751 until sometime in the first decade of the 19th Century. It was generally, but not exclusively, used by those gun-makers who were also contractors to the Board of Ordnance, for barrels used on guns for commercial sale. The mark consists of a Crown over crossed sceptres, (the Ordnance View mark) struck twice, one over the other. It is often found on military pattern arms, and should not be mistaken for the King's Proof.

Proof Marks. See KING'S PROOF.

Rammer. Ordnance term for civilian term ramrod. Until 1748 all arms (excepting some experimental muskets in the mid-1720s) were made with wooden rammers. From 1748 metal rammers (see STEEL RAMMER) were introduced on new-production Land Service infantry muskets. Older arms in serviceable condition were gradually converted from wooden to metal rammers. The Ordnance used the terms "iron" and "steel" interchangeably in describing rammers.

Reinforce. Heavy rectangular upper section on the inner forward part of the lockplate which forms the inner area of the pan and serves to support the steel axis-screw and the rear sidenail.

Rough-Stock. The initial stage of constructing an Ordnance firearm. The appropriate components are issued to the contractor for rough-stocking, and his workforce fits the barrel and the lock to the rough stock, and cuts/bores the ramrod channel.

Set-Up. The final stage in assembling an Ordnance firearm, in which rough-stocked pieces and appropriate components are issued to the contractor for setting-up, whose work-force then fits the brass furniture, sling swivels/bar to the stock, and finishes off the stock and furniture. When the setters-up have completed their work, a complete firearm exists, ready for final inspection and receiving into Ordnance Stores.

Sidenail. Ordnance and gunmakers' term for lock-screw.

Sidepiece *(Sideplate, counter-lock plate).* A plate fixed to or inlaid into the flat of the stock opposite the lock chiefly to reinforce the stock at this point, support the sidenail heads and prevent damage to the wood by excessive tightening of the sidenails.

Sidepiece Flat. Opposite the LOCK FLAT, presenting a parallel flat surface on which the SIDEPIECE is mounted opposite the lock.

Single-Bridle *(lock).* A lock fitted with only one bridle, the internal one supporting the tumbler.

Sling-Bar *(Saddle-bar, swivel bar).* On carbines for mounted troops, a rod with flattened terminals pierced for screws fitted to the left side of the stock to which a shoulder-sling can be attached to carry the weapon in a leather bucket or scabbard while the trooper is mounted.

Steel *(Battery, frizzen).* The L-shaped piece on a flint lock serving as the striker for the flint and also as the pan-cover. Known in the 18th century as the "hammer," and in modern America as the "frizzen." Steel, and only very rarely "frizzle" were alternative 18th Century English terms. Steel is used here to avoid confusion with the correct original term, "hammer."

Steel Rammer. Although the ramrods generally introduced from 1748 were metallurgically iron followed by untempered steel, these were superceded at some unspecified date prior to 1767, (through the efforts of contractor William Grice) by tempered steel ramrods. Steel is used throughout this study to avoid confusion.

Swell. The ball-shaped or oval-shaped bulge on the fore-end of the stock level with the TAILPIPE, intended to give the left hand a better grip. The form developed from ball-shaped on the earlier patterns to oval by the Pattern 1756.

Tailpipe. The lowest of the several ramrod pipes, fitted with a tail to protect the very thin wood where the rod enters the covered part of the rammer channel. Sometimes called the entry-pipe.

Tang. A strap or projection from a main body. The strap-like extension on a breechplug butt; upper and lower (front and rear) extensions of a trigger-guard and the forward supporting extension of a buttplate, &c.

Threads. The Ordnance term for the double border-lines engraved on the lockplate, cock body, and other parts of the lock.

Thumbpiece. Ordnance term for what is often called on civilian arms the "escutcheon" or "initial-plate." Intended as an ornament, reinforcement for the wrist or grip, and for the engraving of company and "rack" numbers of guns within a unit.

Toe. The bottom or lower edge of the butt and buttplate, at the opposite end from the HEEL. On the STEEL, the downward projection of the pan cover which rests against the upper surface of the FEATHER-SPRING and holds the steel in the closed position.

Trigger-Plate. A flat brass bar with a slot through which the blade of the trigger passes, which has an internal boss at its front into which the lower end of the barrel tang screw is threaded. This piece is replaced on the Light Dragoon Pistols, the Light Infantry Carbine and the Sea Service Musket and Pistol by a square iron nut.

Trumpet Pipe *(Long Fore-pipe).* A long tapering ramrod pipe with a short flared mouth used as the upper, first or forepipe for most arms fitted for a steel rammer, to guide it into the ramrod channel; also used on some wooden rammer carbines for mounted troops for the same reason; for these see COMPOSITE PIPE.

View Mark. The second part of a set of gun-barrel Proof Marks, indicating that the barrel has passed careful inspection after being fired with the heavy proof charge. On Ordnance barrels this is represented by a Crown over a pair of crossed sceptres stamped into the barrel below the Proof Mark. See KING'S PROOF, which is understood to mean a complete set of these two marks.

Introduction

All British regulation (that is, made for the Board of Ordnance, as opposed to being made for regimental colonels) military small arms produced during the eighteenth century were divided into two broad categories: Land Service and Sea Service. Under the former heading were included infantry, dragoon and marine muskets, all types of carbines, wallpieces, rifles, and pistols. In the latter category were the ship's company or Sea Service musket in long-barrelled bright finish and shorter barrelled blacked finish, the musketoon, blunderbuss, the seven-barrelled gun and the Sea Service pistol.

The designation "pre-Land," used in previous publications as a chronological guideline to describe those weapons made prior to the adoption of the "Ordnance System" of manufacture after 1715, is misleading in that it suggests a time when there was no "Land Pattern" category. In terms of the period from 1689 forward there was always a Land Service and a Sea Service division in Board of Ordnance small arms.

From about 1710 conscious efforts were made by the Board of Ordnance to simplify, control and regulate the supply of small arms for the British armed forces, and from 1714 a new system in which the Board replaced the London Gunmakers Company as the key agency of design and control was gradually brought into effect. This is now known as the Ordnance System to highlight this change.

However, until the War of the Austrian Succession (1740-48) there existed two concurrent means of arming the British land forces. The elder of these centred upon the colonel of an individual regiment as the source of design and procurement of the small arms carried by his regiment. The somewhat later of the two systems was based upon the Board of Ordnance, who purchased arms from the London gun trade more or less to broad specifications given to the trade by the Board. Each contract between the Board and the gun trade was subject to discussion and compromise, and quality control was, until the completed arm was received by the Board's inspectors, divided between the manufacturers and component inspectors appointed by the Board. At the outbreak of war in 1739 an official inspection of the arms of all British regiments stationed in Britain was carried out, and on the basis of its findings the army was almost entirely re-armed with Ordnance-produced muskets during 1740-1. Cavalry regiments retained a degree of independence for some years to come, but by the time of the Seven Years' War (1756-63) this had been eroded to the point where their individual preferences as to details were produced as official patterns by the Ordnance, as for instance for the 15th (Eliott's) and 21st (Royal Foresters) Light Dragoons. This was also true for regiments stationed in Ireland.

This situation did not apply to the part of the army stationed in Ireland, who were usually armed by the Irish Board of Ordnance, and maintained a certain degree of independence in matters of detail, especially in the mounted branch of the service, until after 1783. When a regiment was taken from the Irish Establishment and placed on the larger British Establishment, usually for service abroad, it often involved the re-arming of the regiment with arms produced for the British Board of Ordnance, their Irish-made arms being left in Ireland. A reversal of this procedure occurred in 1774-6, when the regiments being sent to North America, almost always via Cork, were re-armed with muskets made for the Irish Board of Ordnance to ease the demands on the London Board who were hard-pressed to meet the needs of so many regiments in the face of rapid embarkation requirements and inadequate shipping space.

Until 1768 all Guards and line infantry (i.e. ordinary marching regiments without permanent quarters like the sedentary Guards regiments) muskets issued by the Ordnance had 46-inch barrels, and from the appearance of 42-inch barrels for dragoon muskets in 1744, were known as Long Land Muskets to distinguish them. From the early 1770s the line regiments were gradually re-armed with the newly adopted lighter and handier 42-inch barrelled Short Land Musket, but the Guards regiments retained the traditional and more elegant Long Land Musket until the 1790s (except that the Guards Brigade serving in North America during the American War were supplied with Short Land Muskets as replacement arms in 1780). Grenadier companies of line regiments also retained the Long Land muskets for most if not all of the American War period. Prior to 1744 the dragoons carried infantry muskets, but in common with the other branches of the mounted service there was much individual regimental initiative taken in the area of small arms, and some regiments carried muskets with shorter barrels, generally 42-inches in length. The standard pattern musket first produced for dragoons in 1744 was gradually replaced by a carbine of carbine bore (i.e. .66 calibre) after 1770. There was a single pattern of carbine produced for cavalry after the Pattern 1718 and prior to 1756, only two examples of which, dated 1743, have been identified at the time of writing; and there was one Land Service pistol which, when the pattern was changed from 1738, was produced in both carbine bore (.66 calibre) and pistol bore (.56 calibre). This is the basic framework of the Land Service series within which occurred the several technical changes we will be describing.

Just when any particular regiment received new arms depended upon the condition of their presently held arms, and the nature of the service in which they were, or were about to be, employed. Thus, the North American phase of the Seven Years' War (the French and Indian War) was viewed in London as largely involving colonial, provincial troops, and newly-and/or-locally raised regiments would form the nucleus of the British forces in that theatre. The oldest and best regiments were held for service against Continental European enemies. So, at a time when the steel ramrod was being introduced on all new-production infantry muskets, the infantry arms sent to North America, and those with the troops, were, with very few exceptions, fitted with the older wooden rammer. With the coming of the American Rebellion, the attitude changed; America was now seen as an area to be retained rather than conquered, and there was no immediate threat of a European involvement. Thus, many regiments sent to North America after 1773 were re-equipped with the Short Land Musket earlier than they might have been had they remained in garrison in Britain. But provincial (Loyalist) troops were still largely equipped with wooden rammered muskets until 1778. In the 19th Century a fixed span of 12 years was settled upon for the service-life of a line infantry musket, but in the 18th Century there was no fixed period, and a musket would remain in the hands of a regiment until there was a perceived need for a change, however long that might be.

The Board of Ordnance had its small arms manufactured for it on the basis of need. The manufacturing procedure is illustrated in Plate 1, where it can be clearly seen how the Board, with its storerooms for both components and complete arms, served as the focal point for the production initiative. But there was no steady programme of production, although there is evidence of a certain amount of "busy-work" being carried out by the small workforce within the Tower itself. Apart from pattern-arms, a few experimental pieces, and several specific short runs of limited issue pieces, this did not involve arms manufacture as such. There were periods when neither components nor arms were being made, and other periods when there was a tremendous push to manufacture both components and complete arms. Components were used up, or nearly so, before new batches were contracted for, and it was at the time of such new contracts that changes or modifications to design were made. Old arms were broken up, and usable components returned to storage bins, but the brass furniture, which was manufactured in complete sets, was normally returned to the founder for re-casting, and re-supply in complete sets, or to make up the numbers of missing pieces for complete sets for a specific production run. Hence mixed patterns of furniture will not be found on otherwise normal Ordnance-produced arms (with one specific exception noted below). It is this "fits and starts" situation which makes it both reasonable and clarifying to assign dated pattern-designations to the major productions of the Board.

It was standard Board of Ordnance policy to issue old arms first, and not to issue newly made arms until the old arms in store had been exhausted. This practice is clearly illustrated in the Royal Warrant authorizing the adoption of the Short Land Musket for Line Infantry of 1768. Such orders were followed by the Board as vigorously as possible, often in the face of considerable opposition from senior army officers. It was also standard practice to issue wooden-rammer arms for North American service, keeping the supply of steel-rammer arms for troops being sent to the European Continent. This was continued, with specific exceptions, until the entire army was re-equipped with steel-rammer arms. The first troops to be sent to serve in America who were equipped with steel-rammer muskets as a normal practice were those who went from 1765 onward. Wooden-rammer muskets already in store in America were issued to Loyalist provincial regulars and to Loyalist militias until late in the war.

There is very little evidence to support the view that the British Government sent arms made by the Board of Ordnance prior to the Pattern 1730 to North America. Weapons closely resembling some of these earlier types but made from a combination of purchased ex-Ordnance and privately made civilian parts were shipped over by commercial firms. The weapons discussed in this work are those carried by troops sent to North America between 1737 and 1783, or shipped to them as replacement arms while in America.

The Basis for the New System

Three dates offer themselves as a possible basis for a pattern-date designation: (1) the date a design was officially adopted; (2) the date the new design was first produced as a complete arm; and (3) the date of first issue of the new design. There are problems with all three of these options. In many cases the records do not make it clear when a new design originated. In some cases a new pattern was adopted some years before any steps were taken to produce it. In other instances there is no indication of when the decision was made to adopt a design for future production. The date when a newly produced arm was first issued to the troops varies widely, maybe as long as a dozen years from the time of first production, and the date is often not clear from the records. The only remaining possibility and the one most clearly delineated by the records is the date of first production as a complete piece. Even this is not fool-proof since some technical details are not clearly recorded, but these cases are exceptional and this is by far the most workable option. It is also the option which most clearly reflects the production method and sequence.

The basis upon which pattern-dates have been assigned to the production of muskets is that of *the year in which complete arms of a particular description began to be set up.* (See glossary) This means that reasonable supplies of components were already accumulated by the Board of Ordnance in its Tower of London storage facilities before issuing them to the rough stockers to begin the actual process of assembly. The process of accumulation usually began as much as a year before the beginning of the assembly processes. Until assembly was achieved, however, none but the pattern pieces would exist (with the exception of dated locks for the period prior to 1765). Therefore, it is this final stage of production, the setting up, which has been selected as the focal point.

The system described below may seem complicated and perhaps confusing to those who have grown used to the inadequate, imprecise and often misleading methods of identification which have been in use for many years. But the facts are that the new system closely reflects the actual production of Ordnance small arms, and is an accurate portrayal of when the various patterns appeared in complete form, as well as clearly indicating when changes were made and official alterations performed. The old systems, based almost entirely on examination of the arms rather than on detailed production records, or upon collector's terminology, were reasonably accurate as far as they went as a general guide but they failed to recognize, identify and date the important changes in detail, or to indicate at what level (i.e. Ordnance, regimental, or private) these changes were made. This new system remains open to revision in some areas, subject to the examination of additional specimens and documentary material. Examples of a number of weapons identified in the documents remain to be located and examined, and these are noted in the text.

Wherever the Board of Ordnance had a specific name for a particular weapon, I have used this name either as the title or as the basis for the designation of a particular style of arm, adding only the word "Pattern" and the appropriate date. Several lengthy descriptive names such as "Long Land Musket of the King's Pattern" have been shortened, in the manner normally used by the Ordnance, to "Long Land Pattern."

What, then, constitutes a sufficient change in the design of a weapon to justify an alteration to the original designation? Given that the arms consist of four basic features: barrel, lock, stock, and furniture, a complete change in the basic designation is made when two or more of these basic components are noticeably altered in design. Official modifications are shown by the use of either a stroke / or parentheses ( ) depending upon when the modification was made. The stroke / indicates modification at the time of original manufacture, such as the use of a new pattern lock on an otherwise old pattern weapon (e.g. Pattern 1756/77 Sea Service Pistol, where the only, but significant, change is in the lock). The parentheses ( ) indicate a modification made subsequent to the date of original manufacture, either by the Ordnance workshops or at regimental level; this would include the several modifications involved in converting from wooden to steel rammers.

This is the clearest way of indicating both the date of the change and the importance of it, without creating a whole list of dates which would lead to misunderstanding of the processes of manufacture, and misinterpretation of the status of the object.

In no instance is the ( ) indicator applied to modifications made privately at some indeterminate date and unrecorded either in Ordnance or Army/Naval records.

Readers whose minds and approach have been conditioned by the rigid parameters of modern computer usage may note the occasional slight changes in the rigidity with which the general system is applied in particular situations. This has been done sympathetically with the benefit of the modern student in mind, in accordance with the rules in use when the weapons were being manufactured, and is entirely in keeping with the less rigid standards applied to the usage of most "systems" in the Eighteenth Century.

The pressures on the "Ordnance System" generated by the demands of the American War (1775-83) created an increased number of minor changes in the design of muskets which require a more detailed breakdown of designations for the accurate identification of weapons produced under a system which was breaking down in practice. Several of these permutations have yet to be identified at the time of writing and additional designations, or changes to existing ones, may result when examples are identified and examined.

Recognized Patterns Not Included in the Work

This study is designed to include all those recognized patterns of British military small arms manufactured for the Board of Ordnance from the post-1715 period until the close of the American War in 1783, and for which there is evidence of actual use by British troops serving in North America between 1737 and 1783. There were a number of patterns, especially carbines and pistols, produced during this period for a variety of specialist units, which did not see service in America and which have therefore been deliberately excluded from this study. They are listed below and will be described and discussed in detail in forthcoming works.

Muskets
P. 1718 (or "Pattern of the 10,000"), iron mounted with flat plain lock

Carbines
P. 1718 Land Service
P. 1746 Duke of Cumberland's Dragoon
P. 1756 Royal Horse Guards or "Blues"
P. 1756 Light Dragoon
P. 1760 Hales's Light Dragoon
P. 1767 Horse Grenadier Guards
P. 1771 Dragoon
P. 1773 Eliott Light Dragoon
P. 1781 Burgoyne Musketoon

Pistols
P. 1718 Land Service
P. 1756 "Blues"
P. 1776 Horse Grenadier Guards

SMALL ARMS PRODUCTION SEQUENCE
(1728-1783)

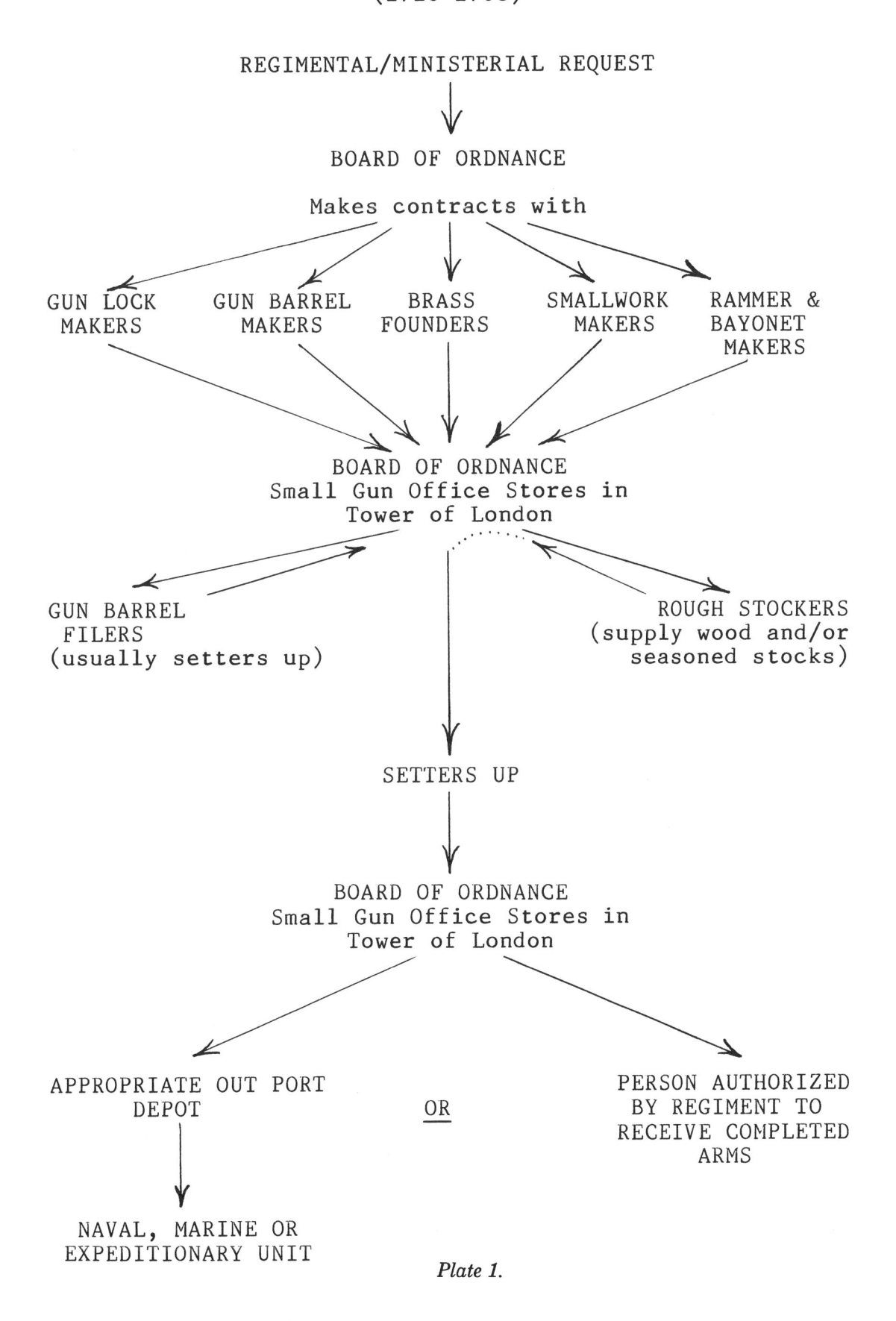

REGIMENTAL/MINISTERIAL REQUEST
↓
BOARD OF ORDNANCE
Makes contracts with

- GUN LOCK MAKERS
- GUN BARREL MAKERS
- BRASS FOUNDERS
- SMALLWORK MAKERS
- RAMMER & BAYONET MAKERS

↓

BOARD OF ORDNANCE
Small Gun Office Stores in Tower of London

- GUN BARREL FILERS (usually setters up)
- ROUGH STOCKERS (supply wood and/or seasoned stocks)

↓

SETTERS UP

↓

BOARD OF ORDNANCE
Small Gun Office Stores in Tower of London

- APPROPRIATE OUT PORT DEPOT
  ↓
  NAVAL, MARINE OR EXPEDITIONARY UNIT

OR

- PERSON AUTHORIZED BY REGIMENT TO RECEIVE COMPLETED ARMS

Plate 1.

Barrels

Like all components of small arms made for the Ordnance in the Eighteenth Century, barrels were made "to the pattern." Therefore, with very few exceptions which will be explained, all barrels produced for Board of Ordnance small arms share certain basic characteristics, which may be assumed to be part of any description of individual patterns of weapon.

There were four standard calibres in which all Ordnance barrels were produced: Wallpiece .98-in.; Musket .76-in.; Carbine .66-in.; Pistol .56-in.

The four categories of barrel (wallpiece, musket, carbine and pistol) conform to basic measurements of width at breech and muzzle within each category. Examination has shown these to be:

Wallpiece	across breech ahead of moulding:	2 1/8" to 2 3/16"
	across muzzle:	1 1/2"
Musket	across breech ahead of moulding:	1 5/16" to 1 3/8"
	across muzzle:	7/8" to 15/16"
Carbine	across breech ahead of moulding:	1 3/16" to 1 1/2"
	across muzzle:	3/4" to 7/8"
Pistol	across breech ahead of moulding:	1" to 1 1/16"
	across muzzle:	11/16" to 7/8"

The larger span on pistol muzzles being due to the use of two calibres, .56" and .66" within one basic pattern.

The first and most noticeable of these common characteristics is that the barrels are secured by round iron wire, known as "pinning-wire," cross-pins, or simply, pins. These were used not only for barrels but for the trigger and much of the brass furniture. The underside of the barrel was fitted with a series of flat studs, usually three on muskets, which were dovetailed and brazed to the barrel. These are variously known as "barrel loops," "tenons," or "pin-loops." With the barrel inlaid and in position in its bed, holes were drilled through the stock, passing through the pin-loops, into which the pinning-wire was inserted, cut off at the proper length for the section width of the stock, and filed flush with the surface of the wood. Exceptions to this general practice occur with the Royal Foresters Carbine and the Pattern 1776 Rifle, whose barrels are held by flat keys (wedges or slides). Another loop of much heavier and thicker construction was dovetailed and brazed to the underside of the barrel between the first and second ramrod pipes on all arms carrying conventional sling swivels, to carry the upper sling swivel screw.

A variation in the use of pinning occurs on the Pattern 1730 Musket where a method known as "double loops" was used. (Plate 2) This involved the use of a pair of loops one alongside the other fitted in the usual way. The tab of the ramrod pipes fitted between the two loops and the barrel pin thereby served to secure both the barrel and the pipe. This system was also used on some of the transitional Pattern 1730/40 Muskets and on the Patterns 1738 and 1746 Long Land and Sea Service Muskets.

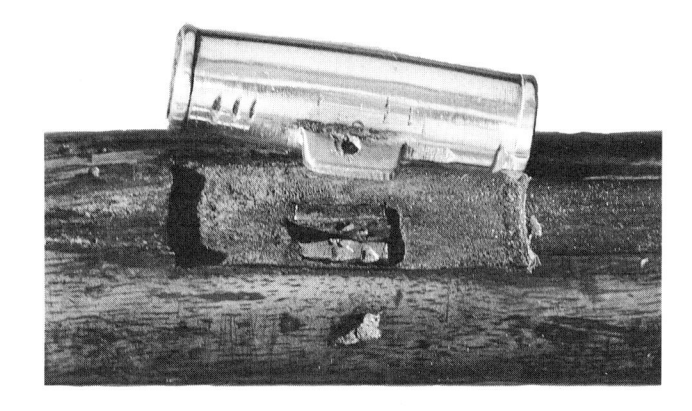

Plate 2. Pattern 1730 "double-loop" system of pinning both the barrel and ramrod pipes with one pin. The slotted loop takes the tab of the rod pipe in the slot. The heavy loop next to the slotted one is for the upper sling swivel screw. Courtesy of the Colonial Williamsburg Foundation.

The second common feature which is found on all Ordnance-made barrels of our period is the baluster-moulding at the breech. This was designed as a reinforcement as well as a decoration and while subject to wide minor variation in shape, the general outline is the same as that shown in Plate 69. The moulding is filed into the upper area of the barrel only, ceasing on the left side where the barrel is covered by the wood, and on the right by a flat filed on the side of the barrel to allow close alignment of the lockplate. The design is often much worn by pitting and frequent polishing by Ordnance staff and soldiers.

The third feature common to musket, fusil and carbine barrels other than Cavalry, is the bayonet-stud, always referred to by the Ordnance as the "sight." (Plate 3) This small rectangular block is dovetailed and brazed on the top of the barrel (except on the Ferguson rifle where it lies underneath in the French manner) at varying distances from the muzzle. The dimensions of the stud increased with the years and improvements in bayonet design, but in general a measurement of 1/4" long by 1/8" wide is most common by the post-1750 period.

The final feature common to all Ordnance-made barrels is their markings, which occur near the breech. There are four classifications of markings found on barrels:

(1) the King's Proof and View Marks
(2) barrel maker's marks
(3) barrel inspector's marks
(4) regimental markings (not always present)

All Ordnance-made barrels should bear the first of these markings, (Plate 4 and 4A) *stamped* on the top, or nearly on the top slightly to the left of centreline of the barrel, about two inches ahead of the baluster-moulding. These are usually struck deeply enough that even heavily cleaned and polished barrels will retain some signs of them. On some early Pattern 1730 barrels and on some Sea Service musket barrels only the Proof Mark will be found; the reasons for this are not clear.

Barrel-makers' marks tend to be present on the majority of barrels until the time of the American War when they are often omitted, perhaps due to the partial relaxation of inspection standards and a certain amount of behind-the-scenes activity amongst the workforces of the barrel contractors, inevitable under the stress of wartime conditions. Some of the "complete arms" contracts from 1778 onward allowed for the use of older barrels on which the original maker's marks were eradicated during their refurbishment. These marks are normally located on the left side of the barrel just ahead of the baluster-moulding, and consist of a pair of initials often with

Plate 4. Proof marks found on Ordnance-manufactured barrels. The "King's Proof" consisting of a Proof Mark and beneath it a View Mark.

(Left) Early type marks: Crowned addorsed GRs over Broad Arrow, and Crowned crossed sceptres. Note also early style crossed sceptres inspector's mark on front of tang. Courtesy of the Colonial Williamsburg Foundation.

(Right) conventional King's Proof Marks ca. 1776. See also Plate 69.

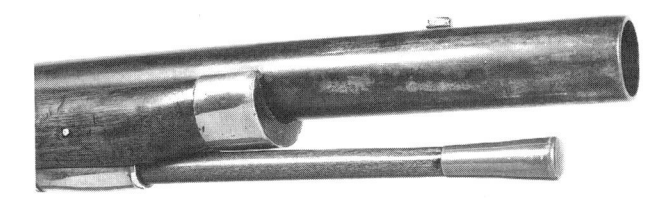

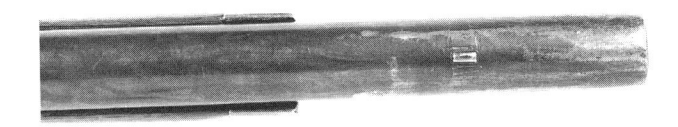

Plate 3. Bayonet stud. Always referred to by the Ordnance as the "sight." This is an early example; from the Pattern 1756 series the stud becomes thicker and almost square. Courtesy of the National Army Museum, London.

Plate 4A. Style of proof marks found on post-Pattern 1730 barrels, an early example of the conventional form on a Pattern 1742 musket; barrel contractors' initials are often found struck between or near these two marks. Also note regimental marking.

Courtesy of the Colonial Williamsburg Foundation.

a star, asterisk or coronet above them. These marks are often not so deeply struck as the proof marks and suffer more from cleaning and pitting. Barrels made in Liège for the Ordnance in 1778-81 will generally have distinctive raised initials in crude relief within a sunken background (*poinçon*) which forms a frame around them (Plate 5). Liège baluster-moulding may also be wider and vary from the precise design followed by English contractors. There are not normally any useful markings on the underside of the barrel apart from finishing and assemblers' marks, in Roman figures. On barrels bearing no external maker's marks it is occasionally worthwhile to examine the underside.

Barrel inspectors' marks take the form of a crowned numeral and are often found in conjunction with a special "view" mark, often appearing at the front of the barrel-tang, in the form of crossed sceptres. The tail of the tang is usually struck with a small crown.

Regimental markings on the barrel were very frequently removed by Ordnance staff when arms were returned into Store from a regiment, or by militia regiments to whom the arms were issued in the later 18th and early 19th Centuries. Originally it was intended that the regimental colonel's name should be engraved along the top of the barrel, (from 1751 the numerical designation of the regiment replaced the colonel's name), the company commander's name on the tang of the buttplate, with the company number or letter and the individual number of the gun within the company on the thumbpiece. This sequence was normally followed on Long Land Pattern muskets. On Marine or Militia muskets, where markings survive, they will be found along the barrel and on the buttplate tang. When the Short Land became standard the barrel markings normally included the numbered regimental designation, while the company number/letter appeared over the individual number of the gun in that company on the thumbpiece. This is also true of most patterns of Land Service pistols. When the marking was carried out by the Ordnance Office engraver the standard format was followed, but where arms were not engraved by the Ordnance prior to delivery to a regiment and that

6

regiment undertook to have them engraved at their own expense, a variety of formats resulted which often makes the establishment of the authenticity of the marking extremely difficult. Some of the markings found today on later Long and Short Land muskets which do not conform to British regimental structures, are probably those of post-Revolutionary War period American militia units.

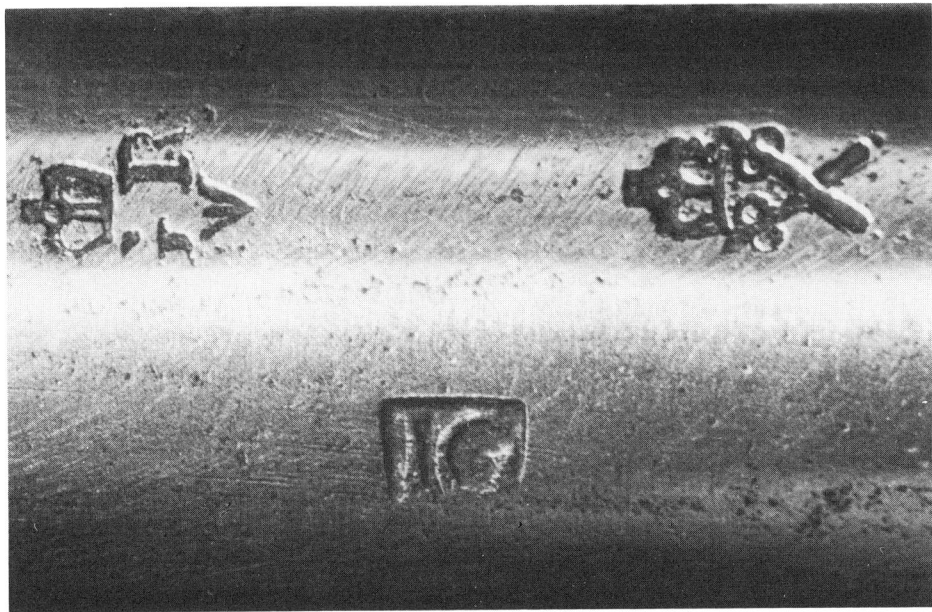

Plate 5. Barrel markings found on Liege-made Short Land Pattern musket barrels, 1778-81.
Courtesy of the Board of Trustees of the Armouries.

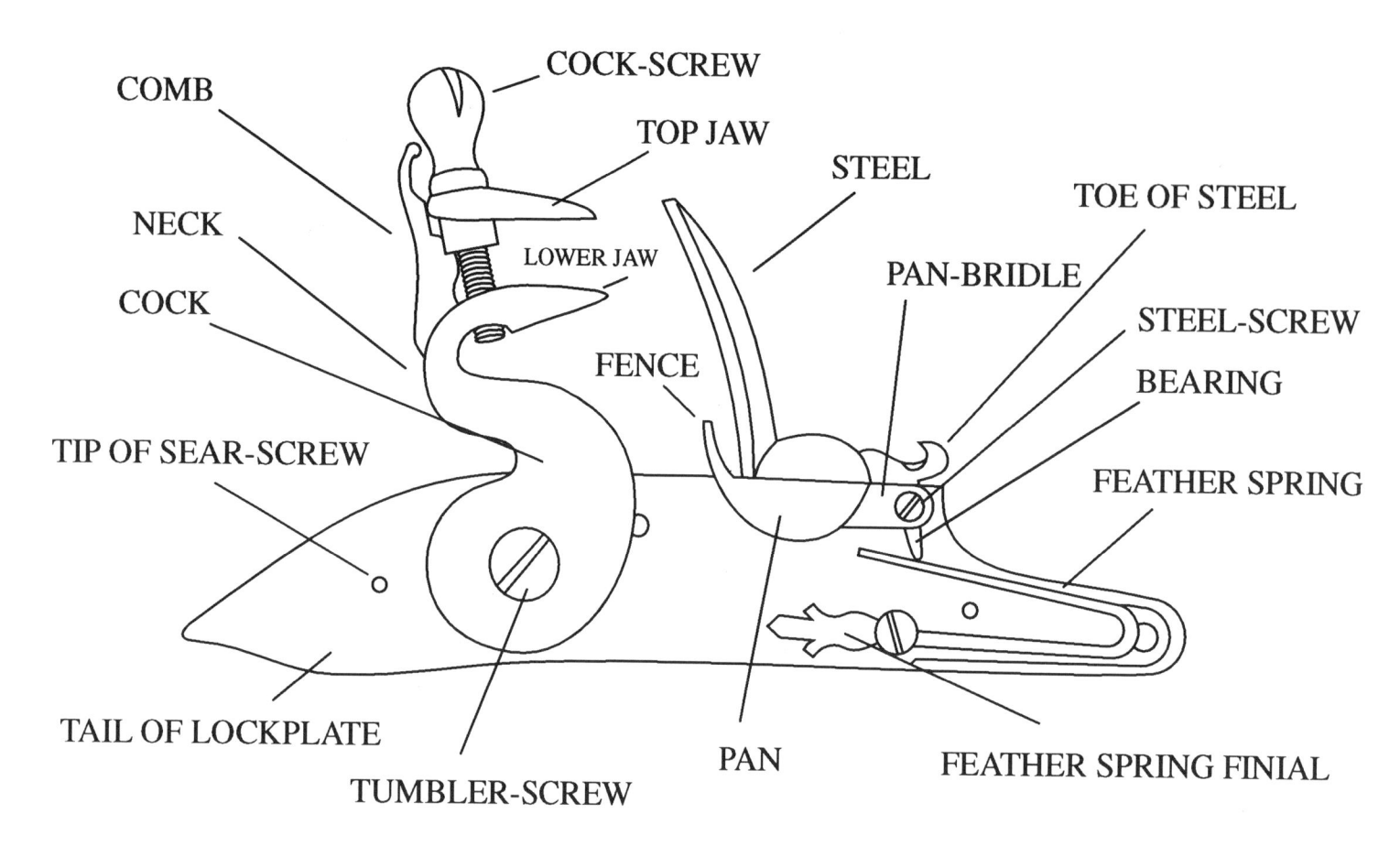

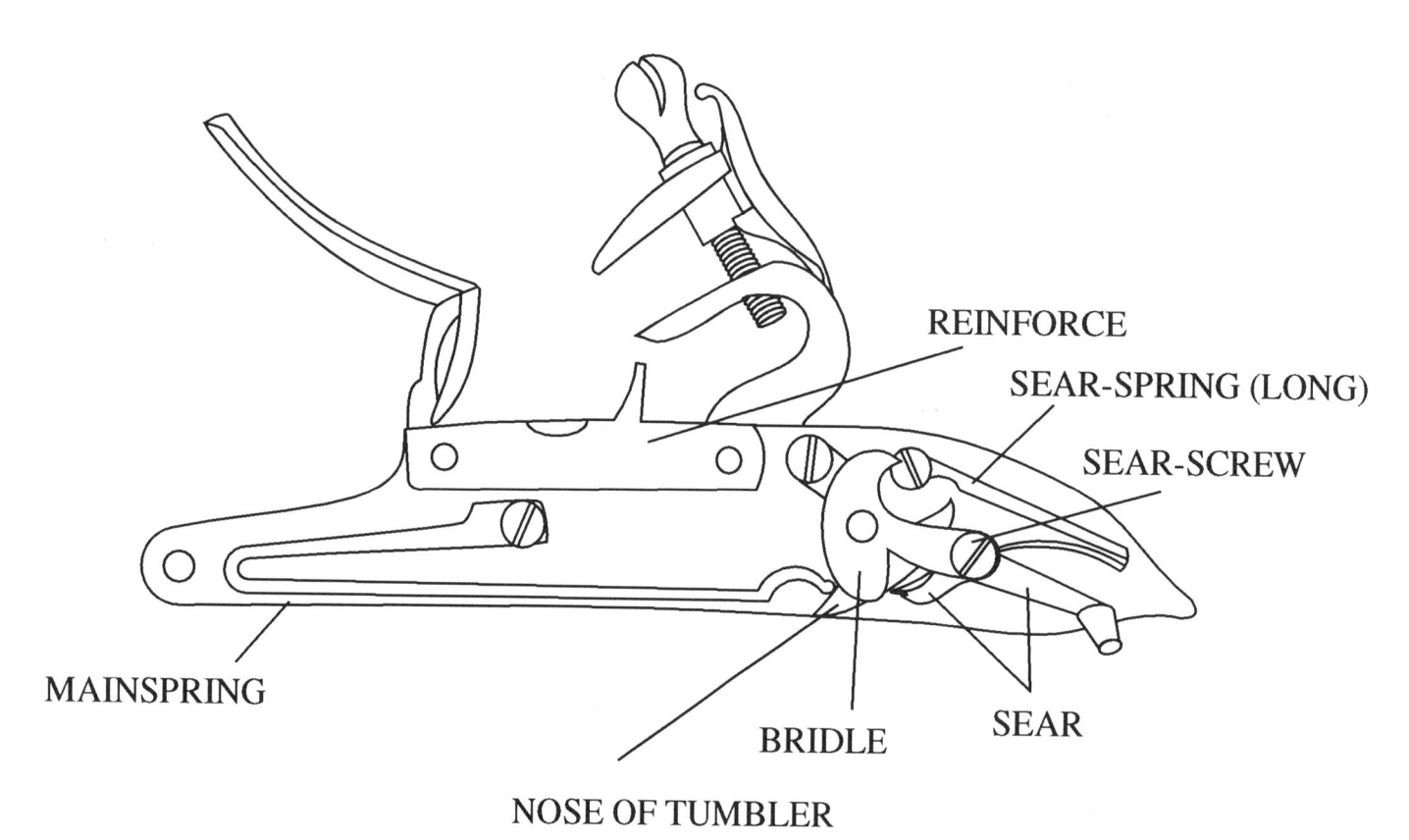

Plate 6. British 18th Century Gunlock Nomenclature.

Locks

During the period covered by this study there were two wallpiece locks, four musket locks, five carbine locks, a rifle lock and six pistol locks used for Land Service arms; and for the Sea Service two musket locks and three pistol locks.

All Ordnance locks made during the period of this study fall into two of five general categories which indicate (1) their surface configuration (convex or flat) and (2) their construction. These are:
 (1) Round or Flat. The term "Extra Flat" was Ordnance shorthand for Extraordinary Flat, referring to the degree of finish.
 (2) Plain, Single-bridle or Double-bridle. These describe locks which have neither an external pan-nor an internal tumbler-bridle; an internal tumbler-bridle only; and both external and internal bridles. A lock with an external pan bridle will always have the internal tumbler bridle.

Markings

All Ordnance-made locks of the period under review bear the same style of external and internal markings. Below and to the left of the pan is *engraved* a Crown over the block-letters GR (the Royal Cypher) while across the tail of the lockplate is *engraved* either TOWER or DUBLIN CASTLE or a lock-contractor's name, above the year in which the lock was delivered into Ordnance Stores. (Plates 7, 8). After 1764 the tail engraving is altered to omit the date and contractor's name, so that either Tower or Dublin Castle alone will be present (Plates 12, 13). Below the pan is *stamped* a small Crown over Broad Arrow (Plate 7), the Government ownership mark, indicating acceptance of the complete lock by the Ordnance inspectors.

Until mid-1777 the lockplate, cock, top-jaw and the back of the steel were engraved with a parallel pair of lines around their edges, known to the Ordnance as "threads" but described here as double border line engraving. The outer of the two lines is slightly heavier than the inner one. After mid-1777 this engraving was omitted from the top-jaw and back of the steel, remaining only on the cock body and lockplate edges.

Internal markings stamped into the lockplate surface are comprised of Ordnance inspector's marks (Crowned numerals) and the initials or mark of the lock contractor and occasionally those of the actual lockmaker or workman. Some locks which are signed externally with Tower and a date (especially Pattern 1727 and Pattern 1740 locks) appear to have been fabricated by the Tower workforce, while others, which were received in the "soft" or not yet case-hardened state, were inspected, polished, and engraved by the Ordnance engraver before being returned to the contractor for case-hardening, and will include the contractor's initials stamped internally. Some late Pattern 1777 musket locks will have the initials IH stamped at the very front of the lockplate ahead of the front sidenail hole; these are the initials of Jonathan Hennem, who provided muskets to the Ordnance in the 1780s and 1790s, and indicate a post-1783 lock.

Wallpiece

The wallpiece lock (Plate 9) is double-bridle with a flat lockplate measuring 8 15/16" x 1 5/8". The pan has a fence and is faceted on its underside with a slightly raised and rounded collar where it joins the plate. The flat ring-neck cock has a bevelled edge, and the throat hole is oval with a curl or lip at the bottom front. The comb is a rectangular-section pillar 5/16" thick with a very slight rearward curve, and a rounded top. The top-jaw is slightly oval and is slotted at the rear to fit around, and move vertically along the comb. The cock-screw is both slotted and pierced. The steel is round topped with a central spine down the back, and the heel is in the form of a teardrop with the base curling upwards. The feather-spring has a teardrop finial.

Musket—Land Service

The four designs of lock used in the fabrication of Land Pattern muskets are: the Pattern 1727, Pattern 1740, Pattern 1756 and Pattern 1777.

The Pattern 1727 lock (Plate 10) is a single-bridle lock produced between 1727 and 1743. Lockplate measurements are 6 7/8" long x 1 1/4" wide. Varia-

Plate 7. Ordnance Gunlock Markings. Two versions of the Royal Cypher, an early and late example. Other variations may be seen on the lock illustrations. Note also the Crowned Broad Arrow stamped beneath the pan, the mark of British Government ownership.

Courtesy of the Board of Trustees of the Armouries.

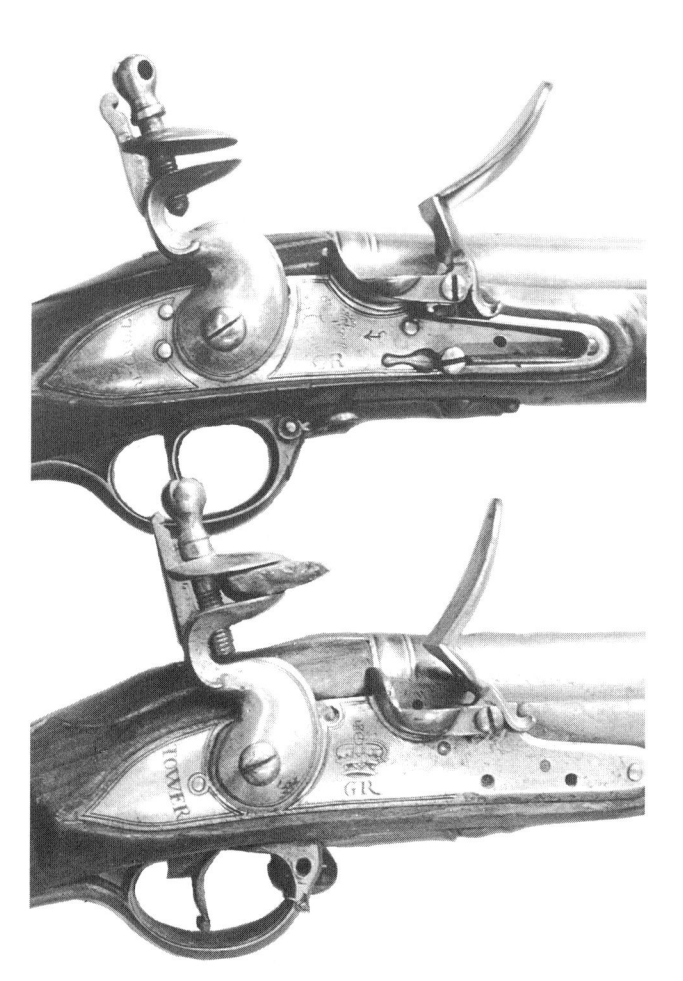

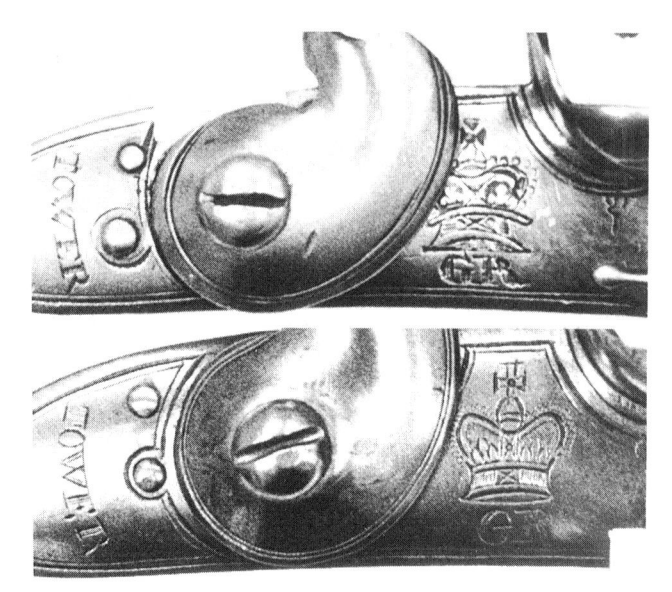

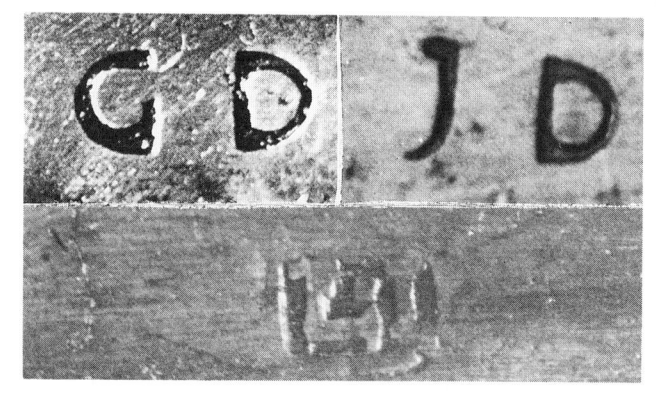

Plate 8. Lock markings on Liège-made locks 1778-82. (Left) Upper is Ordnance-made Short Land with typical (unfortunately faint) markings and typical wartime style of comb to the cock. Lower is Liège-made. Note heavily-shaded letters in Tower and oddly-shaped Crown. (Above, right) Closeups show great variety of crowns, and heavily shaded lettering on Liège-made locks; note also incomplete arrow of Crowned Broad Arrow mark on upper example. (Right) Examples of initials stamped inside Liège-made locks.

Courtesy of the Board of Trustees of the Armouries.

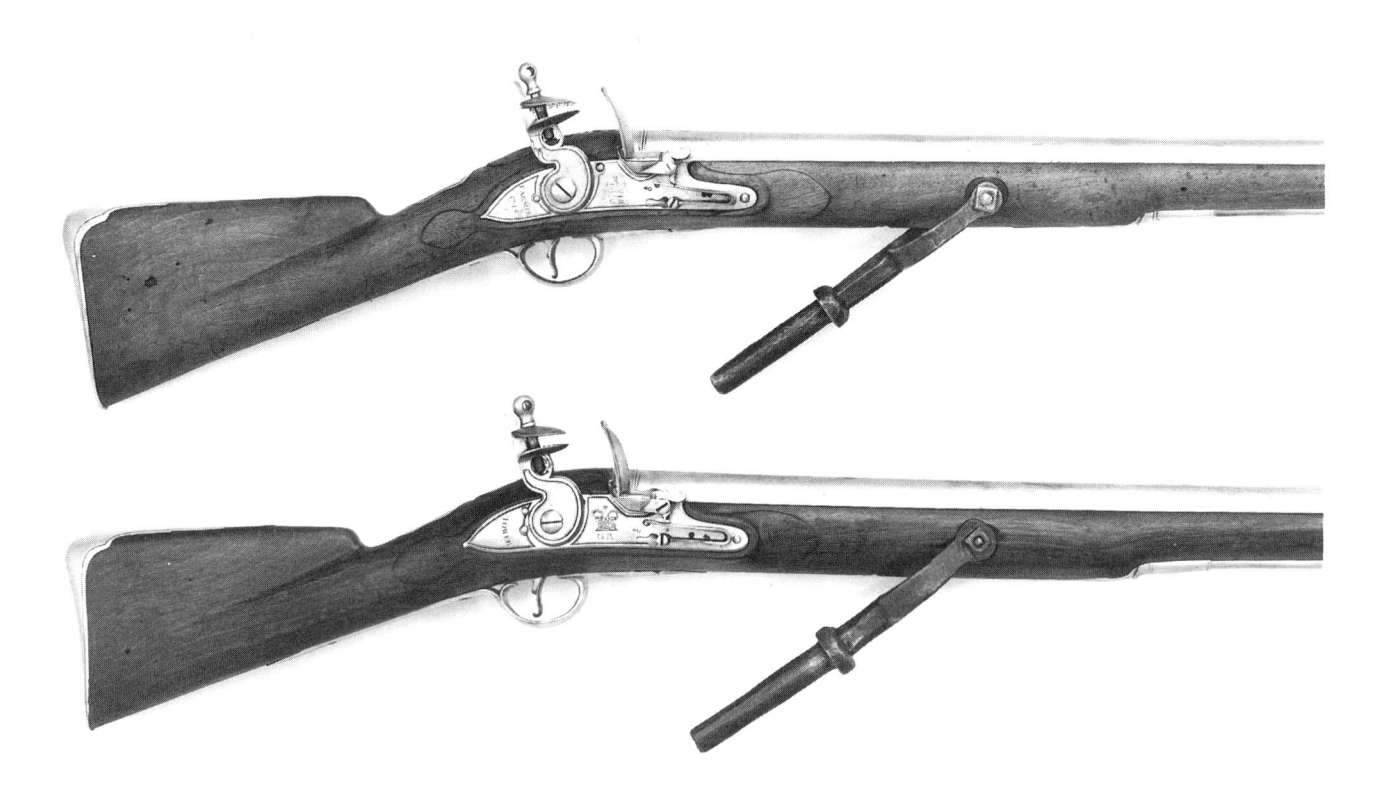

Plate 9. Wallpiece Locks. (Above) Pattern 1737, dated 1744. (Below) Pattern 1777. Only the markings on the tail of the plate and the use of the short sear-spring differentiate it from the earlier pattern.

Courtesy of the Board of Trustees of the Armouries.

tions in length are from 6 13/16" to 6 15/16" but these are rare; variations in width are even less common, only 1 3/16" having been noted. The surfaces of the swan-neck cock and lockplate are rounded, and the tail of the lockplate drops downward at the tail in a manner commonly described as "banana" shaped. This drop amounts to 1/4" below the otherwise straight lower edge of the lockplate. The outer shape of the pan as seen from the side is deep and well rounded, and there is a rounded beading or collar where it joins the lockplate. The mechanism has a long sear-spring, so that its screw comes through the lockplate underneath the body of the cock and is not externally visible, creating a "one screw visible behind cock" appearance. The cock has a comb which, when viewed from the rear is a long oval, or "leaf-shaped," measuring between 7/16" and 9/16" across at its widest point, with a tight curl forwards at the tip. The front face of the comb has a vertical slot in which a stud on the rear of the top-jaw slides. The top-jaw is nearly circular in form. At the neck of the cock at the rear of the underside of the lower jaw, there is a reinforce collar or lip where the cock-screw comes through the jaw, a feature which is unique to this pattern. The cock-screw is slotted but not pierced, and the head is slightly flattened or mushroom-shaped. The finial of the feather-spring is a large and well defined trefoil. There is full double border line engraving.

The Pattern 1740 lock (Plate 11) differs from the Pattern 1727 chiefly in having a pan bridle, making it a double-bridle lock. The cock also lacks the reinforce or lip at the neck where the cock-screw comes through the lower jaw; the point where the pan joins the lockplate no longer has the raised rounded collar. The pan is also visibly shallower as seen from the side. Pattern 1727 locks are found on Pattern 1730/40 muskets with dates as late as 1743. The Pattern 1740 double-bridle lock with the "banana" configuration to the tail was last made in 1750.

The Pattern 1756 lock (Plate 12) represents a considerable visual change in design from the Pattern 1727 and its modification of 1740. The lockplate ceases to have the "banana" tail outline, which is now replaced with a virtually straight lower edge to the point where it tapers up to the tail. Lockplate measurements vary between 6 7/8" and 7 1/16" in length, with the norm being 7", and in width between 1 3/16" and 1 1/4". It was manufactured between 1756 and 1777. Beginning in 1765 large numbers of these locks were re-worked by Ordnance lock contractors (chiefly William Grice) and the Board's engraver, so that undated Tower marks will be found on locks as early as the Pattern 1740.

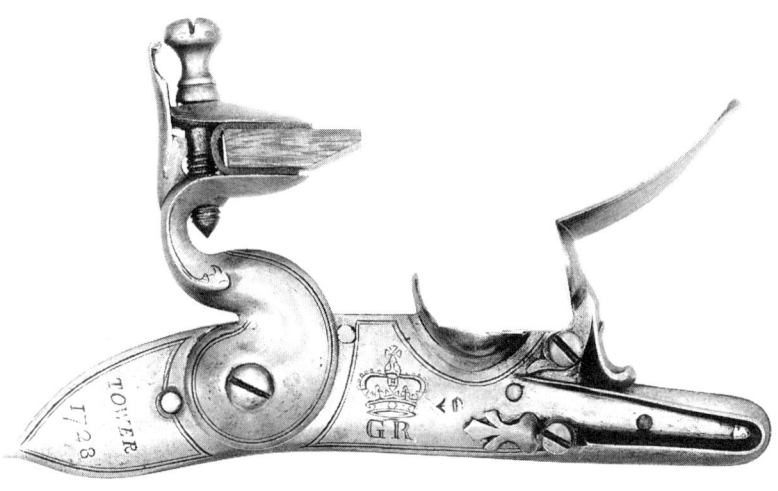

Plate 10. Pattern 1727 Land Service Musket Lock (top, left & right). No pan bridle, making it a "single-bridle" lock, referring to the internal tumbler (above); note positioning of the long sear-spring. Note the raised and rounded collar where pan joins plate, and the reinforcing lip on the underside of the lower jaw (right). Note the variations in the engraving of the Crown, and the early form of Crown in the stamped Crowned Broad Arrow mark.

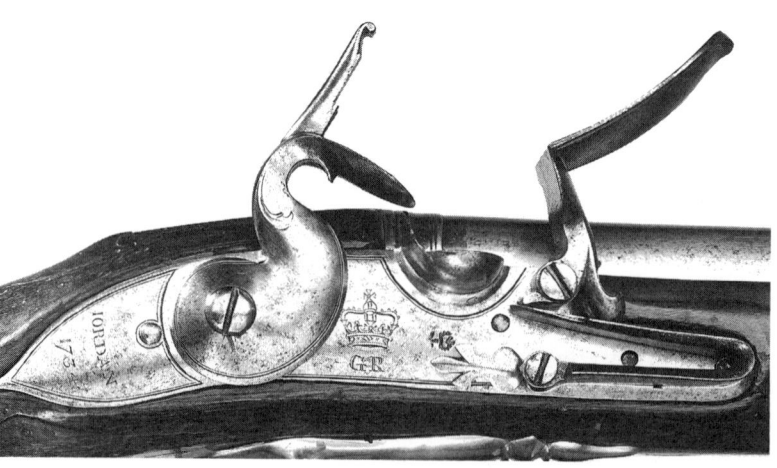

Courtesy of the Board of Trustees of the Armouries

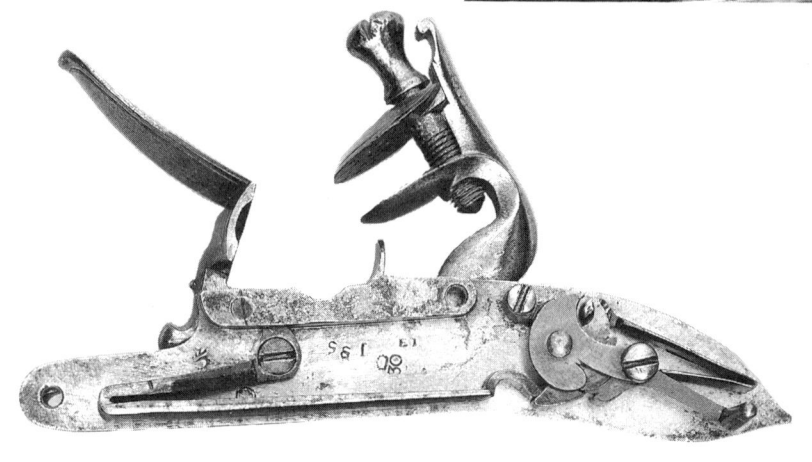

Courtesy of the Colonial Williamsburg Foundation

Courtesy of the Colonial Williamsburg Foundation

Courtesy of the Colonial Williamsburg Foundation

Courtesy of the Trustees of the National Museums of Scotland.

Courtesy of the Colonial Williamsburg Foundation.

Plate 11. Pattern 1740 Land Service Musket Lock. (Top) A 1741 example: the pan now has a bridle, making it a "double-bridle" lock. The pan is also shallower and lacks a collar where it joins the lockplate. The underside of the lower jaw no longer has a reinforcing lip. The tip of the tail is missing.
(Bottom) The last year of production of the Pattern 1740 lock: a small number were produced by James Farmer in 1750.

Plate 12. Pattern 1756 Land Service Musket. (Above and right) a typical example external and internal views. Note the long sear-spring. The lower edge of the lockplate is almost straight. Two variations (below) of markings on Pattern 1756 Dublin Castle locks, (bottom) being the later of the two styles.

Courtesy of the Colonial Williamsburg Foundation.

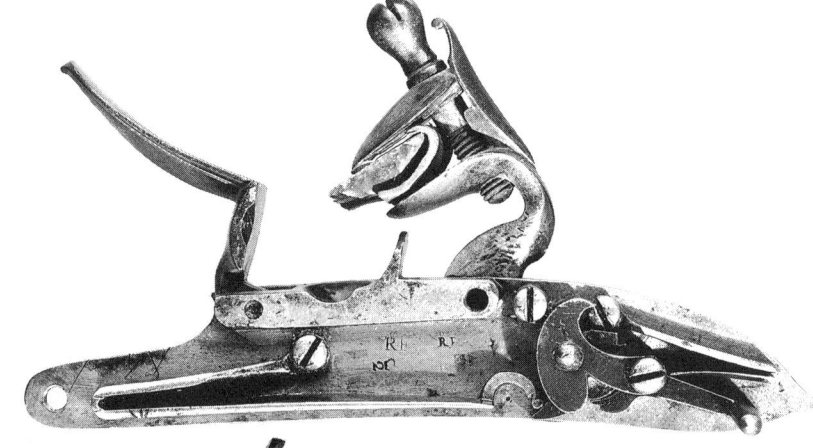

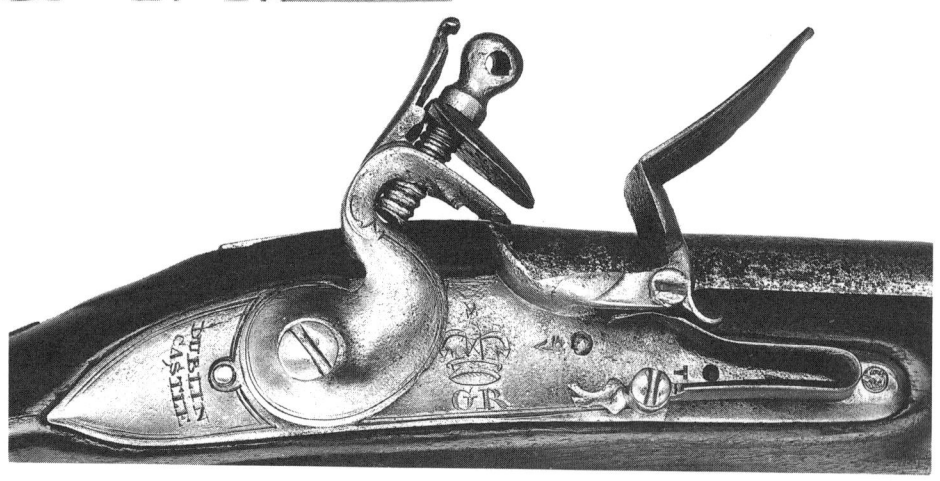

14

The Pattern 1777 lock (Plate 13) is instantly recognizable by its having two screws showing through the lockplate, one above the other, to the rear of the cock, the result of adopting the short sear-spring, so that the screw holding it was no longer concealed by the cock. Its other features include a simplification in the design of the feather-spring finial from a trefoil to a teardrop pattern, and the omission of the double border line engraving on the top-jaw and the back of the steel. The comb of the cock is also of an entirely new shape, simpler, stronger and cheaper to manufacture under the stress of wartime demands. It is now a very slightly curved pillar, rectangular in section, about 1/4" thick at the front where it is widest, with a plain rounded top and a notch chisel-cut into the front at the top to simulate a curl. The top-jaw is now altered to an oval shape and is slotted at the back to fit around, and move vertically along the comb, which is tapered wider towards the front. This made it harder for the jaw to become separated from the cock when changing a flint or cleaning the lock.

Pattern 1777 locks made from the early 1780s to the early 1790s have a heavier comb with a much wider and more pronounced curl (Plate 14).

Plate 13. Pattern 1777 Land Service Musket Lock, wartime production, 1777-82. Note the straight pillar comb with crudely formed notch at the top front. Use of a short sear-spring now shows two screw-ends through the tail of the lockplate. The feather-spring finial is teardrop-shaped, and the two border lines have been dropped from the back of the steel and the top jaw.

Courtesy Clinton M. Miller.

Plate 14. Pattern 1777 Land Service Musket Lock, post-1782 to 1795. Better finished overall. Note heavy well-curved comb of the cock with well-developed notch, the filing details on its base, and the engraved flourish at the neck.

Courtesy of the Board of Trustees of the Armouries.

Musket—Sea Service

Throughout the period covered by this study Sea Service muskets were normally fitted with what was known as a "Flat Plain Lock," that is, one with a flat lockplate and cock, and without a bridle over the tumbler or a bridle on the pan. There were two significant variations in the Sea Service musket lock during this period.

The Pattern 1718 lock (Plate 15) is characterised by having three sidenails, two in the normal positions and the third through the tip of the tail. The flat lockplate and ring-neck cock have very narrow bevels to their edges, and the pan has three facets or bevels on its underside. The lockplate measures between 7 11/16" and 7 5/8" long by from 1 1/4" to 1 5/16" in width. A long sear-spring is used, so that only one screw shows through the lockplate behind the cock. The ring-neck cock has a rectagular-section pillar comb with a plain rounded top, about 1/4" thick. The oval top-jaw is slotted and fits around the comb. The throat hole is oval with a curl or lip at the bottom front. The cock-screw is both slotted and pierced. The face of the steel is roughly hexagonal in shape, and is flat-topped, with a faceted back and a heel in the shape of a teardrop with the base curled upwards. The finial of the feather-spring terminates in a leaf-shape with a central spine. Markings are the same as on Land Service locks, but there is no double border line engraving.

The Pattern 1757 lock (Plate 16) abandons the third sidenail for the more conventionally positioned two, and also drops the use of the flat-topped and faceted-back steel in favour of the rounded-top version with a central vertical spine along the back. The toe of the steel is less robust and has less of a curl to it. The curl at the lower front of the throat-hole is less pronounced.

There were no Sea Service musket locks manufactured between 1771 and late 1777, so it is assumed that the musket lock underwent the modernizations in design now classified as the Pattern 1777, although at the time of writing no example has been examined. From 1778 most of the Sea Service muskets supplied *complete* by various contractors (as opposed to being made up under the Ordnance System) were fitted with Pattern 1756 or 1777 Land Service musket locks. The former, where necessary, had their markings reworked to show merely Tower across the tail (Plate 71).

Plate 15. Pattern 1718 Sea Service Musket Lock, in use with minor finishing variations until 1756.
Courtesy of the Board of Trustees of the Armouries.

Plate 16. Pattern 1757 Sea Service Musket Lock. Only two sidenails are used to secure the lock; the top of the steel is now rounded and the back has a single central spine.
Courtesy of Valley Forge National Historical Park.

Carbine—Round

Carbine locks follow the general progress in design and style of the musket locks, with the banana-shaped lockplate being discontinued on new production in 1756. At the time of writing only one example of a post-1730, pre-1750 (Jordan 1743) carbine has been available for examination, and the design of the lock conforms closely to the Pattern 1740.

The Pattern 1756 Carbine lock (Plate 17) is, once again, a scaled-down version of the musket lock of the same year. Lockplate measurements are 6 1/16" to 6 1/8" length by 1 1/16" width, with only minor variations. This pattern was used for all carbines using round locks manufactured between 1756 and 1777, with the exception of the Pattern 1760 Eliott Carbine.

The Pattern 1760 Eliott Carbine lock (Plate 18) closely follows the design of the Pattern 1756 Carbine lock, but is fitted with a gravity-operated safety-catch making it the latest example of a "dog-lock" in British service. The tip of the teardrop-shaped catch engages in a notch on the lower rear edge of the cock body. It proved to be a superfluous and unpopular feature and most of them were removed and the holes and notches filled in.

The Pattern 1777 Carbine lock followed the design modifications of the musket lock of the same date, with its short sear-spring (two screws showing through the lockplate behind the cock), teardrop feather-spring finial, pillar comb and oval slotted top-jaw. The pillar comb is about 3/16" thick.

Carbine—"Extra Flat"

An entirely new form of carbine lock first appeared on the Royal Horse Guards ("Blues") Carbine of 1756 (and pistol as well) with a flat bevelled-edge lockplate and swan-neck cock, and a faceted pan. These were known as "Extra Flat Locks" for carbines and pistols, the "extra" being short for extraordinary. They cost more than the conventional rounded locks and were used only for specialized arms, in particular the "Blues" and the "Royal Foresters" carbine and pistol, only the latter of which was used in America.

The Pattern 1756 Extra Flat lock measures from 6 1/4" to 6 3/16" long by 1 3/32" wide. The swan-neck cock has an almost straight pillar comb 1/4" thick, with an oval slotted top-jaw. A long sear-spring is used. The engraving on these locks is normally of a higher than usual standard.

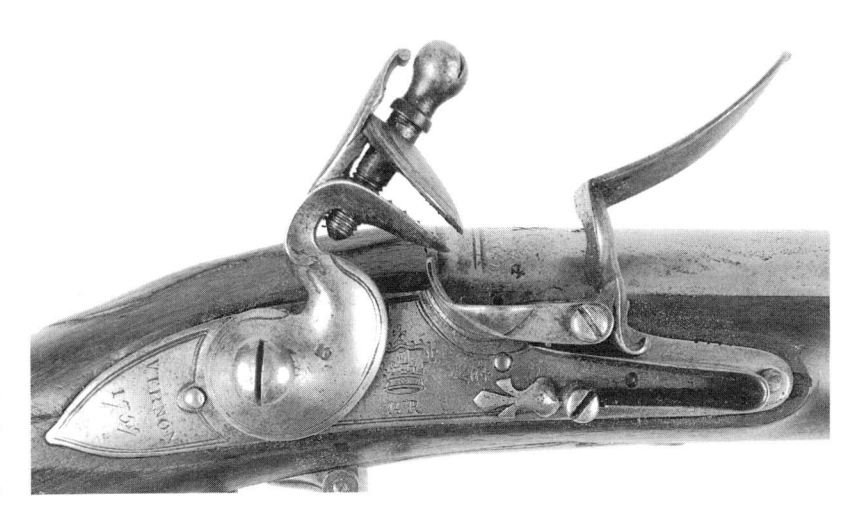

Plate 17. Pattern 1756 Land Service Carbine Lock. The lower edge of the lockplate is nearly straight.
Courtesy of Parks Canada.

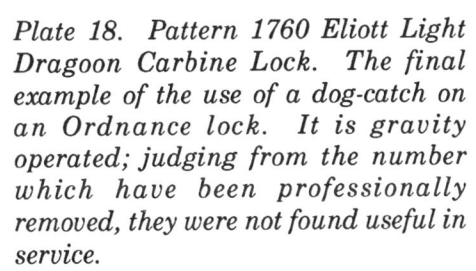

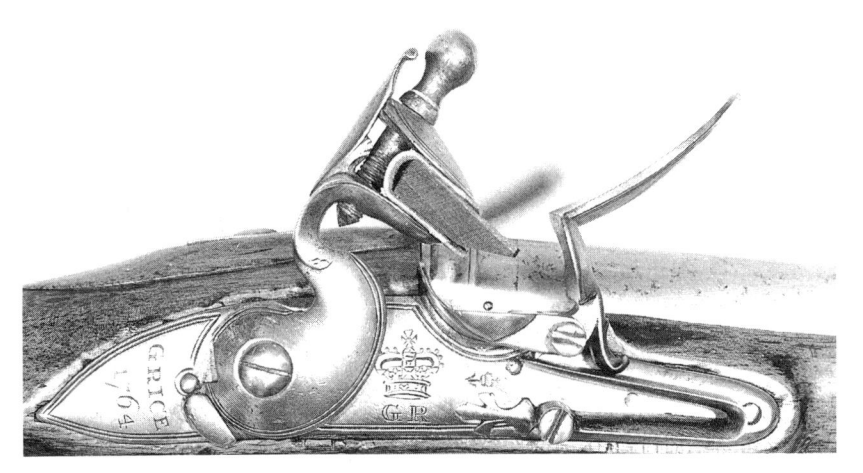

Plate 18. Pattern 1760 Eliott Light Dragoon Carbine Lock. The final example of the use of a dog-catch on an Ordnance lock. It is gravity operated; judging from the number which have been professionally removed, they were not found useful in service.
Photograph I. D. Skennerton, courtesy of the Board of Trustees of the Armouries.

Pattern 1777 Extra Flat lock (Plate 19). The faceted underside of the pan is rounded off, a short sear spring is introduced, the teardrop feather-spring finial replaces the trefoil, and the border line engraving is dropped from the top-jaw and back of the steel.

Rifle—Pattern 1776 muzzle-loading

The lock used on the Pattern 1776 Rifle (Plate 20) is a close copy of the Extra Flat Carbine lock, but is slightly smaller, the lockplate measuring 6" x 1", and not nearly so well made or finished. It has a long sear-spring, but a teardrop feather-spring finial, and a pillar comb with no notch at the top, with an oval, slotted, top jaw. The top jaw and back of the steel have the standard double border line engraving. The quality of the engraved markings is very poor.

Pistol—Land Service

Pistol locks also followed the general design of the musket lock.

The Pattern 1729 Pistol lock (Plate 21) is the first of the round-surface locks in the series, its predecessor, the flat plain Pattern 1718 being used on both Land and Sea Service pistols of that pattern. It is single-bridle with a banana-tail lockplate measuring between 5 3/8" and 5 1/2" long by between 15/16" and 1" in width. The swan-neck cock has a leaf-shaped comb about 3/8" across its widest point, and a circular top-jaw with the stud riding in the vertical groove on the front face of the comb. As on the musket lock of this pattern the underside of the lower jaw has a slight reinforcing lip where the cock-screw comes through. A long sear-spring is used, and there is a trefoil finial to the feather-spring.

Plate 19. Pattern 1777 Extra Flat Carbine Lock. Same changes as for other Pattern 1777 locks: short sear-screw, teardrop finial to the feather-spring, lack of engraved border lines on the back of the steel and top jaw. The underside of the pan is now rounded. Photograph I. D. Skennerton, courtesy of the Board of Trustees of the Armouries.

Plate 20. Pattern 1776 Rifle Lock. Similar to the Extra Flat Carbine lock but smaller and with a plain pillar comb very slightly curved backwards. Does not have improvements of the 1777 series, and the engraved markings are crudely executed. Courtesy of R. J. Whittaker.

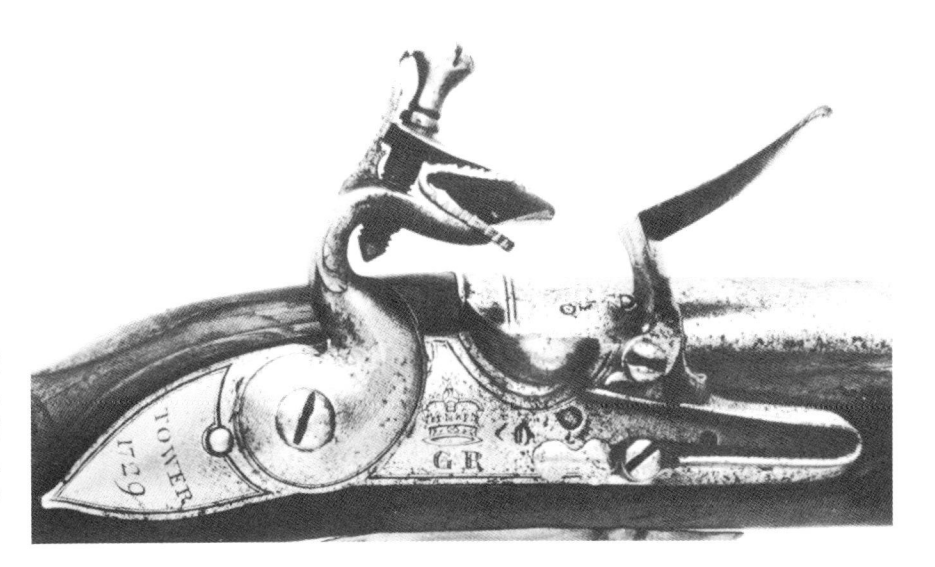

Plate 21. Pattern 1729 Land Service Pistol Lock. Lacks pan-bridle, has large teardrop-shaped feather-spring finial. Used only on the Pattern 1730 Land Service Pistol.

The Pattern 1738 Pistol lock (Plate 22) is the first of the Land Service series to incorporate a pan-bridle in its design. The lower jaw of the cock does not have the reinforcing lip. With these two exceptions, and a trefoil finial on the feather-spring, it is otherwise identical to the Pattern 1730.

The Pattern 1756 Pistol lock (Plate 23) drops the banana-tail design of the lockplate and is slightly longer, averaging 5 5/8" although rare aberrations as short as 5 3/8" have been noted; the width varies less at 1", with 1 1/16" very rarely noted.

The lock used on the Eliott Light Dragoon pistol (Plate 24) introduced in 1759 is unique to this pattern of round lock in having a cock comb of the style described below for the Pattern 1777 locks, and in having the pivot-screw for the steel enter from the inside of the lockplate, with its head countersunk in the reinforce of the plate. The lockplate is smaller than the other pistol locks, measuring between 5 3/16" and 5 5/16" with 5 1/4" the normal length, by 15/16" in width with a few examples as wide as 1".

The Extra Flat pistol lock as used on the "Blues", Pattern 1756 Light Dragoon pistol and Royal Forester's pistols appeared in two forms, the Pattern 1756 and the Pattern 1777. The Pattern 1756 version (Plate 25) has a lockplate measuring about 5 1/4" x 15/16" with a faceted pan. The comb of the flat, bevelled edge swan-neck cock is a straight pillar with a rounded top and no curl or notch at the front. The feather-spring has a teardrop finial. The Pattern 1777 (Plate 26) lockplate measures about 5 5/16" x 15/16" and has the usual features associated with this pattern. The underside of the pan is no longer faceted as on the Pattern 1756; it is now finished in the conventional rounded manner.

The Pattern 1777 Pistol lock (Plate 27) had only extremely limited production prior to 1783 (most of them in 1781), but examples dating to the 1790s show a slightly smaller lockplate measuring 5 5/16" x either 3/4" or 7/8", and having the usual short sear spring, teardrop feather-spring finial, un-engraved

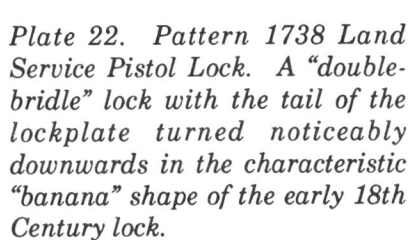

Plate 22. Pattern 1738 Land Service Pistol Lock. A "double-bridle" lock with the tail of the lockplate turned noticeably downwards in the characteristic "banana" shape of the early 18th Century lock.
Courtesy of the Board of Trustees of the Armouries.

Plate 23. Pattern 1756 Land Service Pistol Lock. The only noticeable change from the Pattern 1738 is that the lower edge of the lockplate is now almost straight.
Courtesy of Clinton M. Miller.

Plate 24. Pattern 1759 Eliott Light Dragoon Pistol Lock. First use on an Ordnance lock of an internal steel pivot-screw head, with the screw-end through the pan bridle. The comb of the cock is a straight narrow pillar with a well-developed notch at the top front.
Courtesy of the Board of Trustees of the Armouries.

Plate 25. Pattern 1756 Extra Flat Pistol Lock. Same features as the Carbine Lock of this pattern. Used on the Light Dragoon pistol of this year, and on the Pattern 1760 Royal Foresters Pistol and the "Blues" pistol.

Plate 26. Pattern 1777 Extra Flat Pistol Lock. Same features as for Carbine Locks of this pattern.

Plate 27. Pattern 1777 Land Service Pistol Lock. Similar modifications to those applied to the Musket and Carbine locks of this pattern: crudely-notched pillar form of comb, teardrop feather-spring finial, short sear-spring showing two screw-ends through the tail of the lockplate, and no engraved border lines on the top jaw and back of the steel.

Courtesy of J. Craig Nannos.

top jaw and back of steel, and pillar comb which characterize this pattern; these late examples show a far better developed curl and notch at the top of the comb than the pre-1783 examples.

Pistol—Sea Service

The Sea Service pistol lock, like its musket equivalent, is flat and "plain" with a ring-neck cock, the throat hole being a plain oval; it has two sidenails throughout our period.

The Pattern 1718 Sea Service Pistol lock (Plate 95) measures 5 1/4" x 15/16" with narrow bevelled edges. The underside of the pan is faceted and it has no bridle. The top of the steel is flat (hexagonal when seen from front or back) and the back is faceted. With only minor changes in lines and decoration, as noted below, this design continues in use on Sea Service pistols until superceded by the India Pattern pistol lock.

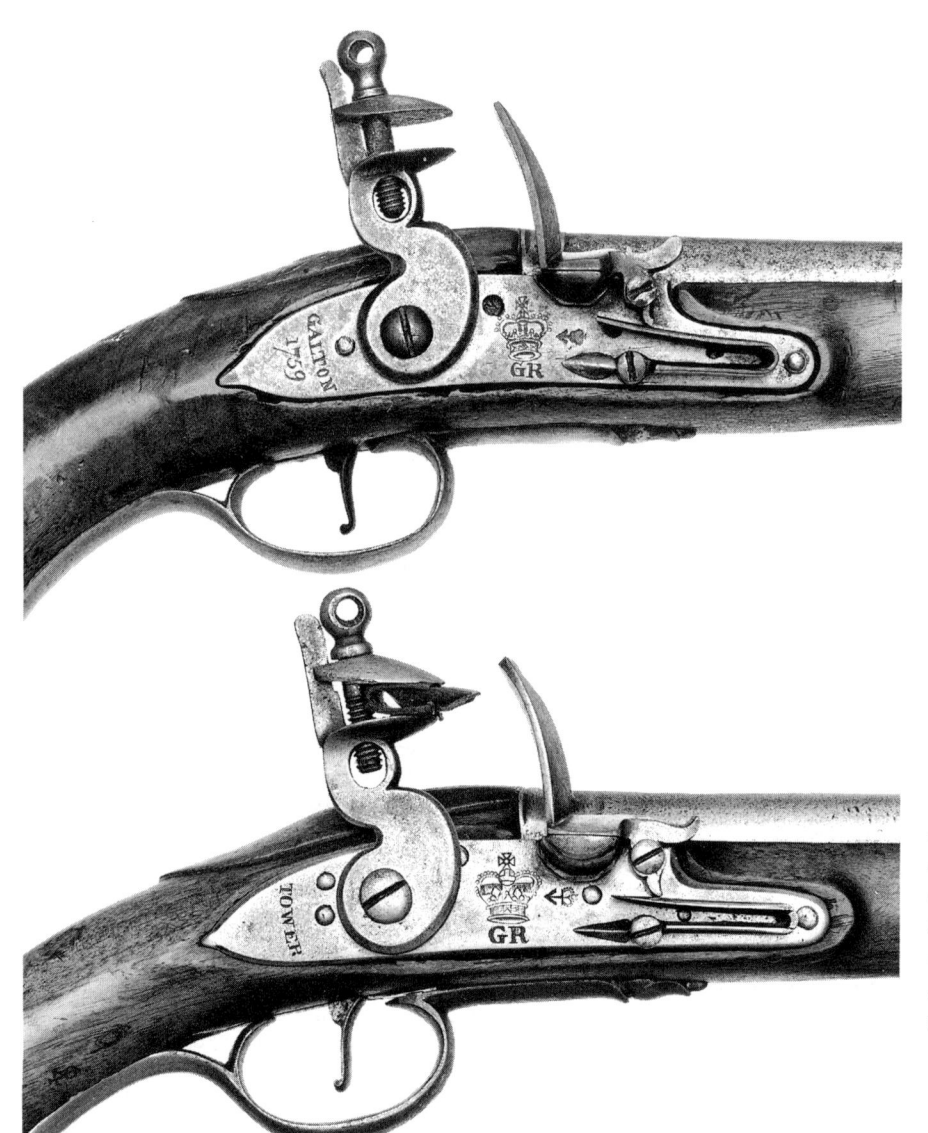

The Pattern 1756 Sea Service Pistol lock (Plate 28) measures 5 1/8" x 15/16", with a fenceless faceted pan and a round-topped steel with a vertical spine on the back. The toe of the steel follows the design of the musket lock, with a teardrop shape having a pronounced upward curl. The cock-screw is slotted and pierced. It has a long sear-spring, and spear-point shaped finial to the feather spring. There is no border-line engraving. This lock is a virtual duplicate of the Pattern 1718 except for being slightly reduced in size and produced to somewhat tighter tolerances in keeping with other Pattern 1756 locks.

The Pattern 1777 (Plate 29) changes to the Sea Service pistol lock include the use of the short sear-spring and the rounding-off of the underside of the pan replacing the earlier facets. The steel is of the conventional round-top form with a central spine down the back, and its toe is less robust with a more tapering curl. The pillar comb of the cock is made slightly heavier in design.

Plate 28. Pattern 1756 Sea Service Pistol Lock.
Courtesy of Clinton M. Miller.

Plate 29. Pattern 1777 Sea Service Pistol Lock. The underside of the pan is now rounded, the feather-spring finial is a spearpoint design, and a short sear-spring shows two screw-ends through the tail of the plate.
Courtesy of Clinton M. Miller.

Land and Sea Service Pattern Furniture

The brass furniture fitted to British military small arms during the Eighteenth Century falls into two broad categories, based on the services for which they were intended: Land Service and Sea Service. Land Service furniture is characterised by being more elaborate in outline, covering more of the surface of the wood, and by being lighter in weight per component than the Sea Service equivalent. Sea Service brass furniture is characterized by its heavy construction, simple outline and by the omission of such "extras" as the fore-end cap, tailpipe and thumbpiece.

Brass furniture made for the Board of Ordnance often bears markings cast into the inner surface of the piece, particularly the Broad Arrow, the initials TH or H (for Thomas Hollier who supplied brass furniture between 1718 and 1754). Assembly marks (see glossary) are normally filed across inner surfaces. Although they look identical externally, ramrod pipes were often file-numbered from I to IV internally.

In the following discussion, "furniture" is taken to include the fore-end cap, ramrod pipes, trigger guard, trigger plate, sidepiece, thumbpiece, and buttplate and will in all cases be described in the same order, beginning with the muzzle of the piece and working towards the butt. The names used for each piece will generally be those used by the Board of Ordnance in describing them, unless the term would create unworkable confusion, when another appropriate term will be used. Variant terms are given in parentheses after the principal term used. The design of the *trigger-plate* remains virtually unchanged and its presence is assumed without being specifically mentioned; its absence, however, will be noted whenever appropriate.

In describing the relative positions of various features the terms "front" and "rear" will be used throughout, understood to be equivalent respectively to "upper" and "lower" and to indicate a position respectively towards the muzzle or towards the butt.

LAND SERVICE

Wallpiece (Plate 30)

There were two groups of wallpieces manufactured during the period covered by this work, one in the mid-1740s and a second smaller group in the late 1770s. There was no significant change in the design of the furniture of the two production periods. No nosecap was fitted and an iron ramrod was fitted throughout.

The two *ramrod pipes* are barrel-shaped and collared, 2" long, 3/4" external diameter and 9/16" internal diameter. The *tailpipe* has a barrel-shaped and collared forward section measuring 1 7/8", a reinforcing moulding and flame-shaped tail section measuring 4 1/16", an overall length of 5 15/16"; the external diameter at mouth is 11/16" and internal diameter is 9/16". The *trigger guard* is 15 1/4" overall, the front finial modified from the conventional Land Pattern to form a flame and the surface is engraved to emphasize this design. There is only one cross-pin, just ahead of the bow, with two small woodscrews, one in the front finial and one at the back of the rear finial. The thumbpiece screw enters the lower tang behind the bow. The bow is 1 7/16" at its widest point. The rear tang terminates in a plain tapering point. The *sidepiece* is Land Pattern, flat and flush with the surface of the wood, 8 1/4" in length, with 4 5/8" between sidenail centres. The trigger axis cross-pin passes through the lower tail of the plate. The disc-outline at the rear of the plate is engraved as a shell and the body has engraved double border-lines. The *thumbpiece* is Land Pattern and measures 3 1/8" x 1 3/8". The *buttplate* closely resembles the Long Land Pattern, except that the tang terminates in a plain rounded point rather than in a ball. The tang measures 7" from the centre of the heelscrew hole to the tip; the first step measures 1 7/8", the second step 1 3/4", and the third step also 1 3/4". The plate measures 6 1/2" from heel to toe and 2 15/16" in width at its widest point. The tang and plate are engraved with double border lines (threads) around the edges and the two screw-holes.

Musket (Plates 31-35)

The following furniture was used on the Long Land, Short Land for Dragoons, Short Land for Infantry, and Marine or Militia muskets.

Nosecap (nose-band, fore-end cap). Until 1737 there was no official metal covering fitted to the forward termination of British musket stocks. Some regimental officers ordered thin sheet-brass strips to be wrapped around the extreme end of the forestock, and these are seen on Pattern 1730 and Pattern 1742 muskets. These sheet-brass additions will be termed *nosebands* to distinguish them from the heavier cast variety.

Between 1737 and early 1741 the Ordnance gunsmiths working in the Tower fitted sheet-brass ("latten") *nosebands* to about 46,500 Land Pattern muskets, using brass wire as rivets. This represents, in theory, all Pattern 1730 production as well as Pattern 1730/40 and early Pattern 1742 production. This feature was abandoned under pressure of the production expansion of 1742 and was not resumed until the close of the war in 1748.

As a result of the introduction in 1740 of an improved pattern of bayonet socket with a reinforcing collar on its lower end, and of the steel ramrod in 1748, the Board of Ordnance in 1748 ordered the first manufacture of *cast-brass nosecaps* for the new production muskets, now designated the Pattern 1748. Many hundreds of feet of sheet brass were also bought to use in adding a measure of protection to already-existing muskets. The nosecap is about 1" long, is inletted around the end of the fore-end and secured by one or two brass rivets. Regimentally fitted nosebands are normally inletted and the ends folded inside the barrel bed and held in position by the barrel. During the period covered by this work, the musket nosecap did not have a downward extension at the rear with a cut-out for the ramrod.

Ramrod Pipes. Until the end of 1756 the cast and swaged ramrod pipes on all Land Service muskets were of the same basic shape, a convex curved or barrel-shaped body with a narrow raised collar at each end, (Plate 31). These are usually about 1 3/8" to 1 5/8" in length (normally all of one length on a particular musket), with an external diameter of 7/16", and an internal diameter of from 3/8" for wooden rods to 1/4" - 5/16" for steel rods. Land Service muskets have three of these pipes as well as a tailpipe. They are secured by a single cross-pin. When the steel ramrod began to be fitted to new-production muskets in 1748, the external shape of the pipes was retained but their external diameter was slightly reduced to around 13/32" at front and rear, with an internal diameter as noted above.

With the introduction of the steel ramrod for infantry muskets in 1748, the Ordnance at first converted existing components by sleeving the upper pipe and adding a circular rod-retaining spring to the mouth of the tailpipe. These conversions proved inadequate and on the Pattern 1756 Long Land Musket and other subsequent new-production arms for steel ramrods, a new elongated pipe, the ***long trumpet forepipe*** was introduced, (Plate 32). This tapering pipe is around 4" in length with a sharply flared mouth ahead of the upper collar and with a collar at the rear of the pipe. The opening of the flared mouth is about 11/16" in diameter, but the internal diameter of the pipe is just over 1/4". This pattern of pipe is held by two cross-pins. The other pipes retain the same external shape but are reduced in diameter as noted above; the rod-retaining spring continued to be riveted inside the tailpipe.

The conventional barrel-shaped pipe created some problems in rapidly returning the rammer to its channel, as it often struck the forward edge and deformed the mouth so that the rod could not enter the pipe. In the spring of 1777 Ordnance gunmaker John Pratt submitted a pattern for the second pipe, which was a *straight-tapered* short pipe, 1 9/16" in length, with the standard collar at each end; the external diameter at the mouth of this ***Pratt pipe***, (Plate 33), is 1/2" and the rear diameter is 13/32". Although approved for adoption in May 1777, they were not produced for the Ordnance until March 1779. Pratt himself became an Ordnance contractor in the meantime and during 1778 was allowed to supply several thousand muskets which *presumably* incorporated his second-pipe design; muskets made under the Ordnance system did not incorporate them prior to the late spring of 1779 at the very earliest.

The ***tailpipe*** protects the entry point of the ramrod into the closed lower area of the ramrod channel. It is shaped in its forward part the same as the other pipes and is usually about the same length with a slightly smaller internal diameter, but added to the back of this basic shape is a reinforcing moulding and a flame-shaped tail covering the thinnest part of the rod channel.

There are two variants of the tailpipe, one for the wooden rammer, and one for the steel rammer introduced on the Pattern 1748. The wooden rammer pipe is larger and longer than the steel rammer version. The wooden rammer version (Plate 31) has a barrel-shaped section about 1 5/8" long and the middle or lip section is short and curled, measuring between 2 3/4" and 3 1/8" including the flame-shaped tail. The internal diameter of the pipe is 3/8". The steel rammer version (Plate 32) measures 1 5/16" in the barrel-shaped section. The central lip section is longer, flatter and with the tail section (which is somewhat narrower in outline) measures between 3 1/4" and 3 3/16" in length. There is a rod-retaining spring riveted to the inside of this pipe and its internal diameter is from 1/4" to 5/16". Both variants are secured by a single cross-pin. The lip and tail section add from 3 to 3 1/4" to the length of the pipe. This pipe is also secured by a single cross-pin.

The Land Pattern ***trigger guard*** appeared in two forms, the first, (Plate 31), used only on the Pattern 1730 musket and some of the very early production transitional Pattern 1730/40 muskets; the second, (Plate 31-33), being the most familiar form used on all subsequent Long Land and Short Land muskets and, in smaller versions, on most carbines and pistols. The Pattern 1730 design, with each finial terminating in a distinctive rounded surface pear-shape outline, is 11 1/2" in length and secured to the stock by two cross-pins, one ahead of the bow and one to the rear of it and by the thumbpiece screw through the upper part of the rear guard tang. The second pattern, although it appeared on some secondary production (such as wallpieces and pistols) and probable pattern arms as early as 1737, is termed the Pattern 1742 trigger guard since this is the first all-new production mainline pattern to use it. It is also 11 1/4" long on Pattern 1742 muskets but may be as short as 11 1/8" on some of the later patterns of Long and Short Land muskets. It is secured in the same manner as the earlier pattern.

The Land Pattern *sidepiece* (sideplate) remains of the same basic outline throughout the period covered by this work (Plate 31-34) but is found with a rounded surface standing proud of the surrounding wood, or with a flat surface inlaid flush with the surface of the wood. All Long Land patterns have the rounded surface variety, as well as the Dragoon muskets and the Pattern 1769 Short Land Musket for Line Infantry, while the Marine or Militia muskets, the Pattern 1776 rifles and later Short Land Infantry muskets have the flat pattern sidepiece. All round-surface sidepieces have the plate recessed for the sidenail heads, while the flat version is not recessed and the heads remain above its surface. Length varies between 6 and 6 1/4" in both versions. The flat version is slightly undercut, the inner surface being slightly smaller than the outer surface, in order to ensure a close fit in the wood.

The Land Pattern *thumbpiece* is of a single design (Plate 31-33) with no intentional variations apart from those inherent in hand-finishing the casting. It is flat and inlaid flush with the surface of the wood, and cast with a curve to fit the contour of the top of the grip. It is secured by a screw from beneath, entering through the rear trigger guard tang near the rear of the guard bow. Its measurements vary between 2 11/16" and 2 9/16" in length, and between 1 1/8" and 1 1/16" in width.

There are two Land Pattern musket *buttplates*, the Long Land, introduced on the Pattern 1730, and the Short Land, introduced on the Pattern 1769. The ***Long Land*** (Plate 31-32) has a tang about 6" long, tapering to a ball-terminal in three steps: the first measuring between 1 3/8" and 1 9/16" with a squared shoulder at the upper end; the second measuring between 1 1/4" and 1 7/16" and the third step 1 5/8" to 1 7/8". The tang is held by a cross-pin. The buttplate itself measures from heel to toe between 5 1/4" and 5 1/2" and is between 2 1/16" and 2 1/4" wide at its widest point. There are two buttplate screws, countersunk and filed flush with the surrounding surface of the brass, one at the point of the heel and the other near the toe of the plate. The Short Land tang (Plate 33) is tapered in two steps, but is only 3 7/8" in length. The first step measures 1 5/16", the second step to the tip 1 3/8". The tang is secured by a cross-pin. The buttplate measures 5 1/8" from heel to toe, and is 2 1/8" at its widest point, being secured with two woodscrews in the same manner as the Long Land.

The ***Marine*** or ***Militia*** musket, which was included under Land Pattern arms for almost all of the period covered by this work, in either wood rammer or steel rammer version, uses Land Pattern furniture with the following exceptions: the ***Pattern 1757 wood rammer*** version has neither nosecap, tailpipe nor thumbpiece, and has the second pattern of sidepiece which is flat and flush. The ***Pattern 1759 steel rammer*** version has both nosecap and tailpipe, but also lacks a thumbpiece. The *buttplate* for both patterns of this musket has a distinctive tang design unique to this pattern (Plate 34), characterized by a tapering two-step design 4" in length, with a 3/8" diameter woodscrew through it 2 5/8" from the centre of the heelscrew, rather than a cross-pin. The length of the first step of the tang is 1 9/16" and of the second, to the tip, 1 3/8". The buttplate measures about 5 1/8" from heel to toe, and is 2" in width at its widest point.

The brass furniture for the two production runs of muskets described as being for Land and Sea Service (Patterns 1738 and 1746), is of a design unique to these muskets. (Plate 35). No nosecap, tailpipe or thumbpiece was fitted. There are three standard Land Pattern *ramrod pipes*. The *trigger guard* measures between 11" and 11 5/16" overall and has a rounded surface. The rounded surface three-screw *sidepiece* measures 7 1/4" overall, and has an oval depression with a raised edge between the centre and rear sidenail. The *buttplate* tang is 4 3/8" to 4 1/2" overall, with three steps measuring 1 1/8", 1 1/16" and 15/16"; the plate measures 5 7/16" from heel to toe and between 2 1/16" and 2 3/16" at its widest point. The inner surface of the buttplate generally has 17 Broad Arrow 46 cast into it.

Carbine

In general most of the Land Pattern furniture for Carbines is of the same design as that for muskets, but made to a reduced scale. It is only with the Serjeant of Grenadier's Carbine and the various regimental carbines which appeared from 1745 (Lord Loudoun's, Royal Horse Guards or "Blues," Eliott's and Royal Foresters') and the Light Infantry Carbine that important variations in furniture design are introduced. The regular service carbines, i.e.

25

those for the Horse (Cavalry), the Artillery and Highlanders, and the Light Dragoon Pattern 1756, all share most elements of Land Pattern furniture in common with certain minor modifications to suit the particular purposes of the pattern. The Cavalry carbine, being stocked to the muzzle and not intended for a bayonet, lacks a nosecap; it also has the front of the trigger guard bow pinched in, and is not drilled for a sling swivel screw. The Cavalry and Light Dragoon carbines have a small section of the rear sidenail recess on the sidepiece cut away to accomodate the rear fastening for the sling-bar.

The "common" furniture for these carbines is as follows:

The *ramrod pipes* for wooden rammer carbines are barrel-shaped and collared, and about 1 5/16" long, with a maximum external diameter of about 7/16-1/2" and an average internal diameter of 1/4"-5/16". On carbines manufactured with steel rammers the internal measurements are somewhat reduced, to between 3/16" and 1/4". On the Pattern 1756 Light Dragoon Carbine, and the Pattern 1779 Cavalry Carbines which were made up for the use of Loyalist mounted militia in the Southern Colonies, the early pattern of long tapered trumpet forepipe is fitted (Plate 38); this is cast in one piece but has the appearance of the joining of a flared-mouth and collared upper pipe to a barrel-shaped and collared lower pipe, to give a double-collared effect in the centre of the pipe. They are about 3 11/16" in overall length.

The *trigger guard* varies in length from 10 1/2" to 11 1/4" and, on those patterns intended for mounted troops and fitted with a sling-bar, the front terminal of the guard bow is reduced to a pillar about 5/16" in diameter with no hole drilled for a lower sling-swivel screw (Plate 36).

The *sidepiece* (Plate 36) is about 5 1/2" long with 3 5/16" between the centres of the sidenails. On those patterns fitted for sling-bars, the rear sidenail recess usually holds the rear of the *sling-bar*, with the head of the elongated rear sidenail on top of it, and the sidepiece recess often has a cut-away section on the left side (towards the muzzle) for the base of the bar. The sling-bar is between 8 5/8" and 8 15/16" long in its straight section, secured by the slightly longer rear sidenail in the recess in the counterboring of the sidepiece, and by a screw through the fore-end into a rounded surface teardrop shaped finial on the front base of the bar. (Plate 38).

The *thumbpiece* (Plate 36) measures about 2 3/8" in length and 15/16" wide at its widest point.

The *buttplate* (Plate 36) is similar to that of the Long Land Pattern musket in having a three-step tapering tang measuring 4 3/4" to 4 7/8", the depth of the plate itself from heel to toe being virtually equal in length and between 1 7/8" and 2" in width at its widest point. The distance from the first to the second step of the tang measures 1 3/8" to 1 7/16", from the second to the third 1 1/16"; and from the third to the pointed tip just over 1 1/16".

The *Pattern 1760 Light Infantry Carbine*, with the exception of the ramrod pipes and the sidepiece, is fitted with furniture of a design used only on the Lord Loudoun Carbine. The sheet-brass *noseband* is between 9/16" and 5/8" wide, secured by an iron rivet, and was either open or closed at the front. The three Land Pattern *rammer pipes* of very thin construction are 1 7/16" long with an external diameter of 7/16" and internal diameter of 5/16". The Land Pattern *tailpipe* is 5" overall. The *trigger guard*, which measures 10 1/2" overall, has a flared front tang 13/16" wide when it steps, and continues in a convex taper for 1 1/16" to terminate in a slight curl with a disc tip (Plate 37). The bow measures 1 1/8" at its widest point and there is no reinforcing forward curl at the rear. The rear tang has a step and curves to a plain pointed finial. There is no trigger-plate and an iron nut inlet ahead of the trigger serves to anchor the barrel tang screw. The *sidepiece* is Land Pattern with a rounded surface, and measures 5 1/2" overall and 3 3/16" between sidenail centres. The *thumbpiece* (Plate 37) is an oval with a trefoil flower-head at the bottom, measuring 2 1/8" x 1". The *buttplate tang* (Plate 37) measures 2 3/4", and has two tapering steps, the first concave and measuring 7/8", the second convex being 1" to the plain pointed tip. The plate measures 5 13/16" heel to toe and is 2 1/16" at its widest point.

The *Pattern 1770 Serjeant of Grenadier's Carbine* with its unique 39-inch .66 calibre barrel, uses conventional Land Pattern, carbine-size furniture for its nosecap, long trumpet forepipe, two rammer pipes, tailpipe, trigger guard and butt-plate. But the sidepiece is of the Eliott Light Dragoon Carbine pattern and there is a unique plain oval thumbpiece (Plate 36).

Of the several regimentally-designed carbines, only the Lord Loudoun, the earliest patterns of the Eliott and the Royal Foresters' come within the scope of this study.

The *Pattern 1745 Lord Loudoun Carbine* (Plate 38), the earliest identified British light infantry carbine, introduces a design of furniture used only on it and the Pattern 1760 Light Infantry Carbine. The sheet-brass *noseband* has a closed front and is 15/16" long, secured by one rivet. The four barrel-shaped and collared *ramrod pipes* are Land Pattern, but vary slightly in length: the upper pipe being 1 7/16" and the second and third pipes 1 3/8"; the tailpipe has a 1 3/8" front section and 1 13/16" rear section. The *trigger guard* measures 10 5/8" overall, the front finial at first flaring to a step, and then curving inwards to terminate in a ball; the rear finial is stepped and curved. It is secured by two pins and the thumbpiece screw. The *sidepiece* is unique to this pattern. It has a slightly convex surface and is roughly triangular in outline. It measures 5 3/4" with 3 1/16" between sidenail centres. The sidenail recesses each have a narrow raised rim around them. The *thumbpiece* is an oval with a trefoil-flower outline at its base, measuring 2 1/8" x 1 1/16". There is no *trigger plate*, a rectangular iron nut serving to anchor the barrel tang screw. The *buttplate* has a very short tang with a single step at 3/4" from the heel, curving for 1 1/16" to a point. The tang measures 2 3/4" from the heelscrew. The plate measures 5" from heel to toe, and 2 1/8" at its widest point.

The *Pattern 1760 Eliott Carbine* (Plate 39) uses the same *ramrod pipes* as the Pattern 1756 Light Dragoon Carbine for wooden rammer, including the composite pattern long forepipe. There is no thumbpiece or nosecap. The *trigger guard*, sidepiece and buttplate are all of a design peculiar to the Eliott. The trigger guard is 10 1/8" overall, with a flaring front tang measuring just over 5/8" wide at the point where it steps and curves for 1" to a disc-tipped point. The guard bow is 1" at its widest point. The rear finial has a step 13/16" from the pointed tip. At 1 1/4" from the rear finial there is a full-width lug cast into the tang, 5/16" thick, intended to be drilled for a lower sling swivel screw, but on most examples noted this has not been drilled. The *sidepiece* is flat and flush with the surface of the wood, measuring 3 7/8" in length with 3 5/16" between sidenail centres. This same pattern is also used on the Eliott Light Dragoon pistol, on the Serjeants of Grenadiers Carbine, and much later on the Baker Rifle. The *buttplate tang* measures 2 7/8" overall and has a large sharp shoulder at its base before tapering to a sharp point in two steps measuring just over 1 1/4" and 7/8" respectively.

At the time of writing no *Pattern 1760 Royal Foresters' Carbine* has been identified. The *Pattern 1776 Royal Foresters' Carbine* (Plate 40) is distinguished by its flat lock and its furniture, which is a combination of Pattern 1773 Eliott (notched nosecap, swell-and-groove rammer and sidepiece), Land Pattern Carbine for steel rammer (ramrod pipes and trigger guard). The *sidepiece* is flat and flush with the wood, having the same outline as the Royal Horse Guards Carbine. The sling-bar is 5" long in its straight section and is held at the rear by the rear side-nail. Unlike the common *sling-bar* this variant has a flat teardrop shaped finial extending slightly downwards and to the rear with a woodscrew through its end. At the front the bar has a figure-eight base plate and a matching design of plate inlet into the right side of the fore-end, with two screws one inch apart passing through the fore-end, the front screw from right to left and the rear screw from left to right. The *trigger guard* measures 8 3/4" overall, with the bow being 1 1/16" at its widest point. The *buttplate tang* is a foreshortened version of the Land Pattern Carbine design with the three steps measuring 1 1/16", 11/16" and 1" respectively.

Rifle

The *Pattern 1776 Infantry Rifle* furniture is a combination of Land Pattern and new designs. The *nosecap* (Plate 41) is iron 1 7/8" long including a rearward extension and held by a screw from the barrel-bed. The short trumpet *forepipe* is 1 3/4" long and secured by a screw from the barrel-bed at the front and a cross-pin at the rear. The middle pipe is cylindrical, 1 7/16" long, with a collar at each end. A slightly curved ramrod-retaining spring is riveted to the inside rear of the forepipe and the front of the middle pipe. The middle pipe is held by two cross-pins. The *tailpipe* is Land Pattern, 2 5/16" long. All three pipes have an internal diameter of about 1/2" to accommodate the heavy iron swivel rammer. The *trigger guard* (Plates 41 and 86) is of the grip-rail type and measures 9" overall, being held by two pins. The *sidepiece* (Plate 41) is Land Pattern with a flat surface and measures 5 1/2", the two sidenails being recessed into the surface. There is no thumbpiece. The *buttplate tang* (Plate 41) is similar to the Short Land Pattern musket design, but longer, measuring 4" overall with three steps measuring 1 1/4", 1 3/16" and 15/16 to the tip.

Sling-swivels are fitted through the fore-end and at the front of the trigger guard bow.

Pistol (Plates 42 & 43).

Until 1756 Land Pattern pistols (today often and incorrectly called the "Heavy Dragoon" pistol) were made only with a 12-inch barrel, fully stocked, and made in either .56 (pistol-bore) or .66 (carbine-bore) calibre. The furniture on these two calibres of pistol was identical and consisted of two ramrod pipes, trigger guard, trigger plate, sidepiece, thumbpiece and a long-spurred buttcap. The ramrod pipes, trigger guard, sidepiece and thumbpiece are reduced-scale copies of the Land Pattern musket furniture. Pistols throughout the period covered by this work were fitted with wooden ramrods having a tapered closed brass cap. The Patterns 1738 and 1756 use the same pattern of furniture as the Pattern 1730 with the sole exception of the trigger guard and buttcap which are unique to the Pattern 1730.

The *ramrod pipe* is 1 1/8" to 1 3/16" long 7/16" in diameter at front and rear with an internal diameter of 5/16".

The *tailpipe* has a barrel-shaped section like the other pipe 1 1/16" long with a lip and tail section 2" long.

The *trigger guard* is 7 3/8" in length (Pattern 1738 is 8") and is unique to this pattern in having a pear-shaped upper finial identical in design to the Pattern 1730 musket guard. All subsequent patterns have the familiar acorn-shaped front finial. It is secured by a cross-pin near the front finial and another near the rear finial, as well as by the thumbpiece screw through the rear tang. The bow is 1" wide at its widest point.

The *sidepiece* has a rounded surface standing proud of the surrounding wood, and measures 4 3/4" in length and is very slightly narrower than on the subsequent patterns.

The *thumbpiece* measures about 2 1/8" x 7/8" and is secured in the same manner as the muskets and carbines by a screw from beneath through the rear trigger guard tang.

The *buttcap* is secured by a woodscrew through the centre of the base of the cap. The rounded base has a raised central moulded boss. A long tapering spur runs up from each side of the cap towards the lock and sidepiece; these are pointed at the front and dovetailed into the wood to secure them; they measure about 4" from the step of the buttcap. The Pattern 1730 has a second mask, the Pattern 1738 has only a single mask.

The *Light Dragoon Pistol, Pattern 1756*. (Plate 44) This new pistol was designed for the troops of light dragoons added to each of eleven regiments of Dragoon Guards and Dragoons early in 1756. Although the single ramrod pipe and thumbpiece are of the Land Pattern, all the other brass furniture is of a new lighter design. The *sidepiece* is flat and flush with the surface of the wood, the outline being adapted from a civilian design popular from the 1720s. The *trigger guard* is both simpler in design and lighter with no contouring on the surface. The *buttcap* resembles that on the earlier Land Service pistol but replaces the long tapering side-spurs with short blunt ones closer in design to those of the Sea Service pistol.

The *Eliott Light Dragoon Pistol, Pattern 1759*. (Plate 44) did not see service in America during the Seven Years' (French & Indian) War but was the chief pistol used by British forces in North America during the American War. The brass furniture of this pattern was much reduced and lightened. There was no nosecap, only one ramrod pipe, no tailpipe, no trigger-plate, no thumbpiece, and a short-spurred buttcap.

The *Light Dragoon rammer pipe* is 1 1/4" long but otherwise of the same dimensions as the Land Service pistol pipe; 7/16" external diameter, with an internal diameter of 3/8" for the shorter and thicker wooden rod.

The *trigger guard* is of a design originating with this pattern and used with variations for several later patterns. It is 6 1/2" in length, with a front finial which flares out from the guard bow, and is then stepped in a convex taper to end in a point capped by a small ball. It is only slightly rounded on the surface and much lighter than the Land Service pattern. The bow is 3/4" wide at its widest point. The guard is secured by a cross-pin through the front, and through the rear tang.

The Eliott Light Dragoon *sidepiece* is that of the Pattern 1756 Light Dragoon pistol and is also used on the Eliott Carbine of 1760. It is flat and flush with the surface of the wood and is 3 1/8" long with 2 3/4" between sidenail centres.

The *Royal Forester's Light Dragoon Pistols, Patterns 1760 and 1776* (Plate 45), saw service with Burgoyne's (16th) Light Dragoons, the Pattern 1776 being set up for the regiment just before they sailed for America in 1776. These two patterns share a common design of furniture based on Land Pattern, Light Dragoon and Royal Horse Guards designs.

There is no *fore-end cap* or *tailpipe*; there is a single barrel-shaped and collared Land Pattern *rammer pipe* 1 1/4" long for wooden rammer.

The Land Pattern *thumbpiece* measures 2" x 3/4".

The *sidepiece* of the Royal Horse Guards pattern, flat with a bevelled edge standing proud of the wood, except for the tail section which is stepped and flush with the wood with a small woodscrew just ahead of the bevel. The plate is 5" long, and all screwheads are recessed in the brass. The tip of the trigger cross-pin is usually visible through the brass.

The Light Dragoon pattern *trigger guard* is 7" overall and held by a pin at the front and a screw through the lower tang.

The long-spurred *buttcap* is of the Land Pattern for pistols with a single plain mask measuring 1 9/16" x 1 3/8", the tapering sidespurs extending 3 1/4" up the sides of the grip.

SEA SERVICE

Musket (Plate 46).

Throughout this period the Sea Service Musket, whether in the long-barrelled "Bright" or short-barrelled "Black" version, was fitted with a wooden rammer and was not fitted with either a nosecap, tailpipe or thumbpiece.

The *ramrod pipes* are barrel-shaped and collared, measuring 1 5/8" long and 9/16" at their widest point, with an internal diameter of 3/8". Three of these were fitted to the long-barrelled version and two to the short-barrelled.

The *trigger guard* is a characteristic feature of Sea Service muskets, being of heavy construction with a well-rounded section, and a large circular front finial 15/16" to 1" in diameter. It measures 9 3/4" overall, the lower tang is 1 3/16" wide and the bow measures 1 3/16" at its widest point. Until 1752 the front reinforce of the bow was not drilled for a lower sling swivel screw on the Black Sea Service muskets.

The *sidepiece* is of two different patterns. The earlier type for three sidenails was in use until 1756; from 1757 onwards a two-sidenail piece, Land Pattern in outline but with a flat surface flush with the wood as was fitted to the Marine or Militia muskets and for the Short Land muskets from 1775, was adopted for the Sea Service muskets. The three-screw form measures 7 5/16" long, 3 11/16" between the front and centre sidenail centres, and 3 3/16" between the centre and rear sidenail centres.

The *buttplate* is formed of flat brass of uniform thickness, and is radiused at the heel for strength and to prevent damage to deck planking. The tang measured from the vertical plane of the plate, measures 3 1/4", the parallel sides having one curved step 2 1/8" long, terminating in a plain rounded tip secured by a wood-screw 5/8" from the tip. The plate measured from the horizontal plane of the tang is 5 7/16" from heel to toe, and 2 1/8" across its widest point. The heel screw is located 1 1/16" below the heel itself.

Seven Barrel Gun (Plate 47).

The furniture of the so-called "Volley Gun" first produced for the Ordnance by Henry Nock during 1779 consists of three ramrod pipes, trigger guard, sidepiece and buttplate.

All three *ramrod pipes* differ from the current Ordnance patterns. The upper *trumpet pipe* measures 3 5/16" overall, and is much more flared and tapered than usual. The *middle pipe* resembles the India Pattern but has a larger and more curved flare with a double collar at the rear and is 1 3/4" in length. The *lower pipe* is 1 7/16" long and has a double collar at each end.

The *trigger guard* is 6 3/4" overall, and has a very short blunt Land Pattern front finial with a screw through it.

The *sidepiece* is 3 5/8" overall with a rounded surface, with 3" between sidenail centres.

The *buttplate* tang is of the standard Short Land Pattern, measuring 3 3/4" overall, the steps being 1 3/8" and 1 1/4" respectively. The plate measures 5 5/16" from heel to toe and 2 1/8" at its widest point.

Musketoon and Blunderbuss.

For Ordnance definitions of these two arms see glossary. Very few examples of either of these Sea Service weapons have been located at the time of writing. In general the furniture follows the standard for Sea Service Muskets as regards pipes, trigger guard and buttplate, but see Part Two for specific examples.

Pistol (Plate 48).

The *Pattern 1718 Sea Service Pistol* remained the basis for production, with only minor variations to the stylistic rendering of the basic design, until 1757. There was a gap in production from 1721 until 1735.

The *Pattern 1718 Sea Service Pistol* is not fitted with a nosecap, tailpipe or thumbpiece. It has a single *ramrod pipe* which is finished either parallel or very slightly barrel-shaped and collared, measuring 1 1/4" long, with an internal diameter of 5/16+". The Land Pattern *trigger guard* measures 7 1/4" long. There is no trigger plate, a square iron nut serving as anchor for the barrel tang screw. The *sidepiece* is flat and flush with the surface, 4 7/8" long with 2 11/16" between sidenail centres. The tail terminates in an upward curl, and a hole through the plate for the stud on the inner surface of the belt-hook (which is held under the head of the rear sidenail) is in line with the front sidenail. The iron *belt-hook* or "rib" as it was known to the Ordnance is flat along its inner surface and slightly convex on its outer surface, flaring slightly outwards away from the pistol at the front. Its overall length is about 8 7/8", and the length of the hook itself about 7 1/4". It is held to the pistol by the slightly over-length rear sidenail which seats in a countersink on the hook's baseplate, and fixed in position by a stud on the underside of the baseplate which drops into the hole in the sidepiece referred to above. The *buttcap* has short rounded spurs on each side, and a plain rounded base.

The furniture of the *Pattern 1756 Sea Service Pistol* is the same as that for the Pattern 1718, described above.

The only variations observed in the furniture of the *Pattern 1756/77 Pistol* are in the sidepiece and the length of the trigger guard, which is 1/4" longer than the earlier pattern at 7 1/2". The *sidepiece* is similar in design but the tail is less swept upwards at the rear, and the hole for the belt-hook stud is higher, and the trigger cross-pin passes through the lower part of the plate, making two holes in the tail.

FLAT

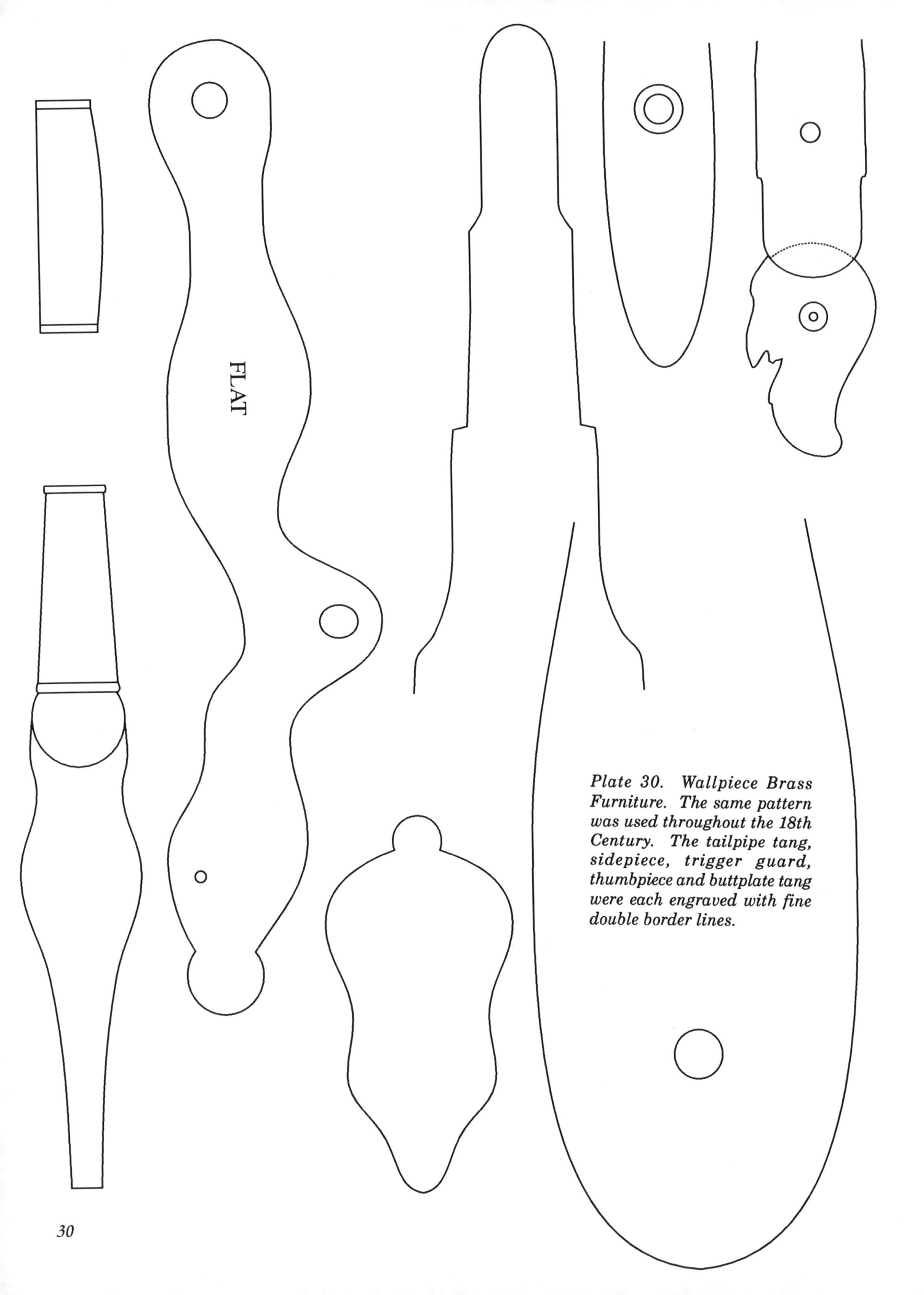

Plate 30. Wallpiece Brass Furniture. The same pattern was used throughout the 18th Century. The tailpipe tang, sidepiece, trigger guard, thumbpiece and buttplate tang were each engraved with fine double border lines.

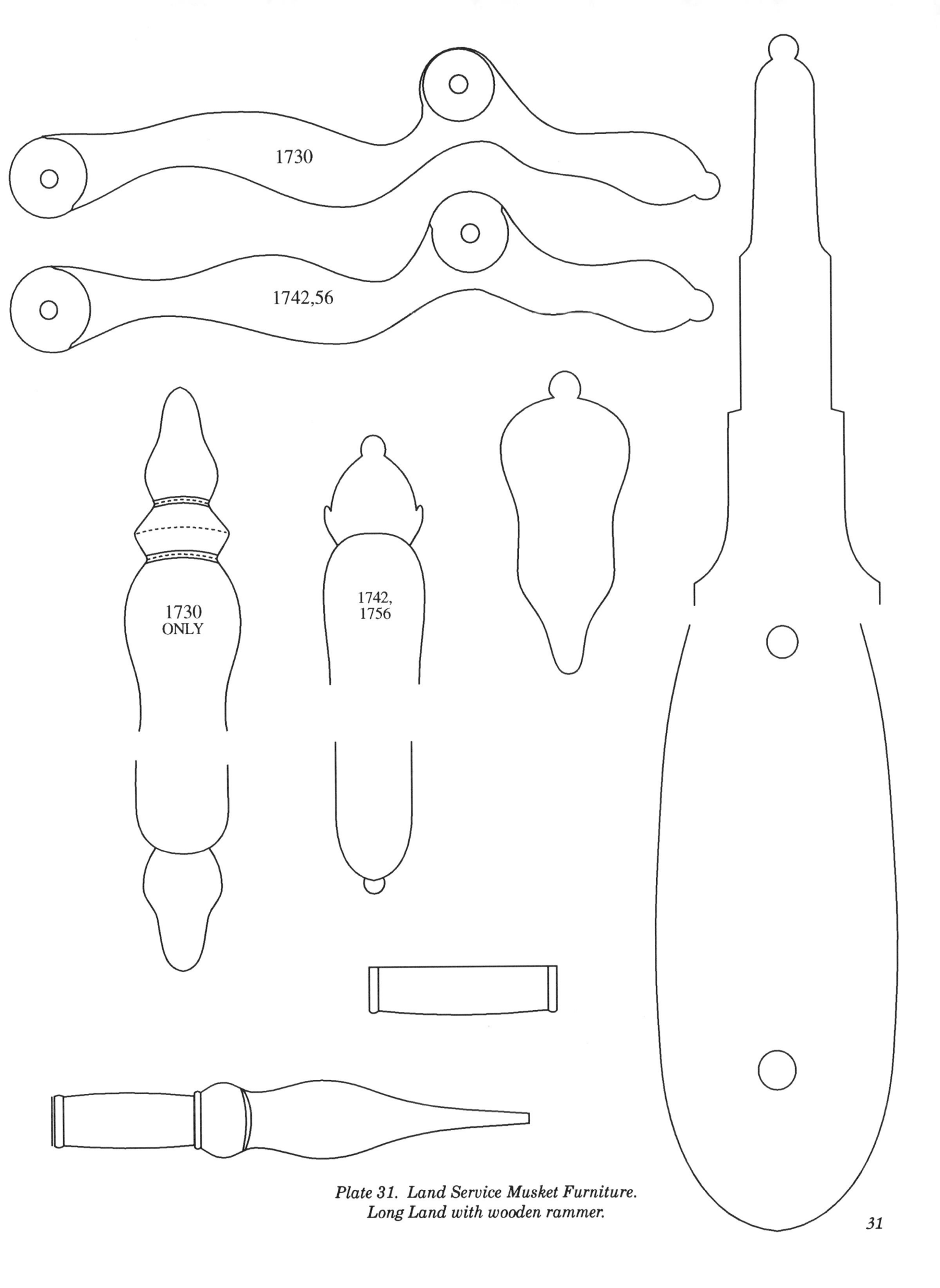

Plate 31. Land Service Musket Furniture. Long Land with wooden rammer.

31

1742, 56

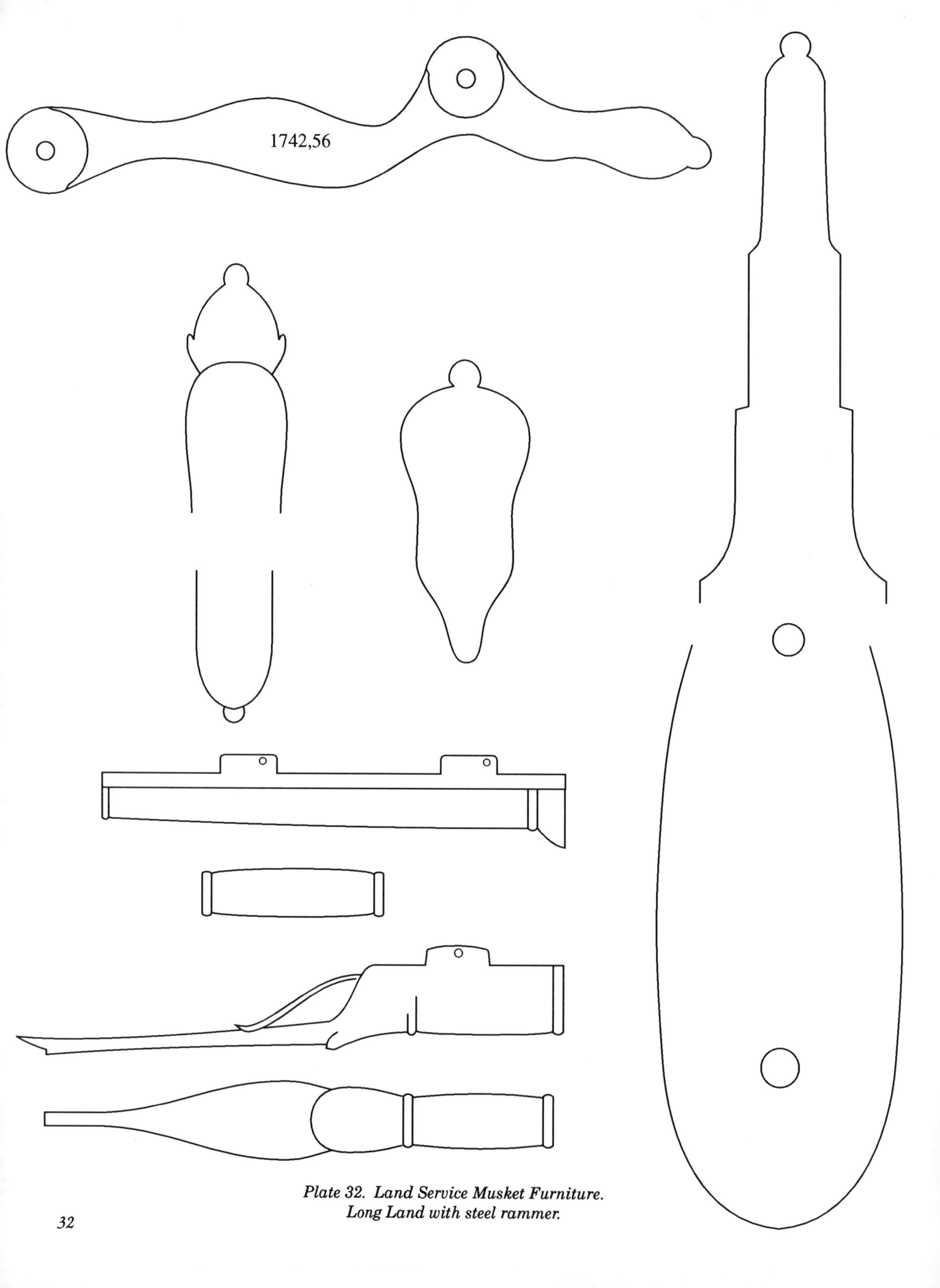

Plate 32. Land Service Musket Furniture.
Long Land with steel rammer.

FLAT FROM
LATE 1775

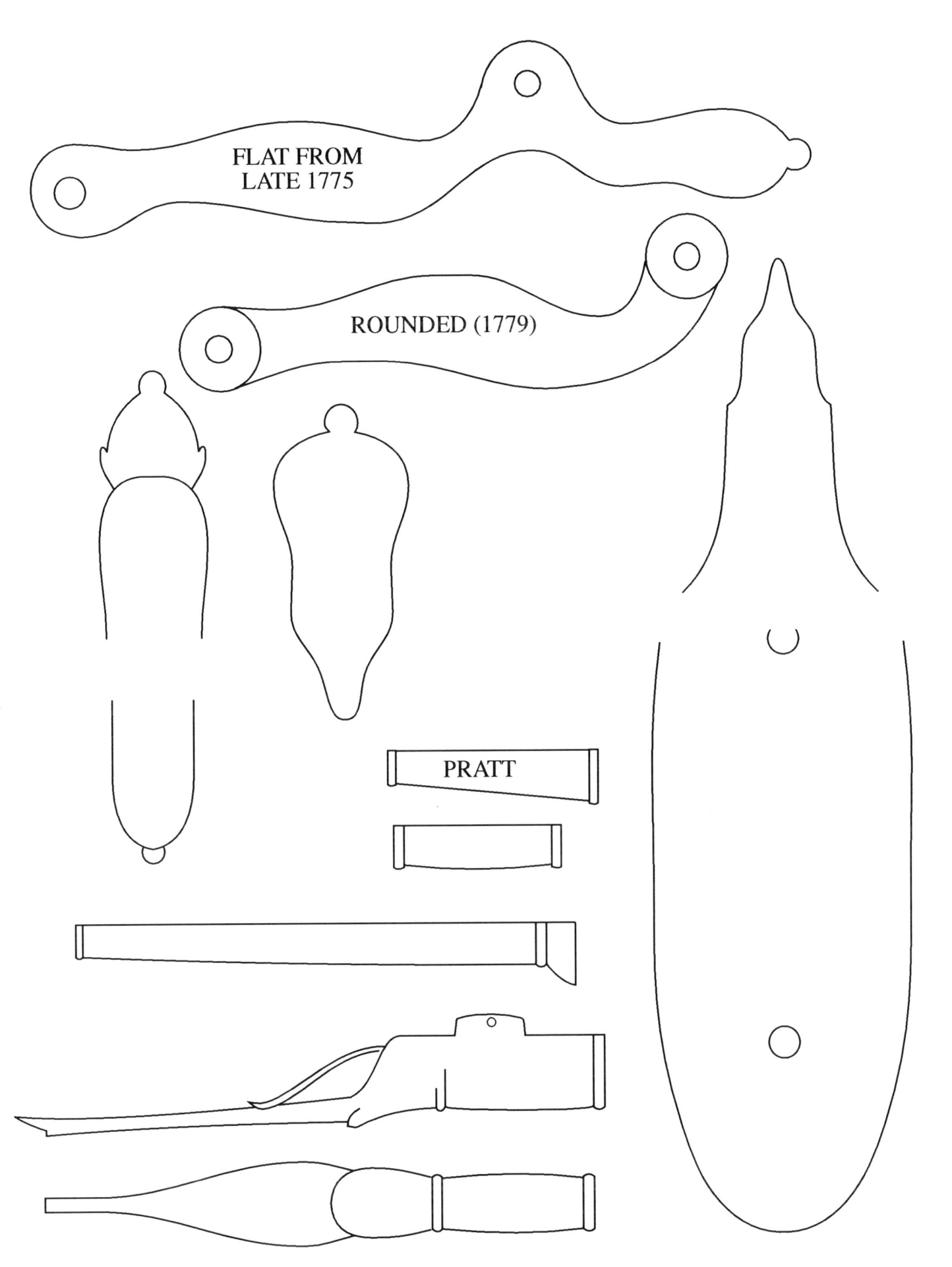

ROUNDED (1779)

PRATT

*Plate 33. Land Service Musket Furniture.
Short Land Pattern with steel rammer.*

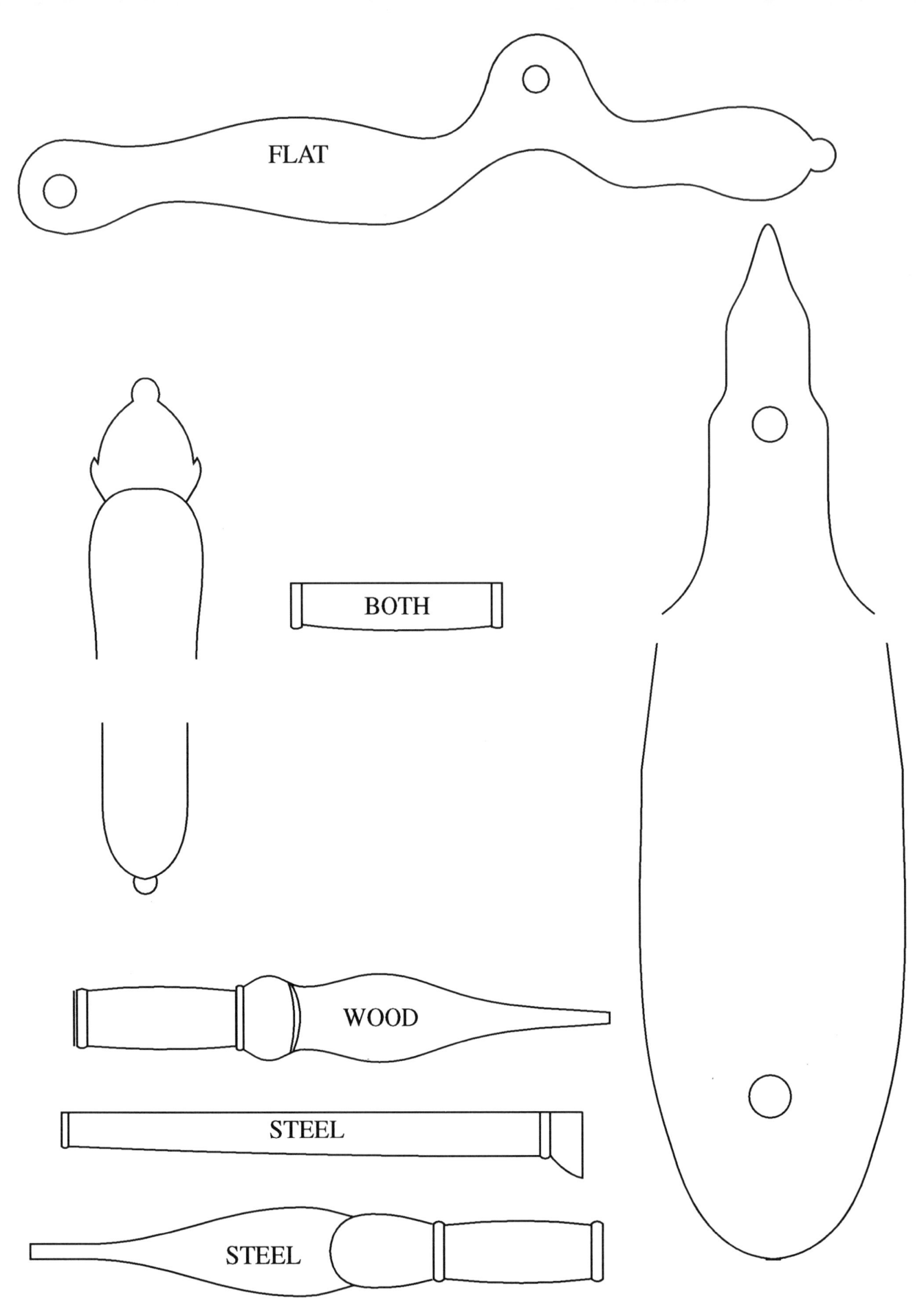

Plate 34. Marine or Militia Musket Furniture, wooden and steel rammer.

34

ROUNDED

RAISED EDGE, CONCAVE

1746
(INTERNAL)

Plate 35. Pattern 1738 and 1746 Long Land and Sea Service Musket Furniture.

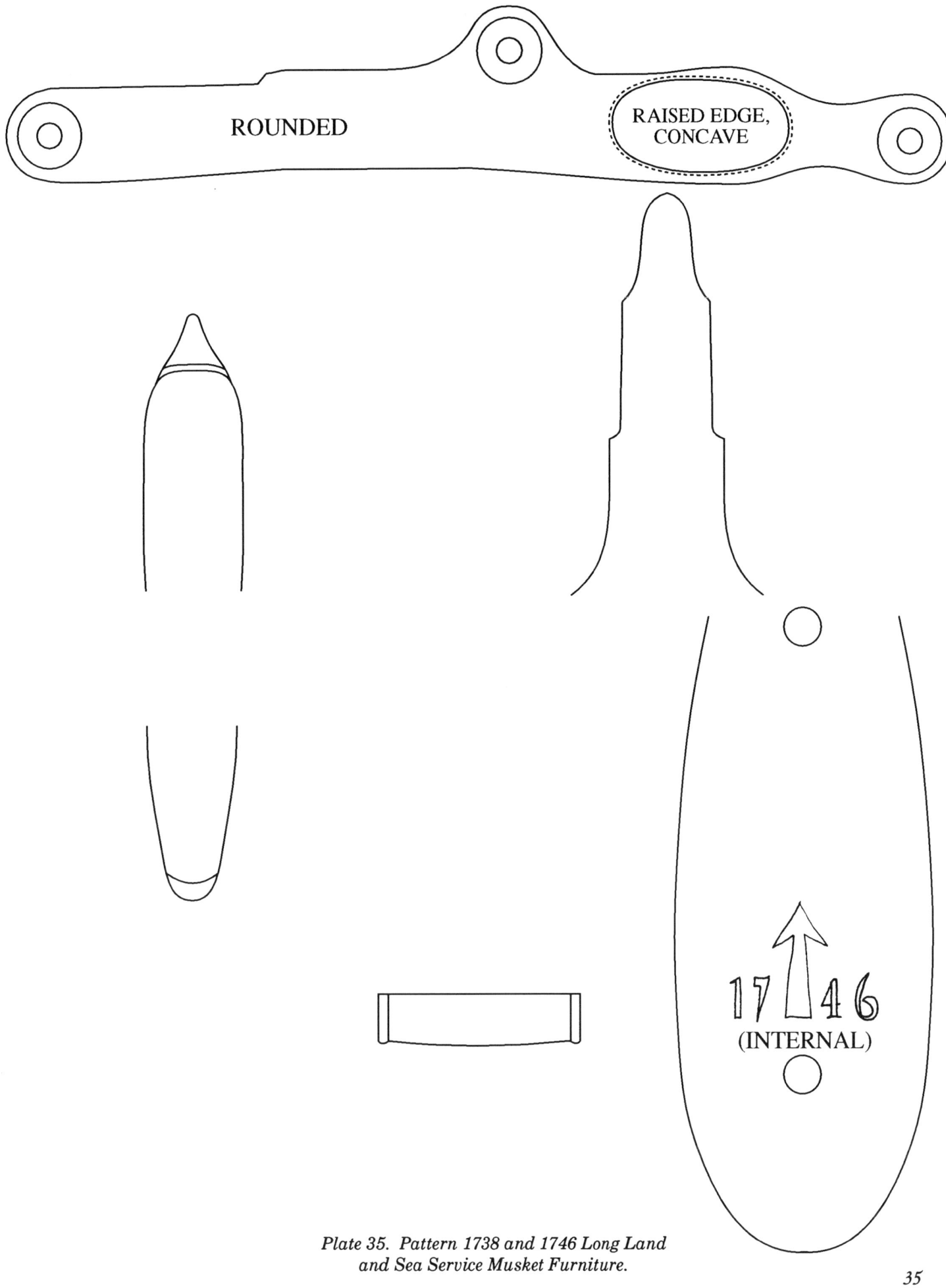

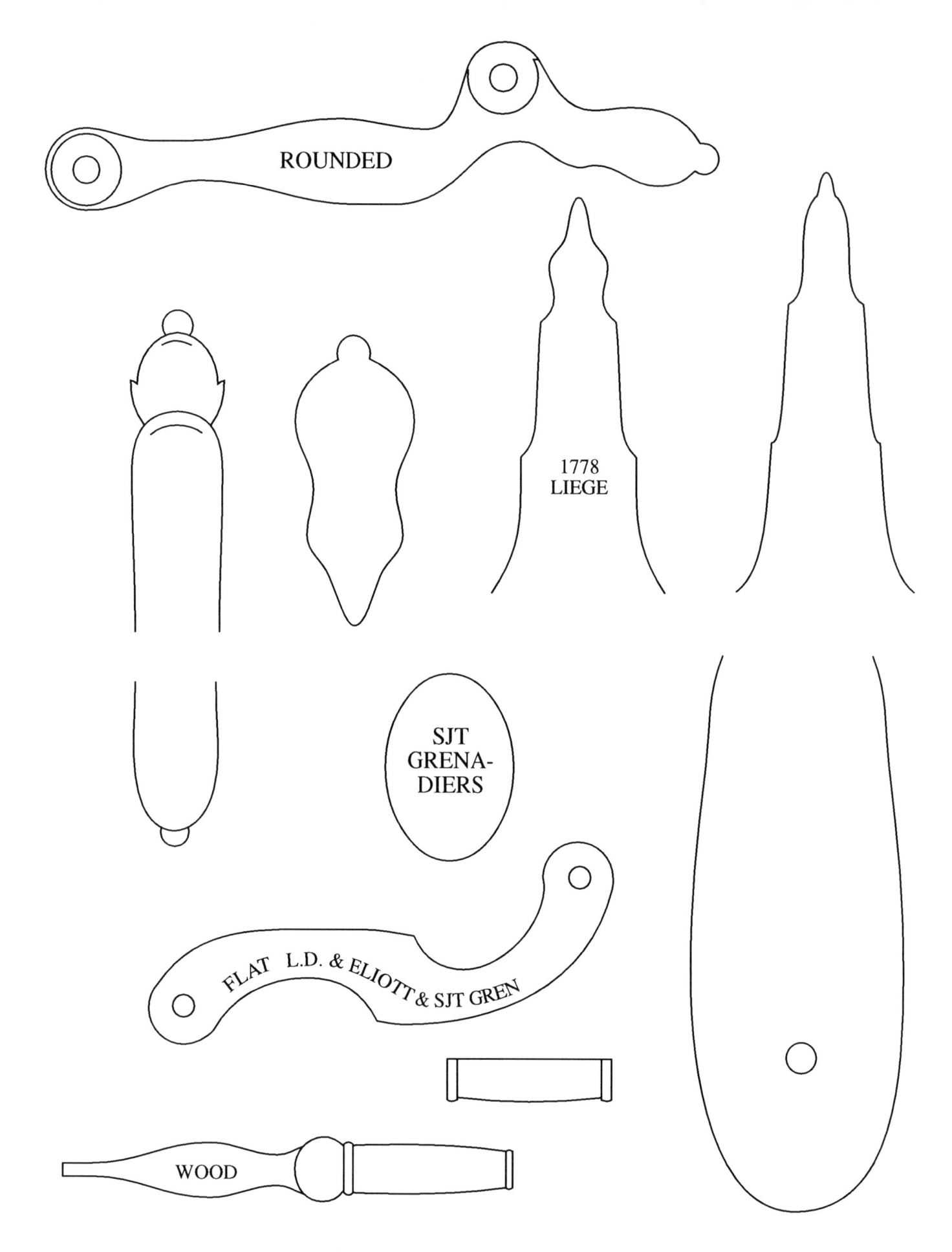

Plate 36. Land Service Carbine Furniture.

ROUNDED

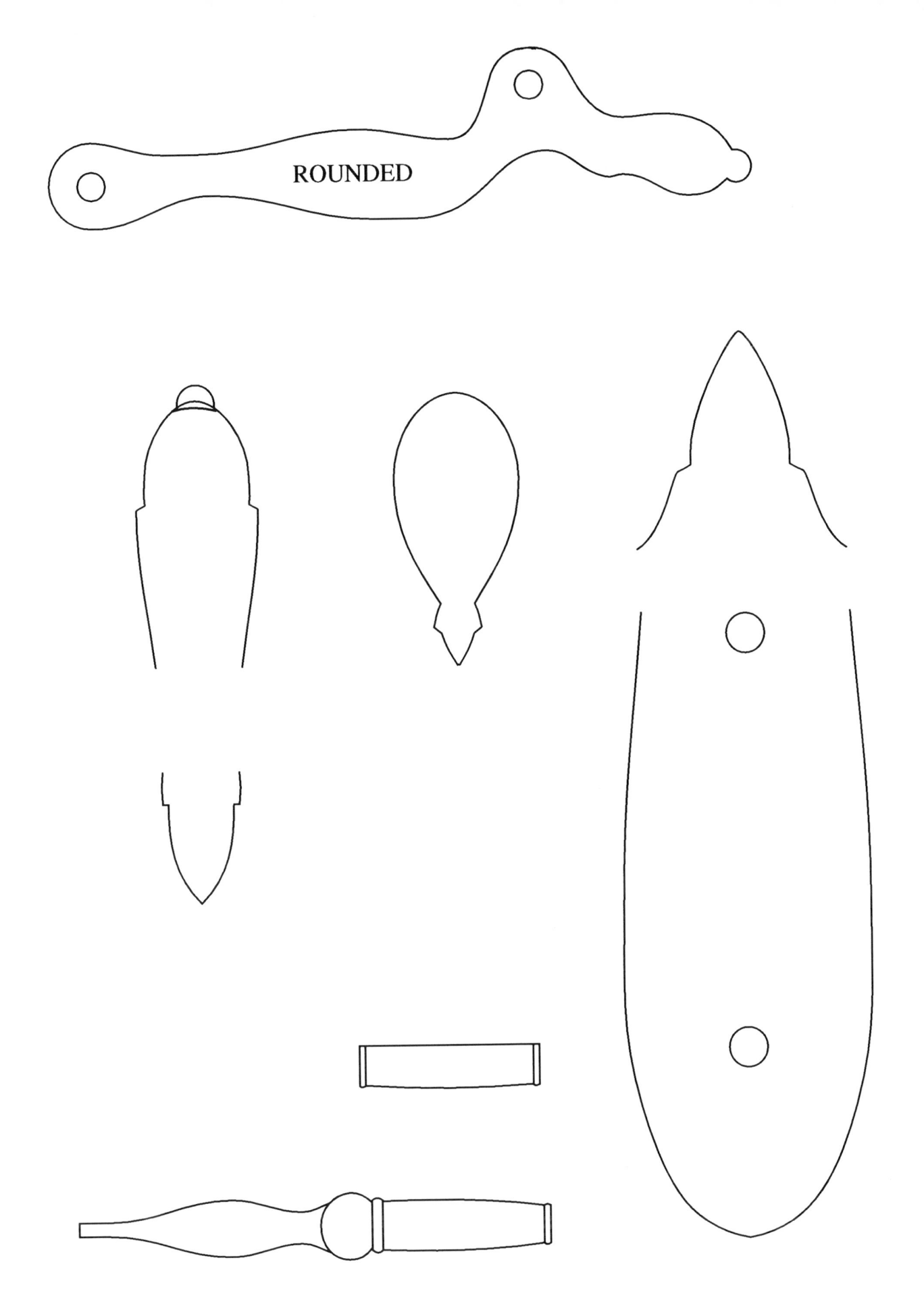

Plate 37. Pattern 1760 Light Infantry Carbine Furniture.

ROUNDED

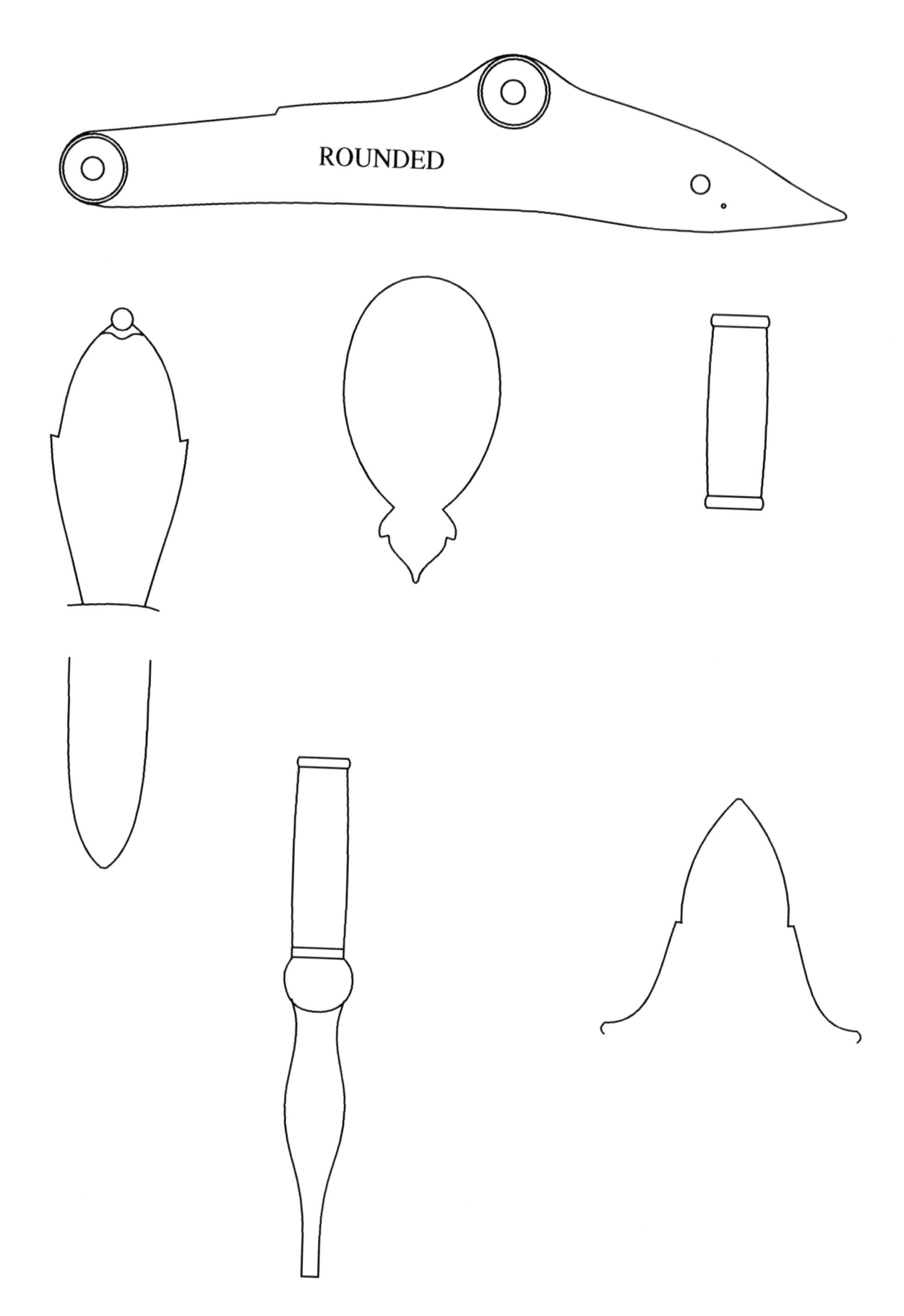

Plate 38. Pattern 1745 Lord Loudoun
Light Infantry Carbine Furniture.

FLAT

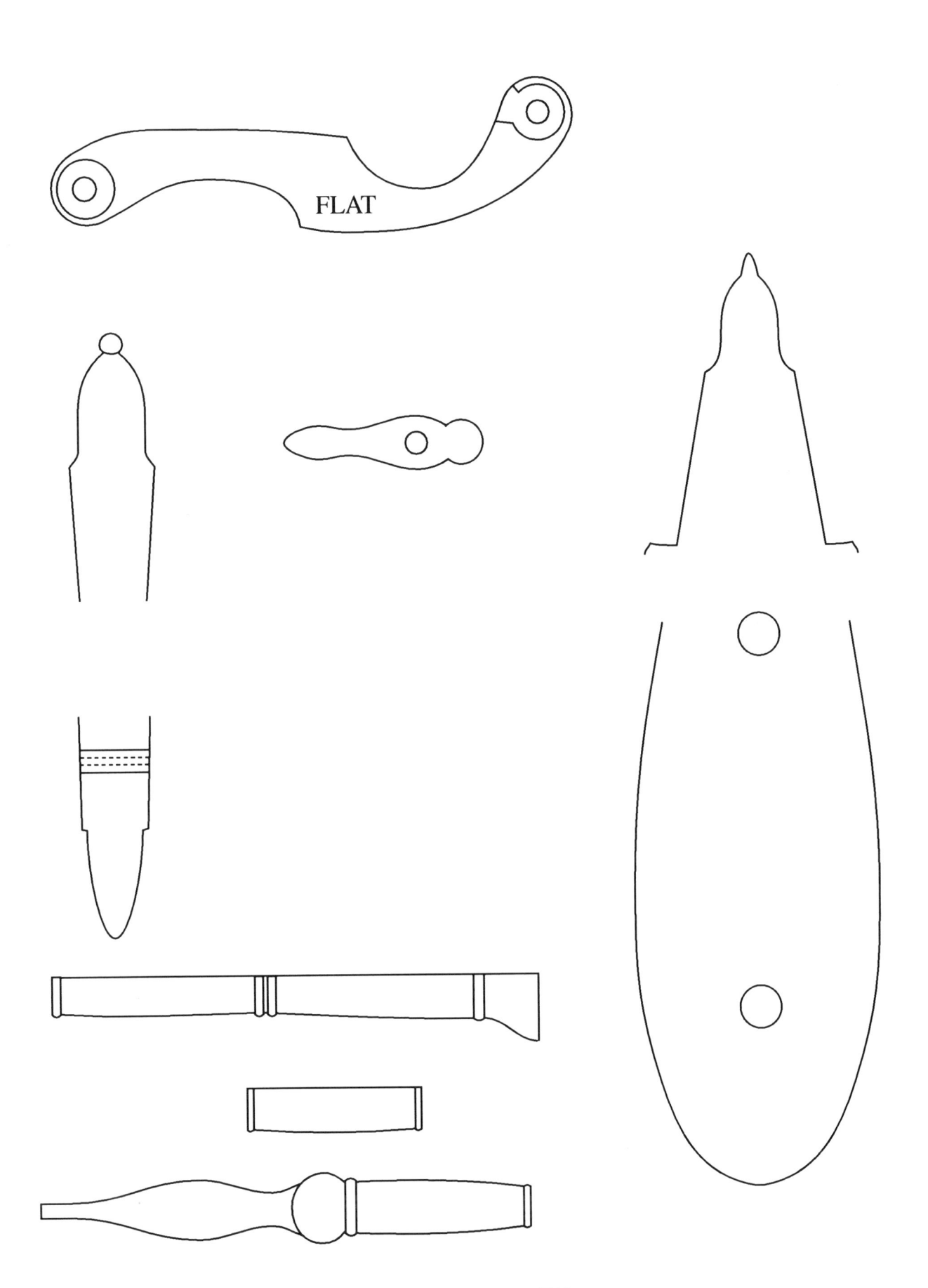

*Plate 39. Pattern 1760
Eliott Light Dragoon Carbine Furniture.*

FLAT

FRONT REAR

Plate 40. Pattern 1776 Royal Foresters Light Dragoon Carbine Furniture.

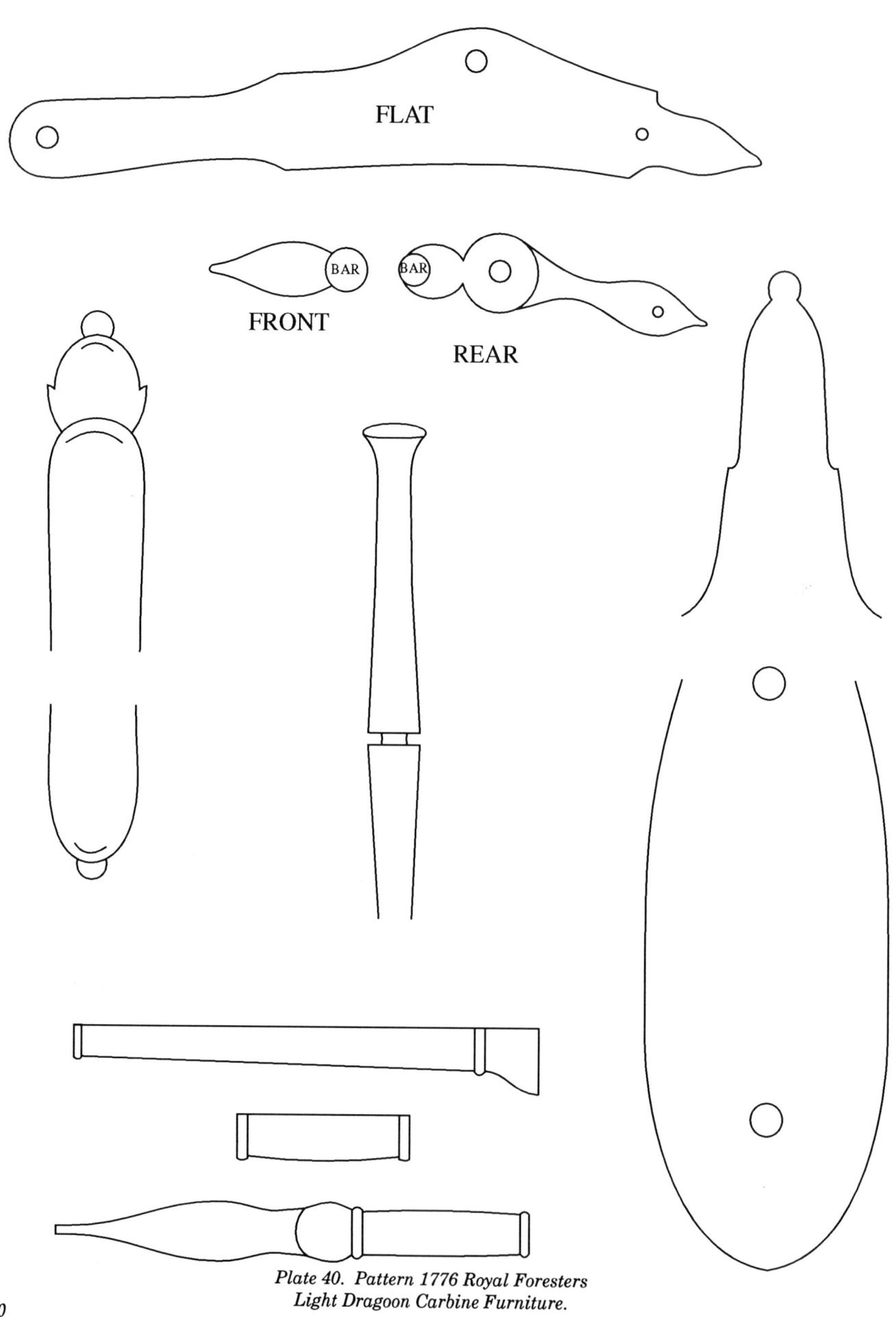

40

FLAT

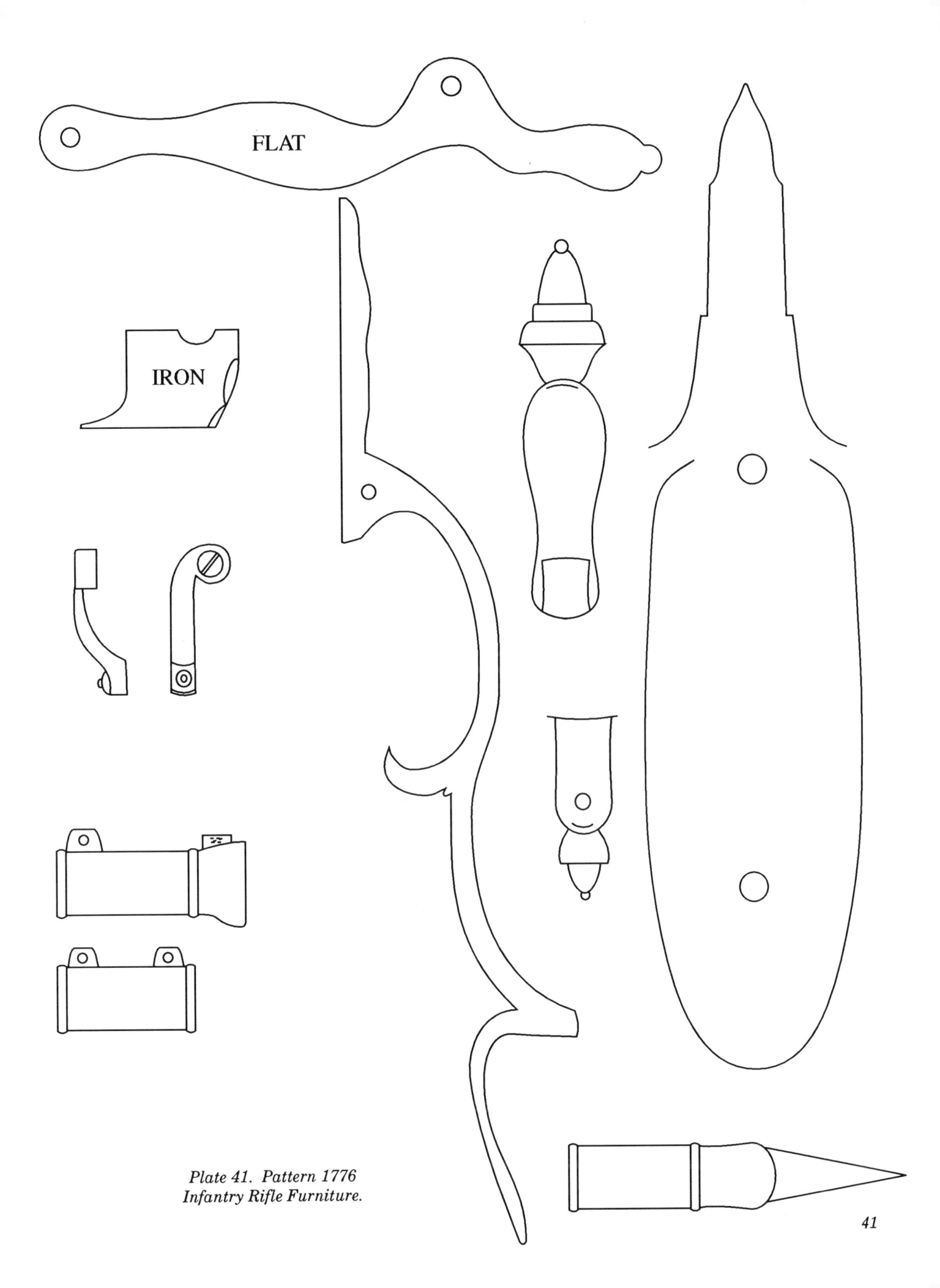

IRON

Plate 41. Pattern 1776
Infantry Rifle Furniture.

41

ROUNDED

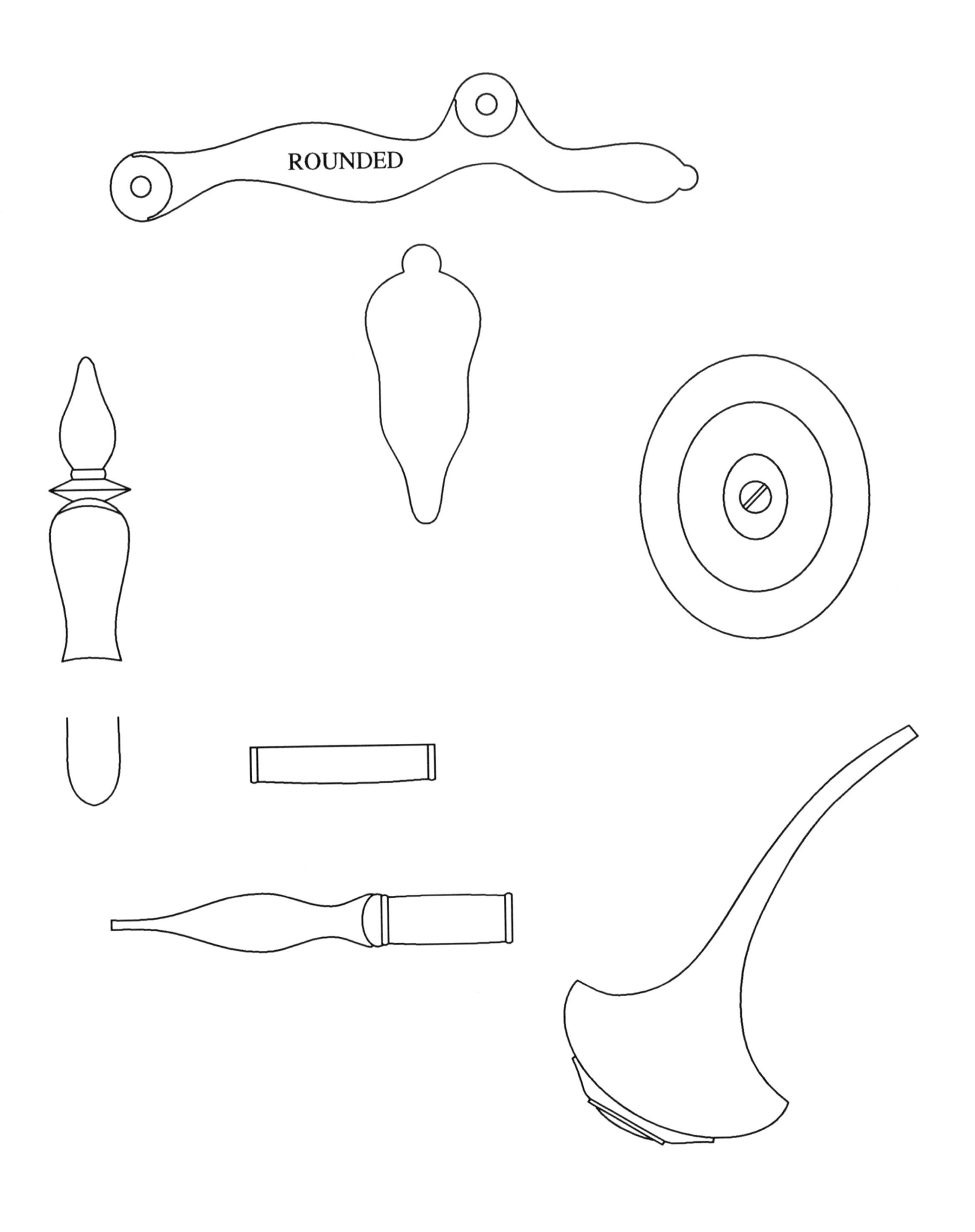

Plate 42. Pattern 1730 Land Service Pistol Furniture.

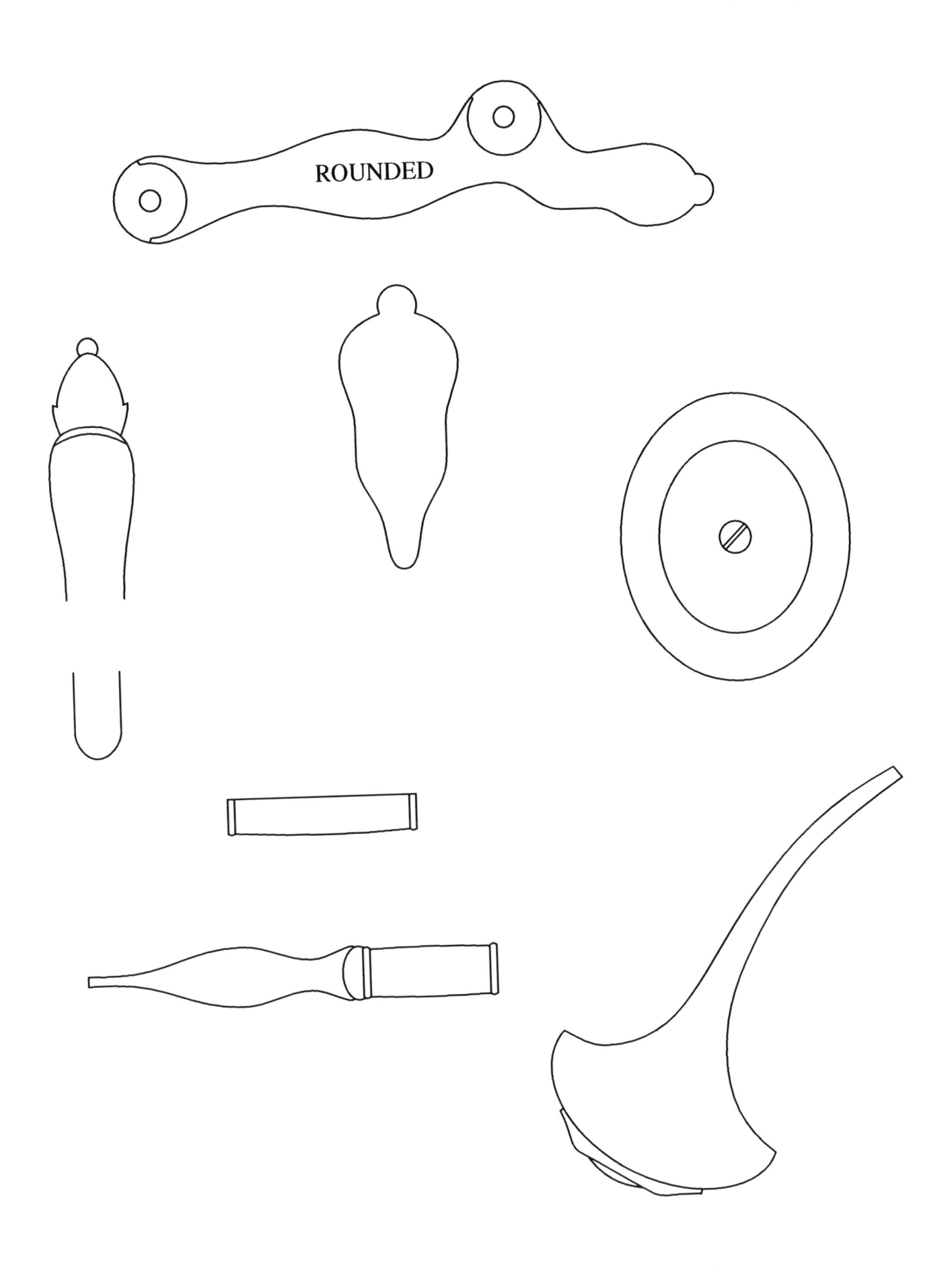

Plate 43. Pattern 1738 Land Service Pistol Furniture.

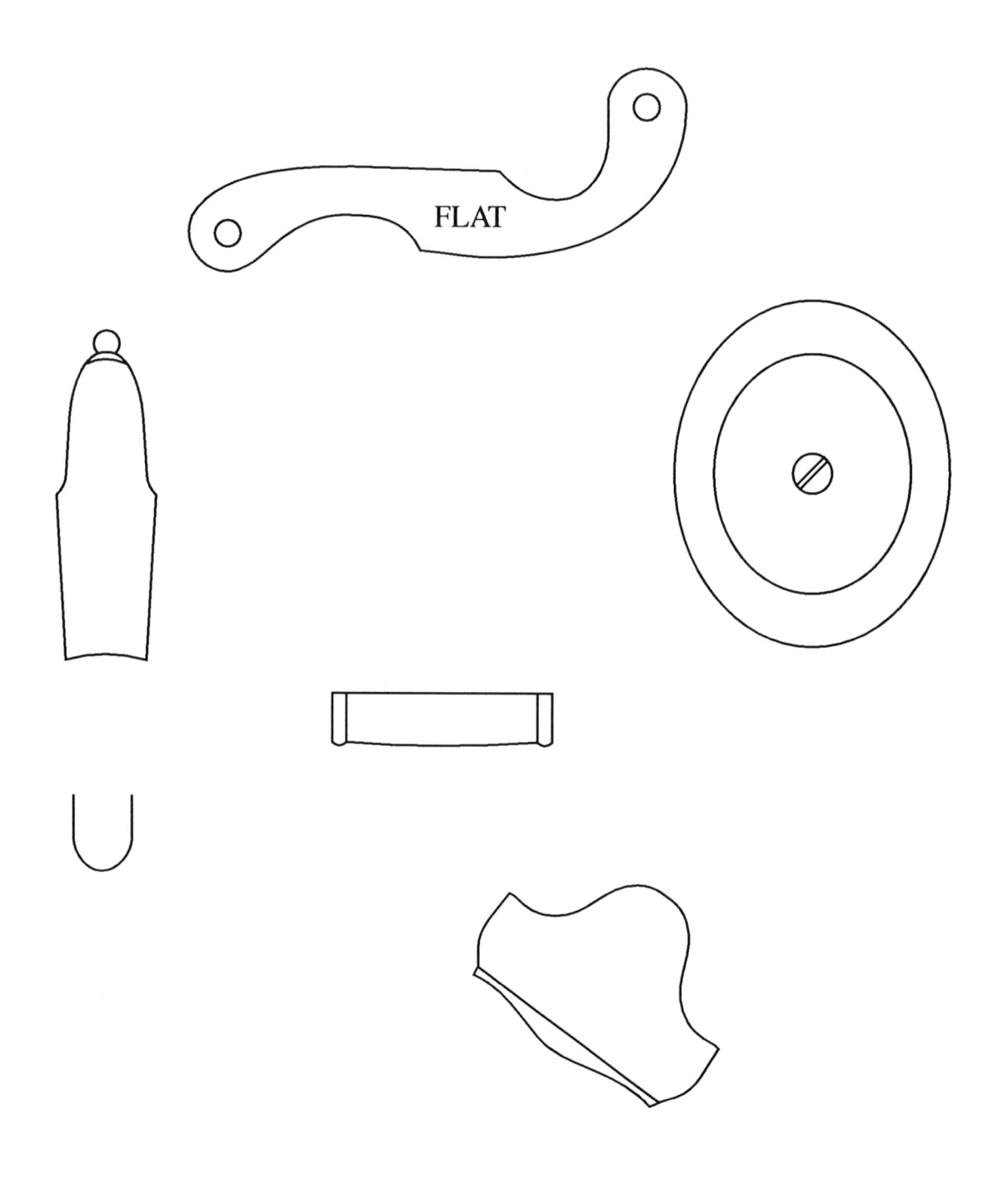

Plate 44. Pattern 1756 Light Dragoon & Pattern 1759 Eliott Light Dragoon Pistol Furniture.

FLAT

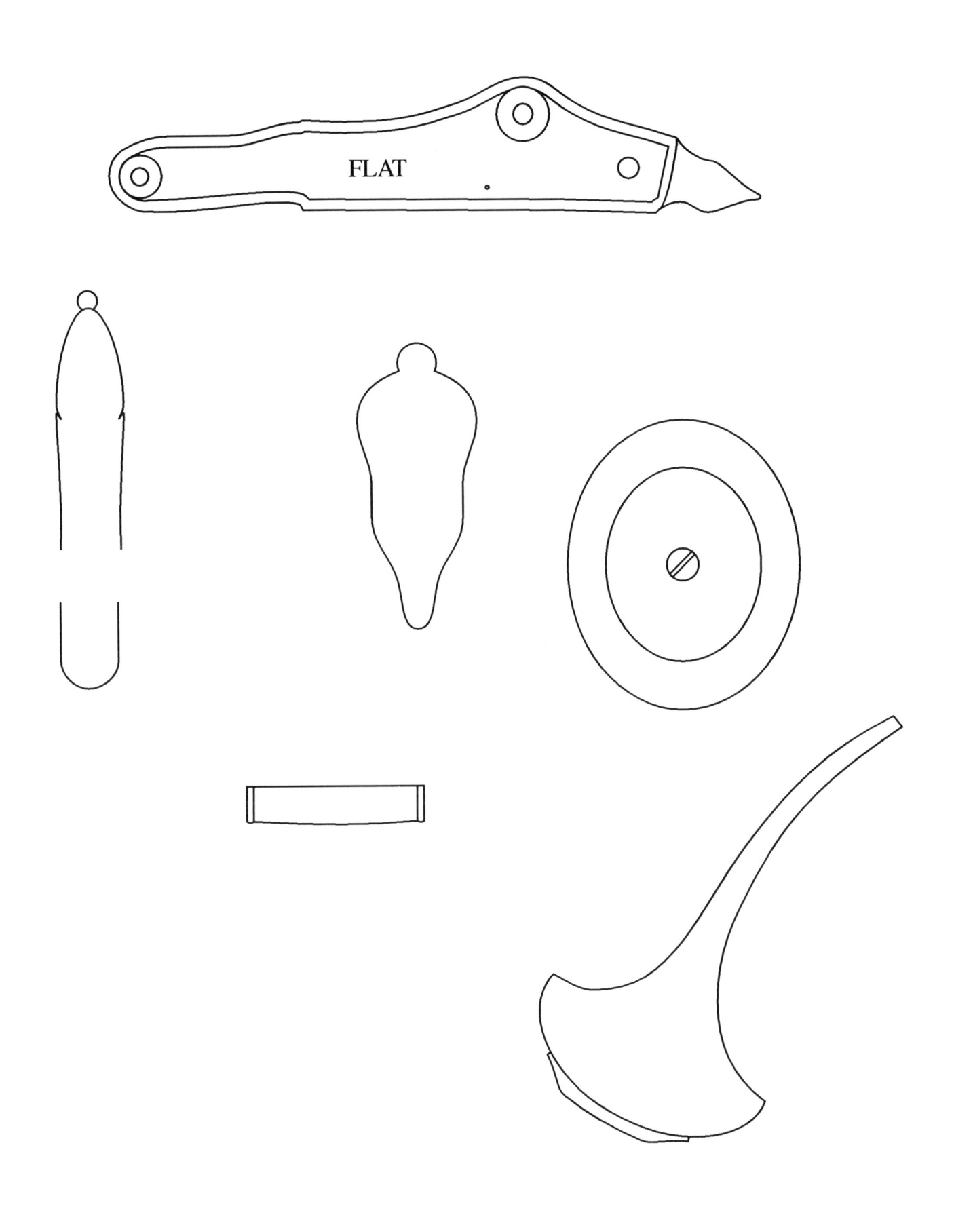

Plate 45. Pattern 1776 Royal Foresters Light Dragoon Pistol Furniture.

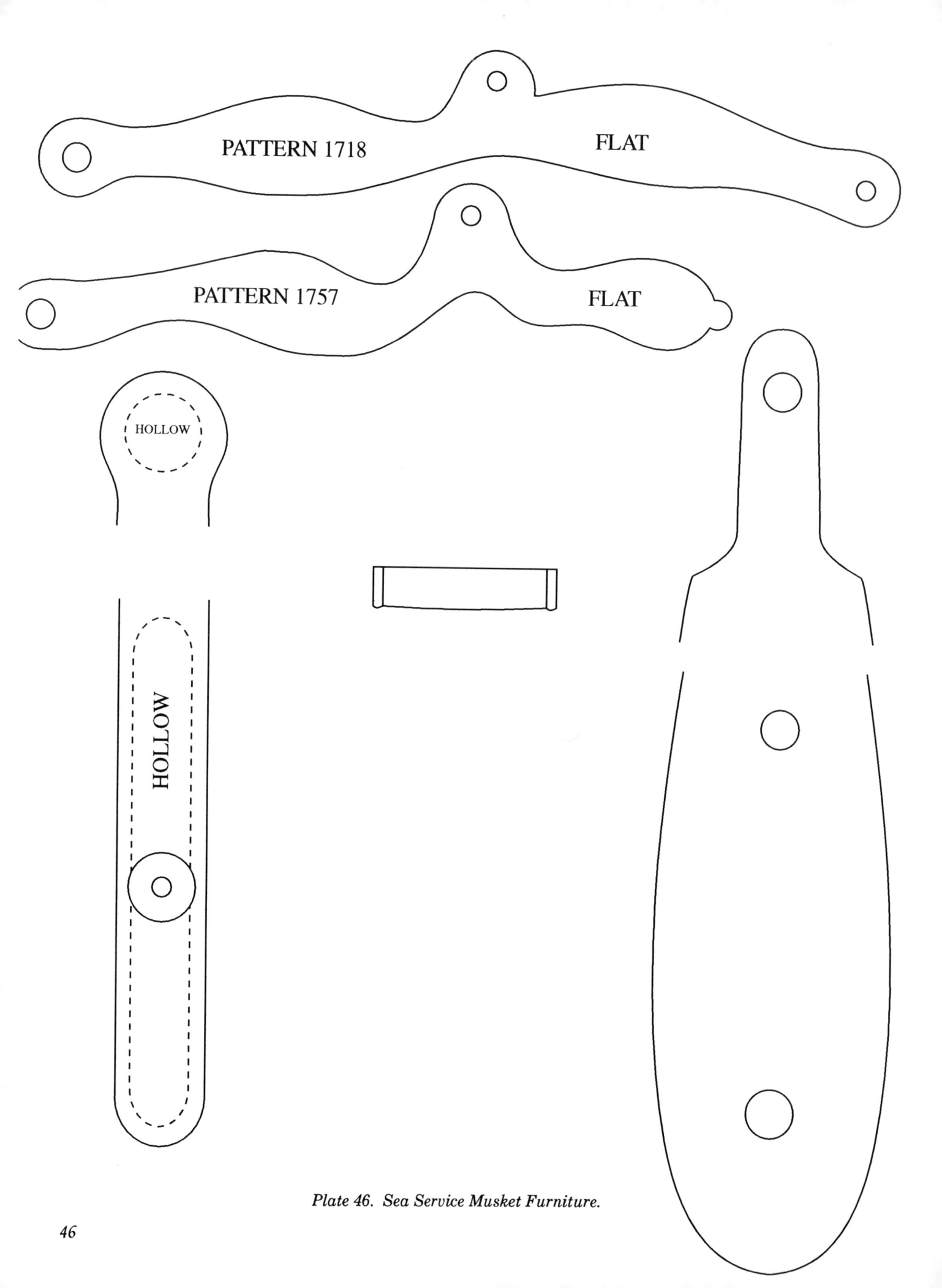

Plate 46. Sea Service Musket Furniture.

ROUNDED

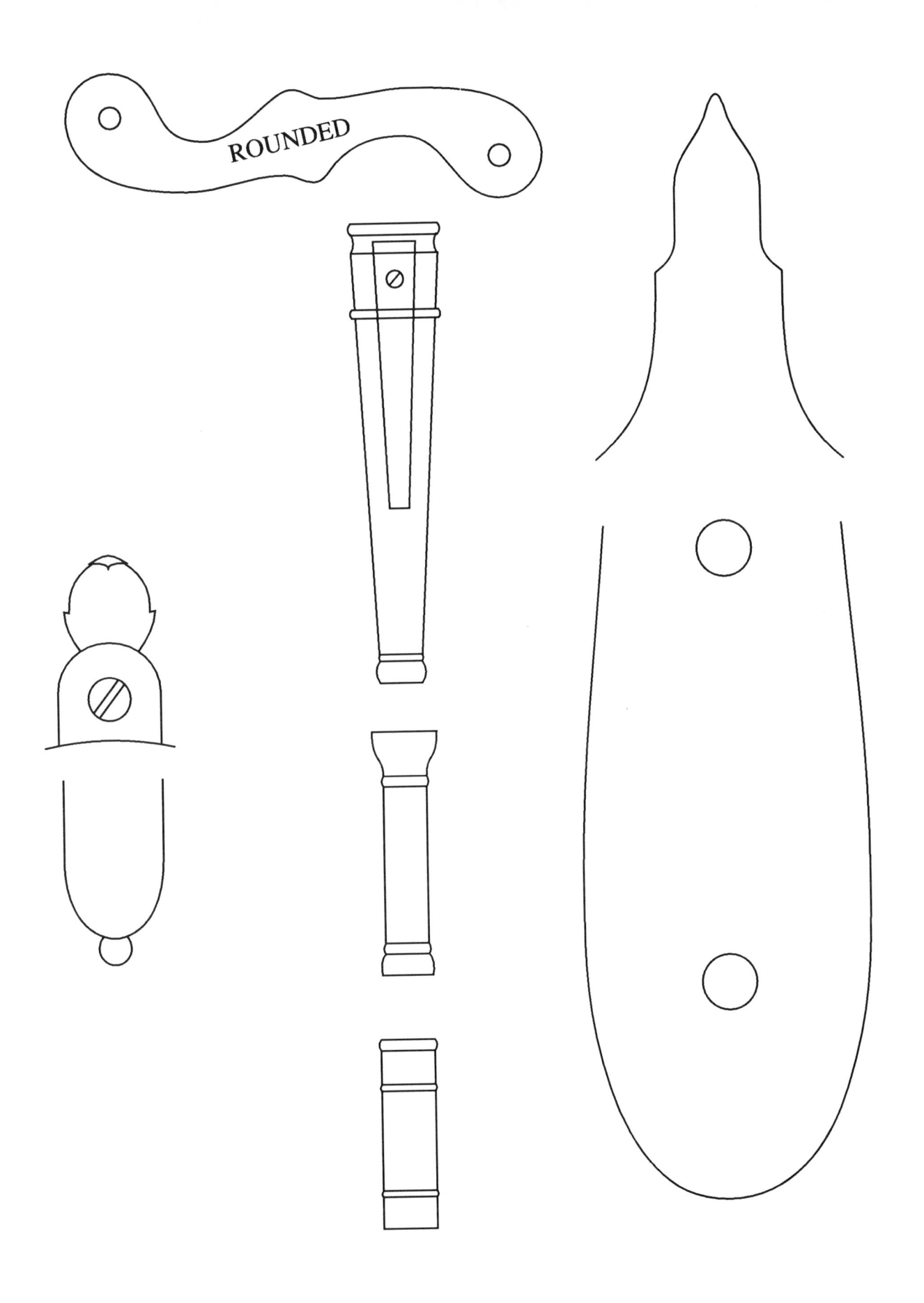

Plate 47. Pattern 1779 Seven-barrel Volley Gun Furniture.

FLAT 1718, 1756

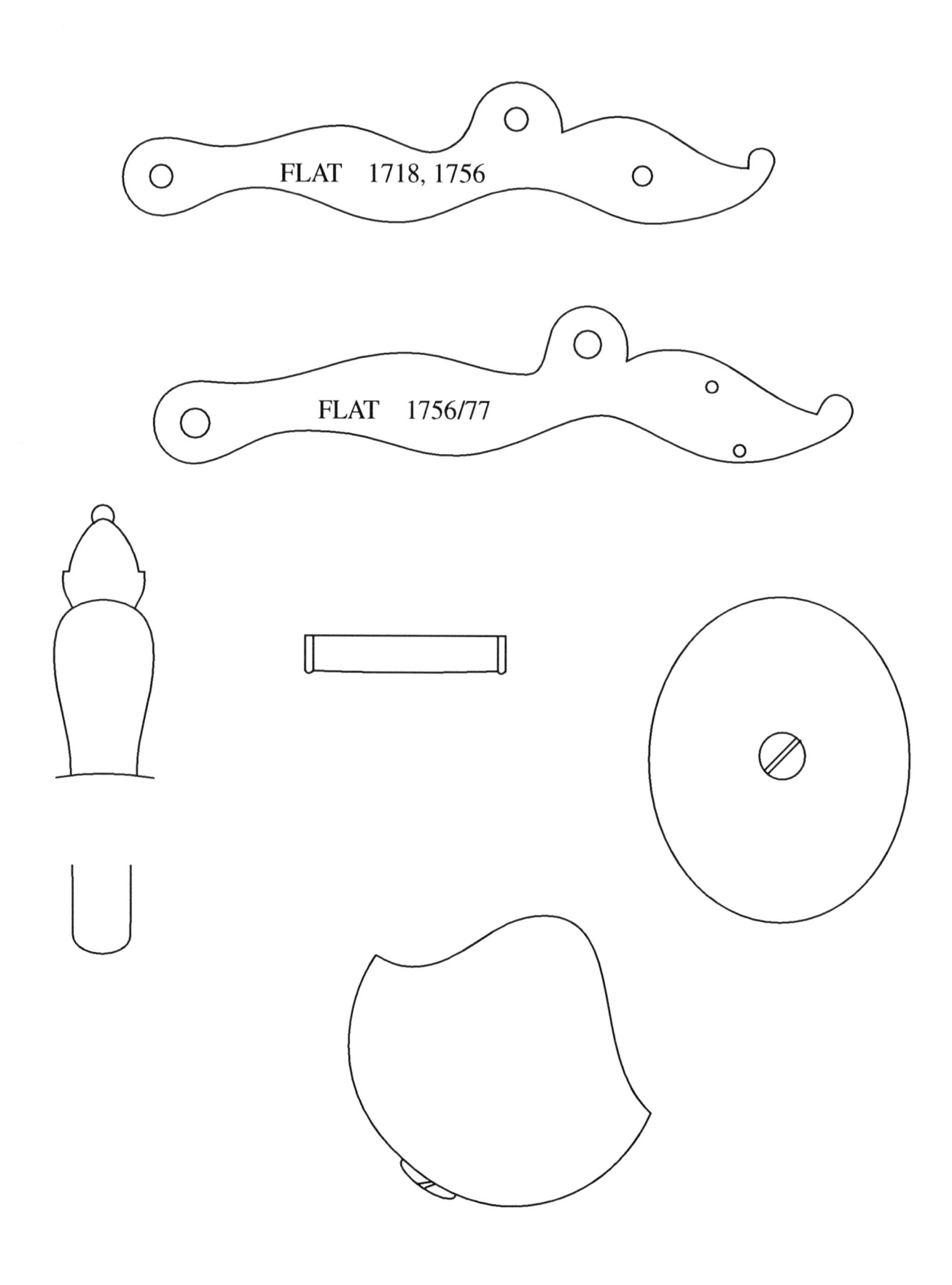

FLAT 1756/77

Plate 48. Sea Service Pistol Furniture.

Stocks

The stocks of all British military small arms made for the Board of Ordnance throughout the period of this study were made from English walnut. The single possible exception to this statement may have occurred on Sea Service muskets set up during the American War from 1778, when some of the complete arms sent in by the contractors *may* have been stocked in beech. Beechwood had been used during the 17th and early 18th century for some Ordnance arms, but its use had ceased by the end of Queen Anne's reign in 1714.

For most of the period covered by this work "wallnuttree" plank was supplied to the Board by the same firm that executed the first stage of manufacturing small arms, rough-stocking. There were price differentials between those arms rough stocked with the contractor's own wood and those rough stocked with the Board's timber. Whether there are any additional inspection markings when contractor's wood was used is not yet known.

Stocks for Land Service wallpieces, muskets and carbines share certain basic characteristics in design. All have what is known as a "handrail" shape to the butt (Plate 49). The lower part of the butt continues to be roughly round in section, the intention being to provide a better grip in thrusting the weapon forward when using the bayonet. The upper part is separated by a sharp demarcation between it and the lower round section, and tapers upwards to the comb of the butt. On stocks made prior to the 1750s this upper or comb area is much fuller and rounder in section than the more straight-sided narrower style adopted in 1756.

A second feature common to Land Service and Sea Service stocks is the swell in the fore-end, located at the point where the tailpipe protects the entry-point of the rammer into the closed section of the ramrod channel. Once again this was intended to improve the grip of the soldier when using the bayonet. There is a certain amount of evolution to the shape of the swell. The earliest patterns have a smaller and more nearly ball-shaped swell, while stocks made from the mid-1740s tend to have a larger, longer and more oval form (both descriptions when viewed from above or below). (Plate 50).

A third feature common to Land Service small arms is the stock carving around the barrel tang and at the front and rear of the flat parallel sections on the sides of the stock where the lock and sidepiece are mounted. These are often called "beaver-tails" but since this description may not be readily identifiable to non-American readers, and since it applies to only one of the several patterns of carving used, the broader term "aprons" will be used here. These carved areas represent the original surface of the stock, with the remainder of the wood cut away from them, leaving surfaces which are both decorative and stronger, acting as a reinforcement to the weakest area of the stock.

Barrel-tang aprons occur in two basic designs (Plate 51). That used on the Pattern 1730 and Pattern 1730/40 Muskets, the Pattern 1745 Lord Loudoun and Pattern 1760 Light Infantry Carbines and Land Service Pistols prior to 1781 is narrow and has a wavy border which (except on the two carbines) directly connects at the front with the carving around the lock and sidepiece flats. That used from the Pattern 1742 Musket onwards is indeed a "beavertail" having a plain elongated oval shape. There is a small flat semi-circular area immediately behind the end of the barrel tang. There is no connection between the tang apron and those on the sides in this second pattern.

The aprons which border the lock and sidepiece flats occur in three variations. The first (Plate 52 a, b) is the most elaborate and is found only on Pattern 1730 and on some of its transitional successors the Pattern 1730/40 muskets and on Land Service Pistols prior to 1781. In this pattern there are elliptical aprons both ahead of and behind the lock and sidepiece, with wavy borders along the underside of the stock on each side which fade out towards the centre and which connect at the breech with the barrel tang apron. The second type (Plate 52 a, c) is found on the transitional muskets and consists of only the rear aprons being of the full elliptical pattern; the front terminals to the lock and sidepiece flats are a plain rounded outline following the form of the front of the lockplate; there are no longer any wavy borders on the underside of the stock and there

49

Plate 49. (Top, left) Handrail Buttstock configuration from 1756. Note the narrower cutting of the handrail and the thinner, flatter form of comb above the handrail. Courtesy of the Board of Trustees of the Armouries.

(Above, left) Handrail Buttstock configuration, pre-1756. Note the full rounded form of the section above the handrail. Courtesy of the Director, National Army Museum, London.

(Top, right) Top view shows full rounded form of comb on most pre-1756 butts.
Courtesy of the Trustees of the National Museums of Scotland.

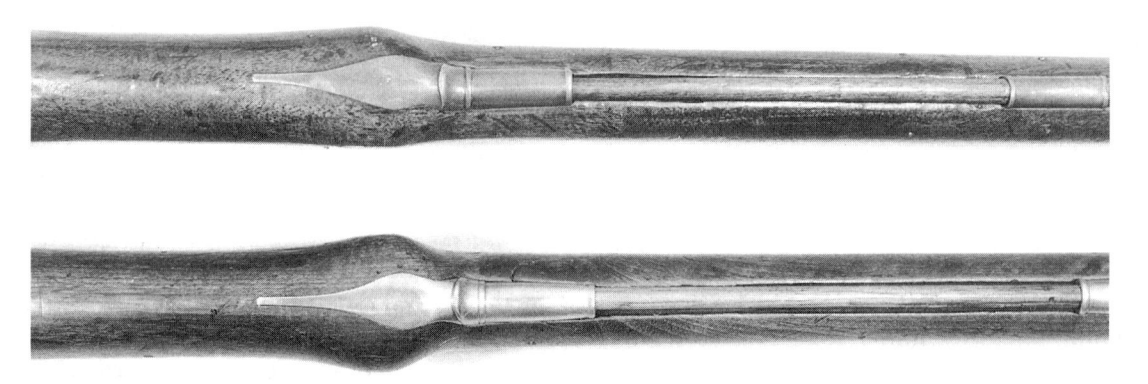

Plate 50. Fore-end swell at tailpipe. Top: late type from mid-1740s. Bottom: early type 1720s until mid-1740s.
Photograph I. D. Skennerton, courtesy of the Board of Trustees of the Armouries.

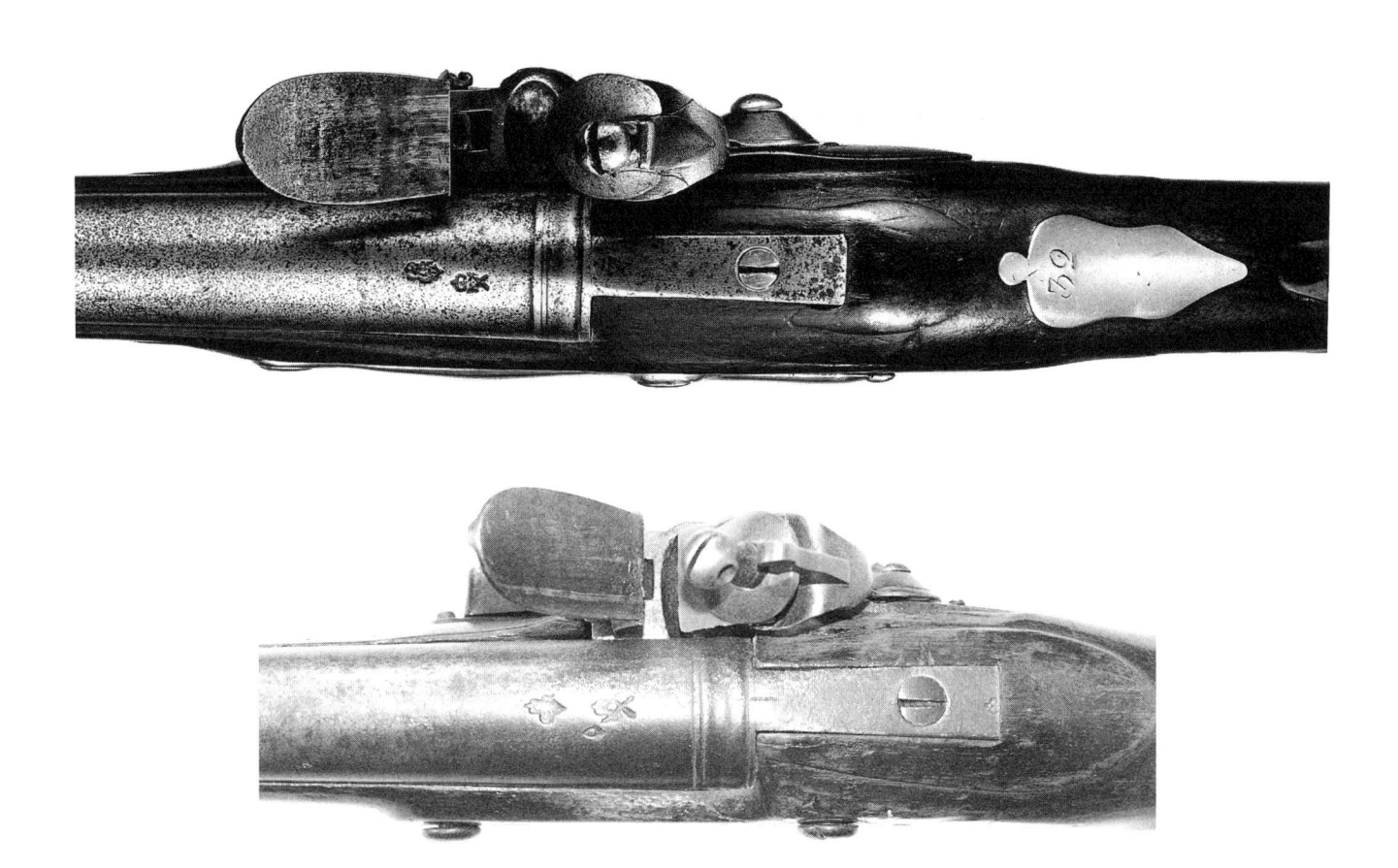

Plate 51. Barrel-tang raised aprons: (Top) Pattern 1730 or wavy outline; used on Pattern 1730 Musket, Loudoun and Pattern 1760 Light Infantry Carbines and Pattern 1738 Land Service Pistol. (Above) Pattern 1742 or oval outline, which was used on all subsequent patterns.
Courtesy of the Colonial Williamsburg Foundation.

is no connection with the barrel tang apron. The final design (Plate 52 c) appears on the fully-fledged Pattern 1742 Musket and continues in use beyond the period of this study on all Land and Sea Service small arms. It consists of a plain rounded termination to the front of the flats as with the previous type and a plain elongated teardrop form to the rear terminations.

As originally manufactured prior to 1737 King's Pattern Ordnance small arms were not fitted with any form of protection for the forward termination of the fore-end. Experience in the field revealed this area as a weak point and some regimental commanding officers paid to have a sheet-brass strip fitted to the wood to help prevent splitting in the manner of some fowling pieces and officer's fusils (Plate 53 b). From 1737 the Ordnance undertook the fitting of these bands, which took the form of the sheet-brass used in the past at regimental level. Many muskets were fitted with this form of noseband by the Ordnance during the period 1737-41, secured with a brass wire rivet (Plate 53 b). With the decision to adopt the steel ramrod for all infantry muskets in 1748, as well as the newly reinforced socket for the musket bayonet which had appeared in 1740, wartime experience had demonstrated that the sheet-brass ("latten") noseband protection was inadequate and a heavier, stronger cast brass nosecap was introduced (Plate 53 c). These appear to have been kept for new-production steel rammer muskets while the sheet-brass nosebands were used on arms converted from wooden to steel rammer. The new cap was held to the stock by a brass rivet, and its design did not change until the adoption of the India Pattern in the mid-1790s.

Inletting, the fitting of the barrel, lock and furniture into the stock, was always of a very high quality on Ordnance arms. Whenever the fit between wood and metal is not very close and even on a piece in otherwise clean and crisp condition, its originality should be closely examined. Locks were always fully inletted, with the internal lock parts outlined in the wood, leaving as much wood as possible for strength. The lock cavity or mortise was not simply hollowed-out with only a ledge remaining around the edge for the lockplate to bear on.

51

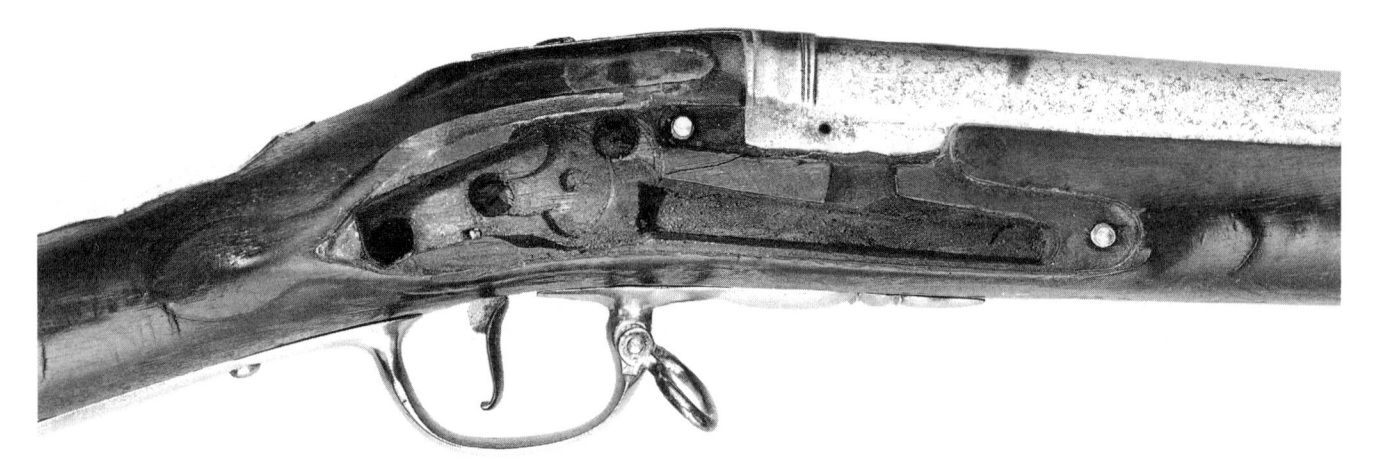

Plate 52a. Lock-and Sidepiece-flat terminal carving. Two oval aprons, note connection with tang apron at top.
Courtesy of the Colonial Williamsburg Foundation.

Plate 52b. Lock-and Sidepiece-flat terminal carving. Note continuation on underside of stock at front and rear of flats. The transitional pattern has only the rear oval apron, the front being plain rounded as on Plate 52c.
Courtesy of the Colonial Williamsburg Foundation

Plate 52c. Lock-and Sidepiece-flat terminal carving. Plain teardrop at rear of flats, in use from ca. 1744.
Board of Trustees of the Armouries

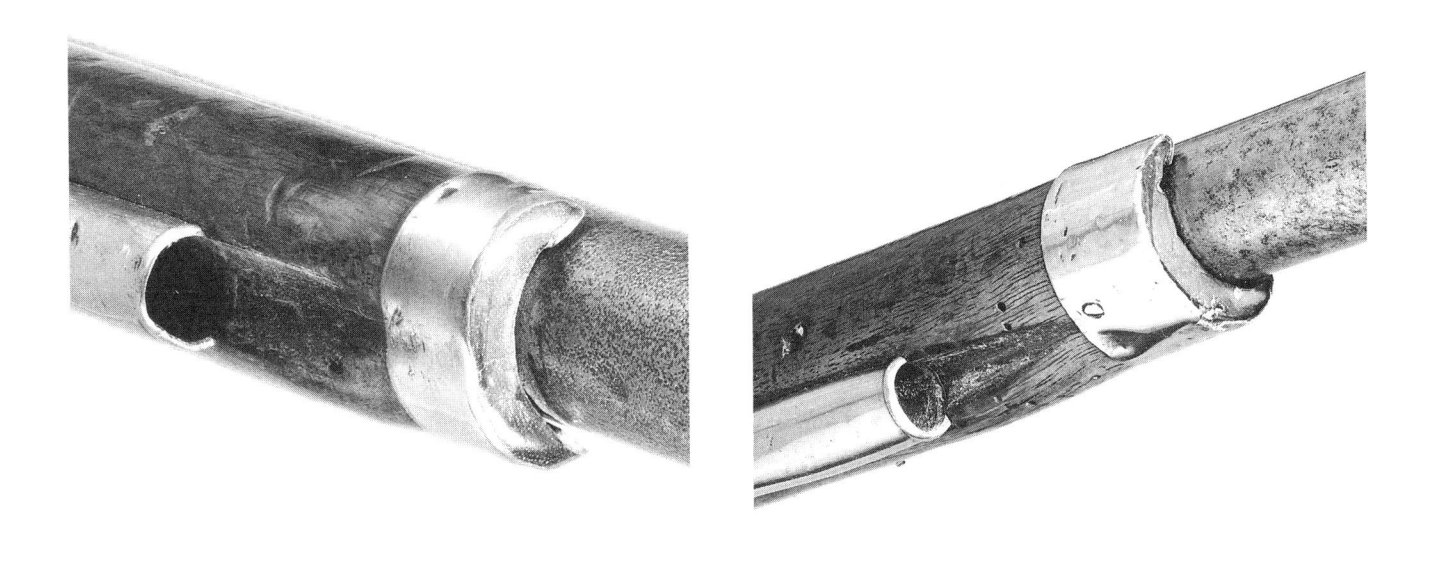

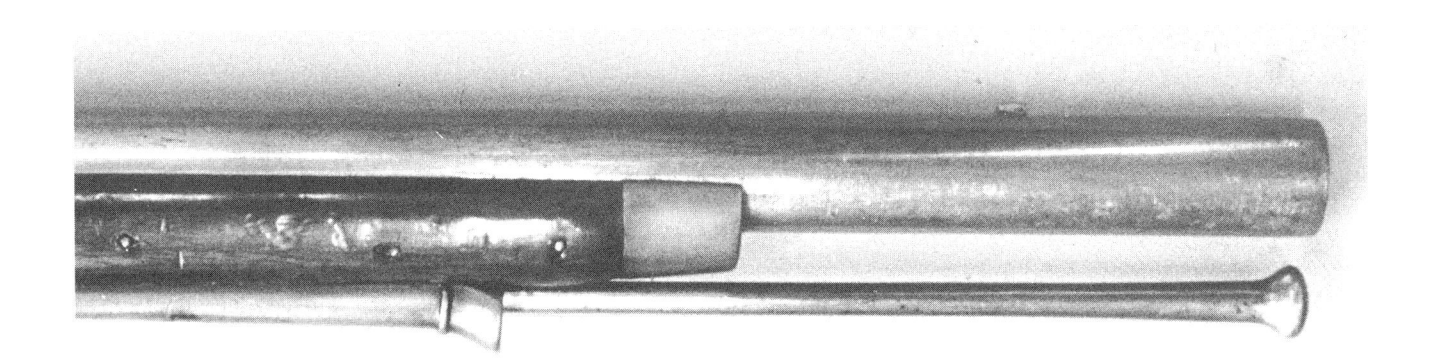

Plate 53. Fore-end Terminals: (a, top) plain for wood rammers; (b, center) nosebands for wooden rammer and conversions to steel rammer; note plain wrap-around and wrap-around with rivet; (c, bottom) cast cap from 1748.

Courtesy of the Colonial Williamsburg Foundation and the Board of Trustees of the Armouries.

Markings

The stock is the component which holds all the other components of a small arm together. As manufactured for the Board of Ordnance, rough-stocking was the initial stage of producing a weapon and "cleansing off" or laying the grain of the wood in final finishing was the last stage. Throughout the process of joining the barrel, lock and furniture to the wood, various inspectors examined their particular area of the process and stamped the wood to indicate their approval of that part of the work. When the piece was completed further marks were added, and when taken into Ordnance Store for the first time a Storekeeper's stamp was added to indicate its official arrival in Government ownership. Although the precise significance of some of these markings remains unclear, their presence on a stock is often crucial to the identification of a military-pattern small arm as an Ordnance product.

Most of the contractors who worked for the Board of Ordnance were gunmakers in their own right and produced military-pattern arms for commercial sale to private landowners for armed tenantry, ship owners, or for the slave trade and particularly for export to colonial settlers. There were many thousands of Long and Short Land muskets and Sea Service arms made up using some ex-Ordnance parts, especially locks and barrels. Some of these had either been condemned and rejected in the process of manufacture, or else were purchased by the gunmakers at the Tower auctions of unserviceable goods. Metal parts such as barrels and locks were often sold into the private sector without bothering to remove the Government markings which would have spoiled the surface and the finish. Government reject stamps used to overstrike markings, especially Proof marks on barrels, did not come into use during the period of this study. In differentiating between an Ordnance piece and an identical piece of commercial nature, stock markings can be crucial in reaching a decision.

Working from the muzzle to the butt, an Ordnance weapon should show the following stock markings:

1. One, two or three small inspector's crowned numbers in the upper area of the ramrod channel, between the mouth and the first pipe.

2. One or two inspector's crowned numbers in the ramrod channel between the last pipe before the tailpipe and the tailpipe. In this area may also be found assemblers' marks such as / or ///, or XXI, III, XVI and so on, and either the name or initials of the setter-up. On rare occasions the name of the rough-stocker contractor, e.g. Loder, Waller, Tucker, &c., may be found, especially on post-1775 arms when additional contractors for this phase of assembly made identification more necessary.

3. A crown and one or two crowned numbers struck in a vertical line immediately behind (below) the rear tang of the trigger guard. On pistols these will be struck in the wood under/below the tail of the lock.

4. The rear of the sidepiece flat often contains one or two initials, stamped in large or small letters, or some form of symbol such as a star or asterisk. The meaning of these marks has not yet been firmly identified but in most cases the initials are probably those of a workman employed either by the rough-stocker or the setter-up.

5. On the right side of the butt a Storekeeper's mark composed of a Crown over the two sets of script initials GR which are turned back-to-back (addorsed) and interwoven. (Plate 54). On pistols this is struck above the tail of the lock. From 1780 a date was added below this monogram.

Weapons which were supplied as complete arms by the contractors under special agreements with the Board during the American War may not display a full set of these markings. Wear and tear and the refinishing of stocks may have removed some or all of them, but the refinishing would have to be much more extensive and thorough than is generally the case to remove all traces of these markings, which were usually well stamped to survive ordinary use and abuse. Ramrod channel markings and those behind the trigger guard tang should always be present, and the Storekeeper's stamp was only very rarely omitted.

These markings should be taken in conjunction with similar markings on the barrel and lock described in their respective chapters, and any weapon which does not show a high percentage of these markings should be considered suspect insofar as its being of Ordnance provenance is concerned.

Plate 54. Storekeeper's stamps on right side of butt on longarms and above rear of lock on pistols. Dates were not used in conjunction with these stamps until the 1780s.

Pattern-Date Designations for British Military Small Arms Used in North America, 1737-1783

WALLPIECES

The salient features of the two patterns produced during the period of this study are a heavy 54-inch .98 calibre barrel with barrel walls just over 1/4" thick at the muzzle, a full length stock often fitted with an oarlock-like swivel pinned through the fore-end, a large flat lock, engraved brass furniture and a heavy iron ramrod.

Pattern Date   **Characteristic Features**

1738 (Plate 55)   54-inch **barrel** with "swamped" form near the muzzle, held to the barrel by four pins, the lower one larger and serving as the pivot for the swivel mount. Heavy steel blade foresight, tang grooved to act as backsight. Heavy iron rammer with flared head.

Flat, double-bridle **lock** with "banana" tail configuration, faceted pan, fitted with long sear-spring (one screw showing through plate behind the cock). Ring-neck cock with teardrop-shaped throat-hole. Teardrop-shaped feather-spring finial. Lockplate, cock, top-jaw and back of steel engraved with double border lines. Dates from 1740 to 1747.

Full length **stock** with swell at tailpipe and handrail butt of conventional British military pattern. Lock and sidepiece-flats have full oval apron carving at front and rear. Most examples were fitted with a heavy iron swivel in the form of an oarlock through the fore-end behind the tailpipe, the stem of which fitted into a ship's rail or fortification wall.

Brass furniture (Plate 30) consisting of three Land Pattern barrel-shaped and collared pipes and tailpipe, trigger-guard with distinctive engraved flame-shaped front finial; Land Pattern thumbpiece and flat two-screw Land Pattern sidepiece, both with engraved double border lines which are also repeated on the three-stepped tang of the buttplate.

1738/78   Same as the Pattern 1738, but fitted with the Pattern 1777 lock having a short sear-spring (two screws showing through the lockplate in rear of the cock) and with TOWER only engraved across the tail.

There are minor finishing variations between this and the earlier pattern and the stocks seem to be somewhat heavier, especially in the fore-end.

These were produced between 1778 and 1782, locks for the 1781-2 production being supplied by Henry Nock.

LAND SERVICE MUSKETS

Long Land Muskets

The salient features of this series are a 46-inch barrel and a long-tang buttplate.

Pattern Date   **Characteristic Features**

1730 (Plate 56)   46-inch **barrel**, with four *pairs* of barrel loops, with the cross-pins also passing through the lugs of the rammer pipes which fit between the two parallel loops. (Plate 2) These "double-looped" barrels are unique to this pattern. The upper sling swivel screw passes through the fore-end and a strong loop on the underside of the barrel in the conventional manner. Wooden rammer with tapered brass cap.

Round, single-bridle **lock** with "banana" lock-plate configuration, and dates on the tail from 1727 to 1743. One screw showing behind the cock (long sear spring). Trefoil feather-spring finial. (Plate 10)

Stock originally made without fore-end cap. Small bulbous swell at tailpipe, very thin-section fore-end wood. Lock and sideplate flats have wide, raised elliptical aprons at each end and the area around the barrel tang has a raised, narrow, wavy-bordered oval apron. The butt, seen in section, has a very full, rounded comb area above the handrail groove.

55

Brass furniture: Three Land Pattern barrel-shaped and collared rammer pipes, and tailpipe. Distinctive Dutch-style trigger guard with thin narrow bow terminals, with a bulbous reinforcement to take the lower sling swivel at the top front of the bow. The front and rear finials are pear-shaped. (Plate 31) Land Pattern thumbpiece and sidepiece with rounded surface. Long Land Pattern buttplate.

1730 (s/r)   Same as Pattern 1730, but *altered* to take steel rammer by brazing liner in upper rammer pipe and rivetting a rod-retaining spring inside the tailpipe. A sheet-brass noseband (Plate 53b) was often fitted at the same time, at Ordnance or regimental level.

1740   Liège contract. Not yet identified but assumed to be based on the current patterns (i.e. 1730/40, 1742) when contracted for in 1740, 1741 and 1745. Issued to marines and other troops who may have served in the West Indies.

1730/40 (Plate 57)   Same as Pattern 1730 *except*: Double-bridle lock OR with single bridle lock with dates from 1740 to 1743. The majority of examples examined retain the basic features of the Pattern 1730, including the double-looped barrel.

Carving at *front* of lock and sideplate flats is the same as 1730 OR a plain curve, the earlier apron now being omitted (Plate 52).

Trigger guard of new stronger design, the first appearance of a feature which becomes the standard for all future Land Service muskets, with heavy full width bow terminals, a reverse-curl at the inner rear of the bow and shorter simpler upper finial terminating in a hazel-nut form. (Plates 31-2)

Examples of this transitional early-wartime production will be found with combinations of the above features such as the older single-bridle lock with the plainer carving, with either the old or the new style trigger guard. But at least one of the new features is present, with the lock dates noted.

1730/40 (s/r)   Same as Pattern 1730/40, but *altered* for steel steel rammer, same as 1730 (s/r).

1742 (Plate 58)   46-inch **barrel**, with three conventional single pin-loops, and the heavier upper sling loop. Wooden rammer with tapered brass cap.

Round *double-bridle* **lock**, the plate with "banana" configuration, with dates from 1742 to 1750. (Plate 11).

Stock carving in front of lock is a plain curve following the outline of the lockplate and about 3/16" wide, with the older elliptical apron at the rear only; by 1744 this rear apron is further reduced to a long narrow teardrop. (Plate 52).

Brass furniture same as Pattern 1730 except for the new stronger trigger guard.

1742 (s/r)   Same as Pattern 1742 but *altered* from 1748 to take a steel rammer by brazing short tubular liner in upper rammer pipe and rivetting a rod-retaining spring inside the tailpipe. A sheet brass noseband was often fitted at the same time.

1742 (56)   Same as Pattern 1742 but *altered* for steel rammer using long trumpet forepipe and the new production heavier cast-brass nosecap.

This conversion of earlier muskets may have been used on the Pattern 1730 and Pattern 1730/42, but none have been reported at the time of writing. Should they appear, designations Pattern 1730 (56) or 1730/42 (56) would be appropriate.

The **long trumpet pipe** was first delivered into store in December 1756.

The presence of a thin sheet-brass nosecap, with either closed or open front, on any of the above arms, could have been fitted by the Ordnance workforce in the Tower between 1737 and 1741, but some were probably fitted by regimental armourers.

1748   Same as Pattern 1742 but *new production* with a steel rammer, narrower rammer channel and cast-brass nosecap. Pipes may be new production smaller diameter, or older larger size with bushing in the forepipe; tailpipe has retaining spring. Only 3887 manufactured between December 1748 and June 1749 by the contractors, but also set up in small numbers by the Tower workforce, 1750-54.

1756 (Plate 57)   The final pattern of Long Land Musket. New pattern lock and stock, with a steel rammer.

Pattern 1756 **lock** (Plate 12) on which the lockplate has straight lower edge, and is now thicker and made to closer tolerances.

Stock re-designed with more wood in the fore-end, the carving around lock and sideplate reduced to a narrow teardrop at the rear. (Plate 52c). Butt is re-shaped with a narrower flat-sided comb above handrail.

Uses the same **furniture** as the Pattern 1742 except for the heavy cast-brass nosecap, and, from December 1756 the long trumpet-shaped upper rammer pipe (forepipe) (Plate 32).

The records indicate that 1,997 Long Land muskets were set up with wooden rammers in 1758-1760. These are probably remnants of Pattern 1742 muskets earlier rough-stocked and only set up during the years indicated.

Short Land Muskets

The salient features of this series are a 42-inch barrel and except for the first of the group, a short-tang buttplate.

Pattern Date   Characteristics

1744 Dragoon.
(Plate 60)   Same as Pattern 1742 but with 42" barrel. Last set up in 1748. Originally known as the "short Land Musquet with Wood Rammer for Dragoons." The introduction of this arm also introduced the use of "Short" in describing Land Service muskets. Made without fore-end cap.

1744/49 Dragoon.
Same as Pattern 1744 Dragoon but new production for steel rammer, using new or bushed pipes, narrow rammer channel. Only 200 set up in 1749.

1757 Dragoon.
Same as the Pattern 1744 Dragoon but with the new straight-line lockplate and stronger stock and simplified stock carving of the Pattern 1756 musket. Made with wood rammer throughout its production. Last set up in 1771.

1769 Line Infantry. 42-inch barrel.
Pattern 1756 lock, furniture and stock design except for the buttplate, whose tang is shorter and very similar to the Marine or Militia musket but with a better defined outline, and held by the conventional crosspin instead of a domed-head woodscrew. (Plate 33).

1769/75
(Plate 57)   Same as Pattern 1769 but fitted with the flat-surfaced sideplate of the Marine or Militia musket. First order for sets of the new furniture dated 25 July 1775, first delivery 21 Nov. 1775. May not have been set up until 1776. (Plate 33).

1777   Same as Pattern 1769/75, but with new, simplified lock design, and a small square iron plate as a ramrod stopper inserted in the stock behind the rammer and beneath the front trigger guard finial from Aug. 1777.

Pattern 1777 **lock** (Plate 13), the lockplate 7 1/16"-1/4" x 1 1/4", but now has a short sear-spring with two screws showing through the plate behind the cock; a teardrop shaped feather-spring finial; the engraving on the top jaw and back of the steel is omitted. The comb of the cock is re-designed to a flat-sided and slightly curved rectangular pillar, with a notch in the top forward edge which simulates a curl. The rear edge of the top jaw is now slotted to move vertically on the new comb.

1778-HP   Same as Pattern 1777, but not made on the Ordnance System and of lower quality finish. The distinguishing feature is a flat-surfaced longer sideplate, and often the Pratt second pipe. These muskets were furnished complete by Hirst from September 1778 until March 1779; muskets supplied complete at the same price were delivered by Pratt beginning in December 1778 until May 1779; some may have the Pattern 1756 lock, but all will have fewer inspector's marks.

1778   Liège contract.
Based on the Pattern 1769/75, but with noticeable variations in contours of the buttplate, trigger guard, thumbpiece and butt. The lock is based on the Pattern 1756 lock. The lock-plate engraving features large crude shaded letters in the word TOWER and the Royal Cypher is very crudely executed. The Government ownership mark beneath the pan usually lacks the arrow beneath the crown. Maker's marks usually in sunken frames are stamped inside the lockplates. The breech area of the barrel will have maker's sunken letter-stamps in frames in addition to the usual King's Proofmarks. (Plates 5, 8, 64)

This is the first of two basic variations obviously stemming from the two patterns supplied by the Ordnance and submitted by the two successive entrepreneurs who handled the contracts for the Ordnance.

1779 (Plate 62) — Same as Pattern 1777, but fitted with the Pratt design of second rammer pipe. These arms, supplied on the Ordnance System, will bear the usual set of contractor's and inspector's markings on all components. All of the Pratt second pipes produced for the Ordnance were supplied on a warrant of 22 Jan. 1779, and the total of 15,000 was delivered in March 1779. This establishes a total possible Ordnance production of 15,000 muskets during the war using the Pratt pipe; others were supplied as complete arms by Pratt himself. These 15,000 muskets are the final pattern musket produced under the Ordnance system during the American War. Given the several varieties of sub-standard arms produced during the war and the Board's traditional practice of issuing the older and lower quality arms for foreign service first, most of these may well not have been issued to the troops until their return from America in the mid-1780s. Some cocks on locks of this Pattern are made with a wider comb and better defined curl (Plate 14), and muskets with these cocks are generally better finished than the arms with the plainer type of comb. Evidence suggests that these are a post-1782 refinement used during the last production of the Short Land Musket from the late 1780s and early 1790s. Some of these cocks were doubtless also fitted as working-life replacements on earlier muskets.

1779-S (Plate 63) — Same as the Pattern 1779 but fitted with a convex S-shaped **sidepiece** (identical to the India Pattern sidepiece). Made outside the Ordnance System, supplied complete by John Pratt between April 1779 and July 1780. (Plates 33, 63)

1779-HP — Same as the Pattern 1779 but made outside the Ordnance System, with fewer inspector's markings and of lower quality workmanship and finish. In June 1779 Hirst and Pratt agreed to supply 8804 Short Land muskets using their own locks and furniture and the Ordnance's barrels and stocks. Hirst supplied his full quota of 4500 between September 1779 and May 1780; Pratt delivered 4098 of his 4304 between August 1779 and January 1780.

1779 Liège contract. (Plate 64) — Based on the 1777 with the simplified lock &c., and with the same style variations as described for the 1778 Liège contract. Most are found with an imitation of the Pratt pipe.

Marine Muskets

Pattern Date   **Characteristic Features**

1738 and 1746 Long Land & Sea. (Plate 65) — 45 1/2" Liège-made **barrel** with four "double-looped" pins which also fasten the ramrod pipes, as on the Pattern 1730 barrels. Wooden rammer. Standard bayonet stud/front sight.

Pattern 1718 flat Sea Service Musket **lock**, with dates either pre-1738, or first half of the 1740s.

No nosecap, tailpipe or thumbpiece. Three Land Pattern rammer pipes. Specially designed trigger guard, sidepiece and buttplate. (Plate 35) Conventionally mounted sling swivels. Archaeological recoveries in the Fort Ticonderoga New York area indicate that this pattern of musket was used during the campaign of 1758.

1748 Marine. 46-inch barrel.
Bridleless ("plain") flat **lock** and cock, signed by Vaughan or Smith only, with dates 1746-1748.

Brass Sea Service **furniture** by Hollier. Fitted for bayonet and sling swivels. Set up in 1748, and 24 in 1749.

1757 Marine or Militia. 42-inch **barrel**.
(Plate 66) Pattern 1756 **lock** and stock designs. All had wood rammers until 1759, when some militia arms were converted at county level, thereafter made with steel rammers for the militia. The Marines began to receive the Pattern 1759 Militia Musket with steel rammer from mid-1768. **Furniture** same as Pattern 1756 Long Land, except: nosecap, tailpipe and thumbpiece are omitted, and the sidepiece, of Land Pattern outline, has a flat surface flush with the stock; the buttplate tang is much shorter and wider, with a two-step taper, and it is held by a woodscrew in place of a crosspin. (Plate 34)

1757/59 Marine or Militia.
(Plate 67) The same as the Pattern 1757 but *altered* to steel rammer from and after 1759. Since this alteration was carried out by county militia armourers and other gunsmiths in the private sector as well as by the Ordnance workshops, a number of variations will be found. The Ordnance modification includes the fitting of a long

trumpet fore-pipe and a tailpipe with rod-retaining spring, while many non-Ordnance alterations merely sleeve the existing short upper pipe and fit the tailpipe and its spring. The 3/8" diameter of the rod channel quickly identifies the piece as a conversion.

1759 Militia.
(Plate 68) Same as the Pattern 1757 but new production fitted with a steel rammer, which meant the fitting of a cast-brass fore-end cap, a long trumpet fore-pipe, and a tailpipe with rod-retaining spring. The four pipes are of smaller diameter for the steel rammer, and the rod channel itself is 1/4" in diameter. 1776 was the last year in which either Marine or Militia muskets were set up.

The above list contains all of the mainstream Land Service and Marine muskets produced between 1730 and 1783. The Pattern 1742 was really a modification of the Pattern 1730, with a bridle added to the pan, a new stronger trigger guard, and simplified carving at the front and rear of the lock and sideplate flats. Production of the Pattern 1748 was aborted by the glut of returned arms and a peacetime Parliamentary budget. The Pattern 1756 represented a much more complete revision with a new stock and lock, and the steel rammer and long trumpet forepipe as standard.

SEA SERVICE MUSKETS

Pattern Date   **Characteristic Features**

1738 Bright (Long)
40 to 46-inch **barrel** finished bright, with bayonet stud/foresight.

Wooden rammer with tapered brass cap.

Flat plain **lock**, Pattern 1718, the lockplate held by three sidenails, with a very narrow bevel; faceted pan. Flat bevelled ring-neck cock with straight rectangular section comb, the throat-hole oval with a curl at the bottom front. Leaf-shaped feather-spring finial. (Plate 15)

Stocked to about 4 inches of muzzle, no noseband. Plain oval raised apron carving at barrel tang. Heavy ill-defined handrail butt with broad rounded comb. Three equal-length barrel-shaped collared pipes, no tailpipe. Flat flush-fitting side piece with almost straight lower edge, curved upper edge and sidenails through front, upper centre and rear. (Plate 46)

Heavy well-rounded trigger guard, the front finial circular in outline and bulbous. (Plate 46) Sling-swivel through reinforce at upper front of bow, and through fore-end. Flat sheet brass buttplate curves around heel of butt, plain rounded tang held by one screw, with a second screw near the toe.

1738 Black (Short)
(Plate 69) 36 to 38-inch **barrel**, with longitudinally draw-filed and blackened finish, small blade foresight. Wooden rammer. **Lock** same as Pattern 1738 Bright. **Stocked** to the muzzle, no noseband. Two equal-length pipes and no tailpipe, all brass furniture same as for Bright version. No sling swivels.

1738/52 Black (Short)
Same as 1738 but fitted with sling swivels and fore-end cut back (no nosecap) to take a bayonet. Alterations done by Tower workforce from 1752.

1757 Bright & Black
(Plate 70) Same as the equivalent P/1738 except in having Pattern 1757 two-screw **lock** and a new sideplate identical in outline to the Land Pattern but flat and inlet flush with the surface of the wood. This pattern continued in manufacture and issue beyond the period of the American War.

1778 Bright & Black
(Plate 71) Same as the equivalent P/1757 except in being fitted with a round Land Service **lock** of either P/1756 or P/1777, and in having fewer Ordnance inspector's markings particularly on the stock. Supplied as complete arms by several London gunmakers. (See page 16.)

CARBINES

All arms in this section will be a nominal .66 calibre, or "carbine-bore" in 18th Century British military usage.

NOTE: Only those patterns which are likely to have been used in North America, or which form the basis for a converted type used in America are listed here.

Land Service

Pattern Date   **Characteristic Features**

1744 Horse (Cavalry)
(Plate 72) 37-inch heavy-walled slightly swamped **barrel** with heavy brass blade foresight.

59

Round **lock** a reduced scale version of the double-bridle Pattern 1740 musket lock with banana-tail configuration.

Stocked to the muzzle, handrail butt. The earlier elaborate form of carving at barrel tang and lock/sidepiece flats is used.

Brass **furniture** consisting of two barrel-shaped pipes and a tailpipe, Land Pattern trigger guard, convex sidepiece, thumbpiece, and Carbine buttplate. **Sling-bar** mounted on left side, held at rear by rear sidenail, and at front by a screw through the fore-end from the right side. Wooden rammer.

1745 Lord Loudoun (Light Infantry)
(Plate 73) 42-inch **barrel**, bayonet-stud sight. Wooden rammer.

Round double-bridle **lock** 6 1/8" x 1 1/8" with "banana" configuration, swan-neck cock, signed BARBAR ahead of cock, no border engraving.

Stocked to 3 15/16" of muzzle with handrail butt, wavy tang apron but plain teardrop side flats.

Brass furniture: sheet-brass noseband, three Land Pattern ramrod pipes and tailpipe for wooden rammer, first use of "light infantry" pattern trigger guard, thumbpiece and buttplate and unique sidepiece. (Plate 38)

1756 Horse (Cavalry)
(Plate 74) Same as P/44 but with straight-line P/1756 lockplate, more robust **stock** with simplified carving at tang and flats.

1779 Cavalry (Horse)
(Plate 75) Same as P/56, except new-made with wood **rammer** and long trumpet carbine forepipe.

1756 Artillery
(Plate 76) 37-inch **barrel**, bayonet stud-sight. First-year production used older barrels. Old pattern "banana" **locks** used until new P/56 locks produced in 1757.

New design of **stock** with thicker fore-end, plain oval raised apron at barrel tang and plain teardrop carving at rear of flats.

Land Pattern brass **furniture** consisting of two barrel-shaped rammer pipes and tailpipe, trigger guard pierced for lower sling swivel at front of bow, sidepiece, thumbpiece and Carbine buttplate. Wooden **rammer**.

1756 (s/r) Artillery
Same as P/56 but altered to take steel **rammer**; retains larger diameter rod channel and pipes, with bushed forepipe and spring riveted into tailpipe.

1776 Artillery
(Plate 77) Same as P/56 but new-made with steel **rammer**, long forepipe and fitted with nosecap. Early productions have Pattern 1756 lock, later have Pattern 1777 lock.

1756 Artillery Officer's Fusil
37-inch **barrel** with hook-breech, held by flat keys.

Engraved brass **furniture**.

1760 Eliott Light Dragoon
(Plate 78) 28 3/8" **barrel**. Iron blade foresight. Pattern 1756 Carbine **lock** but fitted with small teardrop shaped catch at lower rear of cock body, which engages in a notch in the cock body. (Plate 18) Most of these removed and holes plugged, post-1765. **Stocked** to the muzzle, hand-rail butt. Oval barrel-tang apron and plain teardrop at rear of flats.

Brass **furniture** consisting of composite-pattern trumpet forepipe, Land Pattern second pipe and tailpipe for wooden rammer; Eliott pattern trigger guard, sidepiece and buttplate tang. (Plate 39) **Sling-bar** usually but not always found, mounted on left side and held by rear sidenail and screw through fore-end into teardrop shaped rounded baseplate at front of bar. Some examples not cut for bar. Rear guard tang has a raised section across it intended for a lower sling swivel, often found not drilled.

Wooden **rammer**.

If any of these saw service in America from 1776, they would be the version converted to steel rammer in 1772 and with the back-catch removed.

1760/73 Royal Foresters
28-inch round **barrel** held by two flat keys.

Flat double-bridle **lock** with faceted pan and bevelled-edge swan-neck cock.

This is the original Pattern 1760, but altered to take a steel **rammer**. Neither an original nor the modification has been identified at the time of writing.

1776 Royal Foresters
(Plate 79) 28-inch **barrel** held by three flat slides or keys. Steel **rammer** of swell and groove Eliott design.

Flat bevelled **lock** and swan-neck cock, faceted pan.

Stocked to about 3 1/4" of muzzle, handrail butt.

Brass **furniture** consisting of Eliott pattern notched nosecap, Land Pattern long trumpet forepipe, barrel-shaped middle pipe and tailpipe; "Blues" pattern flat bevelled-edge sidepiece; Land Pattern trigger guard without reinforce at front of bow or hole for sling swivel. Land Pattern Carbine buttplate. (Plate 40)

The method of attaching the **sling-bar** on the left side is, apart from the use of the Extra Flat lock, one of the salient characteristics of the type. At the rear the bar is held beneath the rear sidenail and there is a tail on the bar extending downwards and backwards which is fastened to the sidepiece by a woodscrew. At the front the bar has a figure-8 baseplate inlet into the fore-end, and a duplicate plate inlet opposite on the right side; through this plate pass two screws, one from the right and the other from the left side.

1770 Serjeant of Grenadiers
(Plate 80) 39-inch **barrel**. Steel **rammer**.

Round Pattern 1756 Carbine **lock**.

Full **stock** with fore-end length for standard carbine socket bayonet.

Brass **furniture** (Plate 36) consisting of Land Pattern nosecap, long trumpet forepipe and two barrel-shaped pipes and tail-pipe, Land Pattern trigger guard, Light Dragoon sidepiece, plain oval thumbpiece, Land Pattern Carbine buttplate, and conventionally located sling swivels.

1760 Light Infantry
(Plate 81) 42-inch **barrel**. Wood **rammer**.

Round Pattern 1756 Carbine **lock**.

Full **stock** with fore-end length for standard carbine socket bayonet.

Brass **furniture** (Plate 37) consisting of sheet-brass nose band, three Land Pattern barrel-shaped pipes and tailpipe, trigger guard with "Light Infantry" front finial, rounded Land Pattern sidepiece, oval thumbpiece with trefoil outline at bottom, and special pattern buttplate. Conventionally located sling swivels.

These carbines were set up in 1760-2, and may have seen service with light infantry in Germany 1761-2. They were issued to the established light companies of Line Infantry from 1771.

Sea Service

Pattern Date   Characteristic Features

1715 Iron-barrelled Blunderbuss.
(Plate 82) 26-inch three-stage heavy-walled **barrel** with flared muzzle. Bore 1.9-inches across flare. Wood **rammer**.

Pattern 1703 catch-**lock**, with no bridles, faceted pan, hexagonal steel, three sidenails.

Stocked to the muzzle, butt without handrail.

Furniture consists of one brass ramrod pipe, formed sheet iron trigger guard and brass Sea Service buttplate.

1718 Brass-barrelled Musketoon.
(Plate 83) 28 9/16-inch heavy-walled brass **barrel** from reign of Charles II, and with his proofmarks. Bore 2 1/8-inches across flare. Wooden **rammer**.

Pattern 1718 Sea Service **lock**, no bridles, hexagonal steel, three sidenails.

Stocked to 2 9/16-inch of muzzle, oval tang apron, no handrail to heavy butt.

Brass **furniture** consisting of one ramrod pipe, trigger guard and buttplate very similar to standard Sea Service.

1755 Marine Officer's Fusil

Made privately to a pattern on order from the Admiralty initially by James Freeman (1755 only) and thereafter by James Barbar of London, and purchased in batches as required from date of raising until 1762. No further evidence of manufacture. Use in American War not confirmed but probable.

No dimensions listed; brass mounted, with socket bayonet & scabbard, and sling.

1779 Seven-barrel Gun
(Plate 84) Seven 20-inch .52 calibre **barrels**, six mounted around the seventh in the centre. Barrels have Ordnance Viewmarks and right-side one is engraved H. Nock.

Back-action flat bevelled **lockplate** and swan-neck cock, L-shaped featherspring.

Brass **furniture** (Plate 47) consisting of three rammer pipes, two of them (long and short trumpet pipes) unique to this pattern and a barrel shaped pipe at rear; a short-tang trigger guard, rounded Light Dragoon sidepiece, and a buttplate resembling the Short Land Pattern.

RIFLES

Pattern Date   **Characteristic Features**

1776 Ferguson (Breech-loading)
(Plate 85)   34-inch .65 calibre tapered round **barrel**, with bayonet stud on underside. Small blade foresight brazed to barrel, set back level with tip of fore-end to allow for socket of bayonet. Block backsight with pierced leaf dovetailed into barrel. Wood **rammer**.

     Flat bevelled **lockplate** and swan-neck cock, lock held by one short sidenail from right side into breech of barrel.

     Stocked to 4 1/2" of muzzle, handrail butt.

     Brass **furniture** consisting of nosecap, two barrel-shaped rammer pipes and Land Pattern tailpipe, and buttplate similar to the Land Pattern Carbine design. Upper sling swivel just ahead of middle pipe, lower swivel screwed into the sidepiece flat at the point where normally the rear sidenail is located.

     The iron **trigger guard** is attached to the bottom of the vertical cylindrical breechplug, and serves to open the breech by making one counter-clockwise turn to lower the plug for loading. There is a spring-stud in the triggerplate tang which holds the guard in the closed position.

1776 Infantry (muzzle-loading)
(Plate 86)   .65 calibre swamped octagonal **barrel**, with 8-groove angular rifling, length varying between 28 and 29 inches. Fitted with hook-breech, barrel held by three flat keys. No bayonet. Brass blade foresight dovetailed into barrel, two-leaf block backsight with tapered ornamental front finial dovetailed into barrel. Steel **rammer** with swivels hinged on screws threaded into the barrel at each side of the muzzle.

     Lock with flat bevelled lockplate and swan-neck cock, faceted pan.

     Full **stocked** with handrail butt. Conventional sling swivels.

     Iron nose cap cut away for swivel-screws on upper edges; brass **furniture** (Plate 41) consisting of short trumpet forepipe, barrel-shaped pipe with a **long rounded rod-retaining spring** riveted to both it and the forepipe, and a Land Pattern tailpipe, the two lower pipes each held by two pins; flat Land Pattern sidepiece, special pattern trigger guard with grip rail, and buttplate with tang approximating the Land Pattern Carbine buttplate in design.

PISTOLS

Land Service

Pistols were made in two calibres, .56 (pistol-bore) and .66 (carbine-bore). All were fitted with wood rammers.

There were no regular mounted forces serving in America prior to 1776, and no record of pistols being sent out prior to that date by the Ordnance.

Highland pistols, which accompanied the Highland regiments in 1756-7, and from 1775, were privately supplied by the regimental colonels, who were paid money "in lieu" of the pistols by the Ordnance.

The 16th and 17th Light Dragoons went to America at the beginning of the war and both units carried pistols. With the raising of provincial Loyalist cavalry during the Southern campaigns from 1779, a certain number of earlier Land Service pistols were pressed into service to arm them, in addition to carbines and edged weapons.

Since there is neither evidence for, nor a likelihood of, their being used in North America, the Royal Horse Guards or "Blues" pistols are not described here.

Pattern Date   **Characteristic Features**

1730
(Plate 87)   12-inch round **barrel** with no sights. Round *single-bridle* "banana" **lock**.

     Brass **furniture** (Plate 42) of Land Pattern consisting of one barrel-shaped pipe and guard with *pear-shaped finial*, thumb-piece and long-spurred buttcap with a plain double mask.

1738
(Plate 88)   12-inch round **barrel** with no sights. Round *double-bridle* "banana" **lock**.

     Brass **furniture** (Plate 43) of Land Pattern consisting of one barrel-shaped pipe and tailpipe, sidepiece, trigger guard, thumbpiece and long-spurred buttcap with a plain double mask.

1756
(Plate 89)   Same as Pattern 1738 but with Pattern 1756 straight-line lockplate.

     Some of these may have been fitted with Sea Service belt-hooks and used for Southern provincial mounted militia from 1780.

1756/81
(Plate 90)   Same as Pattern 1756 but with the Pattern 1777 **lock** fitted, and with stock carving simplified to include a plain oval barrel tang apron and a simple teardrop form at the rear of the lock-and sidepiece-flats with the front of the flats finished in a plain curve following the shape of the lockplate.

These 12-inch barrelled pistols are usually lumped together today as "Heavy Dragoon" pistols, but there was no such designation in the British Army even after the raising of Light Dragoons in 1756, until 1796. Any of these pistols may have come to America in very small numbers late in the American War.

1756 Light Dragoon
(Plate 91) 10-inch .66 cal. (carbine-bore) round **barrel** with no sights.

"Extra Flat" double-bridle **lock**, the lockplate and swan-neck cock with bevelled edges, the underside of the pan faceted; long sear-spring screw.

Brass **furniture** (Plate 44) consisting of one Land Pattern rammer pipe (no tailpipe), with trigger guard, sidepiece and short-spurred buttcap of the new "Light Dragoon" Pattern. Land Pattern thumbpiece.

1759 Eliott Light Dragoon
(Plate 92) 9-inch .66 cal. (carbine-bore) round **barrel** with no sights.

Round **lock** of design unique to this pattern (Plate 25), with early use of notched pillar comb to the cock with its oval, notched top-jaw; the pivot-screw for the steel enters from inside of lock.

There is no trigger-plate, a square iron nut inlet ahead of the trigger serves to anchor the barrel tang screw.

Brass **furniture** (Plate 44) consisting of one barrel-shaped rammer pipe, Light Dragoon pattern trigger guard and sidepiece, and plain masked buttcap with very short well-rounded side spurs.

1759/78 Eliott Light Dragoon
Same as the Pattern 1759 but fitted with the Pattern 1777 short sear-spring lock.

NOTE: American War-period production. It would appear that of the 684 completed by July 1776, 384 went to Preston's 17th Light Dragoons embarking for America and the balance to Burgoyne's 16th Light Dragoons. These should have Pattern 1759 features throughout, except that the tails of the lockplates will be engraved with Tower only, and will have been set up using repaired pistol barrels, not new-production barrels. They will be Pattern 1759 in all but the tail of the lock engraving.

Those set up in 1778-82 will have the post-1777 features in the locks but are probably otherwise unchanged, and should be called the Pattern 1759/78.

1760 Royal Foresters
(Plate 93) 10-inch .66 cal. (carbine-bore) round **barrel** with no sights.

Flat double-bridle **lock** and swan-neck cock with pillar comb and slotted top-jaw; the undersurface of the pan is faceted. The standard "Extra Flat" Pistol lock.

Brass **furniture** (Plate 45) consisting of one Land Pattern barrel-shaped rammer pipe, trigger guard of Light Dragoon pattern; Land Pattern thumbpiece; "Blues" pattern flat bevelled sidepiece with woodscrew through tail; and a long-spurred and plain masked buttcap.

1760/78 Royal Foresters
(Plate 94) Same as Pattern 1760 but with the Pattern 1777 Extra Flat **lock** fitted, and with a Light Dragoon pattern short-spurred buttcap.

Sea Service

All Sea Service pistols were made in .56 (pistol-bore) calibre.

Pattern Date   **Characteristic Features**

1718   12-inch .56 cal. round **barrel** with no
(Plate 95)   sights. Wood **rammer**.

Flat plain two-screw **lock** with ring-neck cock, the throat-hole being circular; flat-top steel and faceted pan. No engraved border lines.

Brass **furniture** (Plate 48) consisting of one almost tubular collared rammer pipe, Land Pattern trigger guard with hazelnut front finial, flat flush sidepiece and plain deeply rounded buttcap with short blunt side-spurs.

Belt-hook held by the rear sidenail and by a stud on its inside surface into a hole in the sidepiece.

1756 (Plates 96 & 97 upper)
12-inch **barrel** as Pattern 1718.

Similar pattern **lock** but with minor outline changes to the cock, throat-hole now oval, and a round-top steel.

Brass **furniture** of same general design as Pattern 1718 with slightly deeper buttcap.

1756/77 (Plates 96 & 97 lower)
Same as 1756 but with Pattern 1777 **lock** fitted and the sidepiece (Plate 48) has the design of its tail section slightly lower.

Apart from the distinct change in the internal construction of the lock in 1777, the overall design of the Sea Service pistol between 1718 and 1777 is such that it might be argued the distinctions made above are not sufficient to justify any change in Pattern designation between these two dates.

63

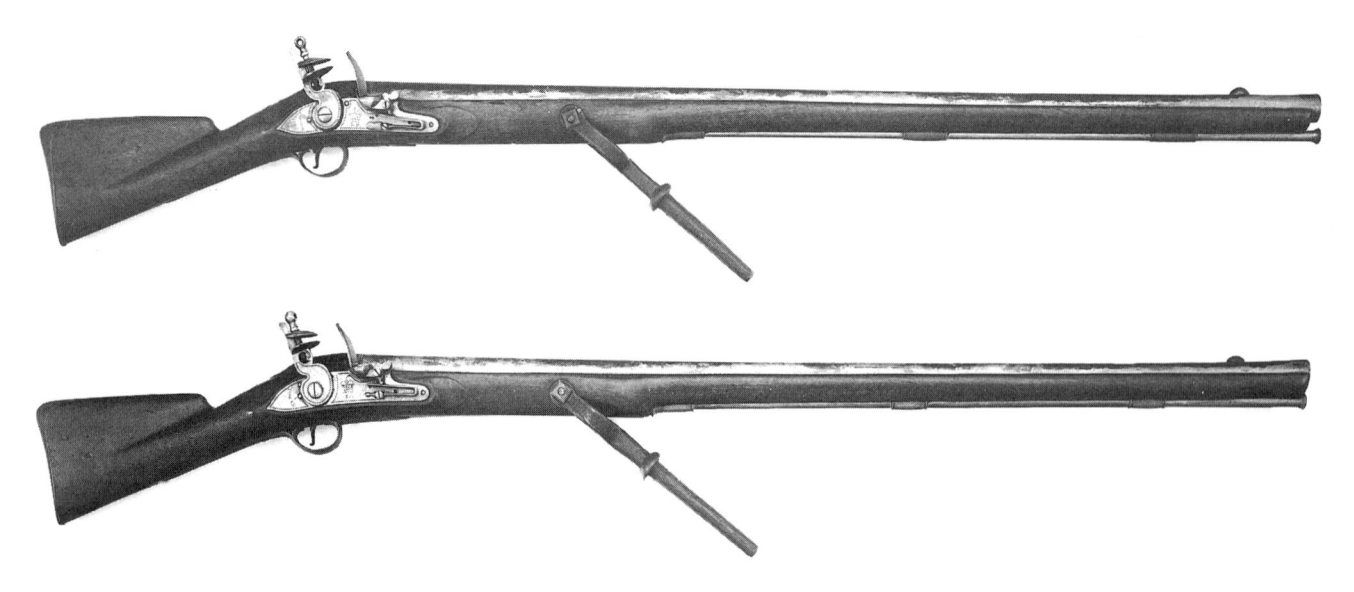

Plate 55. (Upper) Pattern 1738 Wallpiece. (Lower) Pattern 1738/78 Wallpiece. With the exception of the locks, there are no significant differences between the two patterns.
Courtesy of the Board of Trustees of the Armouries.

Courtesy of the Colonial Williamsburg Foundation.

Courtesy of the Board of Trustees of the Armouries.

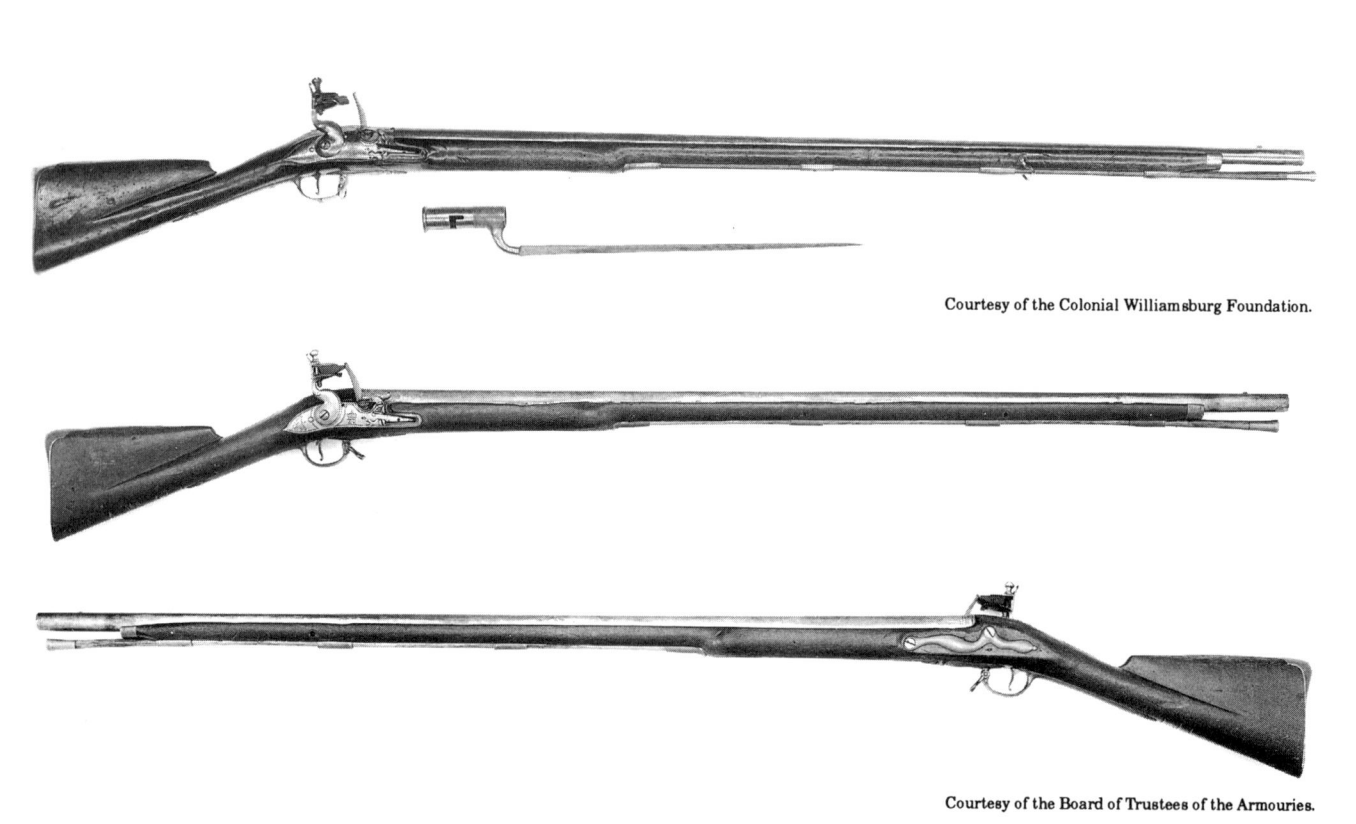

Plate 56. Pattern 1730 Long Land Musket.

Courtesy of the Trustees of the National Museums of Scotland.

Courtesy of the Colonial Williamsburg Foundation.

Plate 57. Pattern 1730/40 Long Land Musket. The example on top combines the new form of trigger guard and cock, with all other features, including the 1741-dated lock, remaining of Pattern 1730. The lower example combines the old stock carving with the Pattern 1740 double-bridle lock and the new pattern trigger guard.

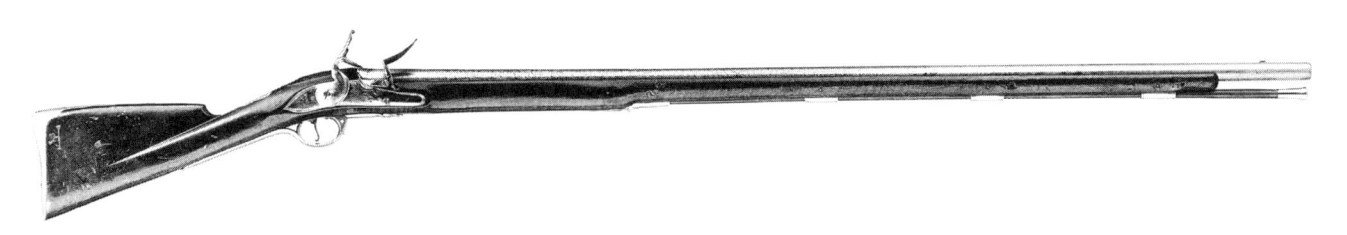

Courtesy of the Colonial Williamsburg Foundation.

Plate 58. Pattern 1742 Long Land Musket.

65

Plate 59   *Plate 60*   *Plate 61*   *Plate 62*

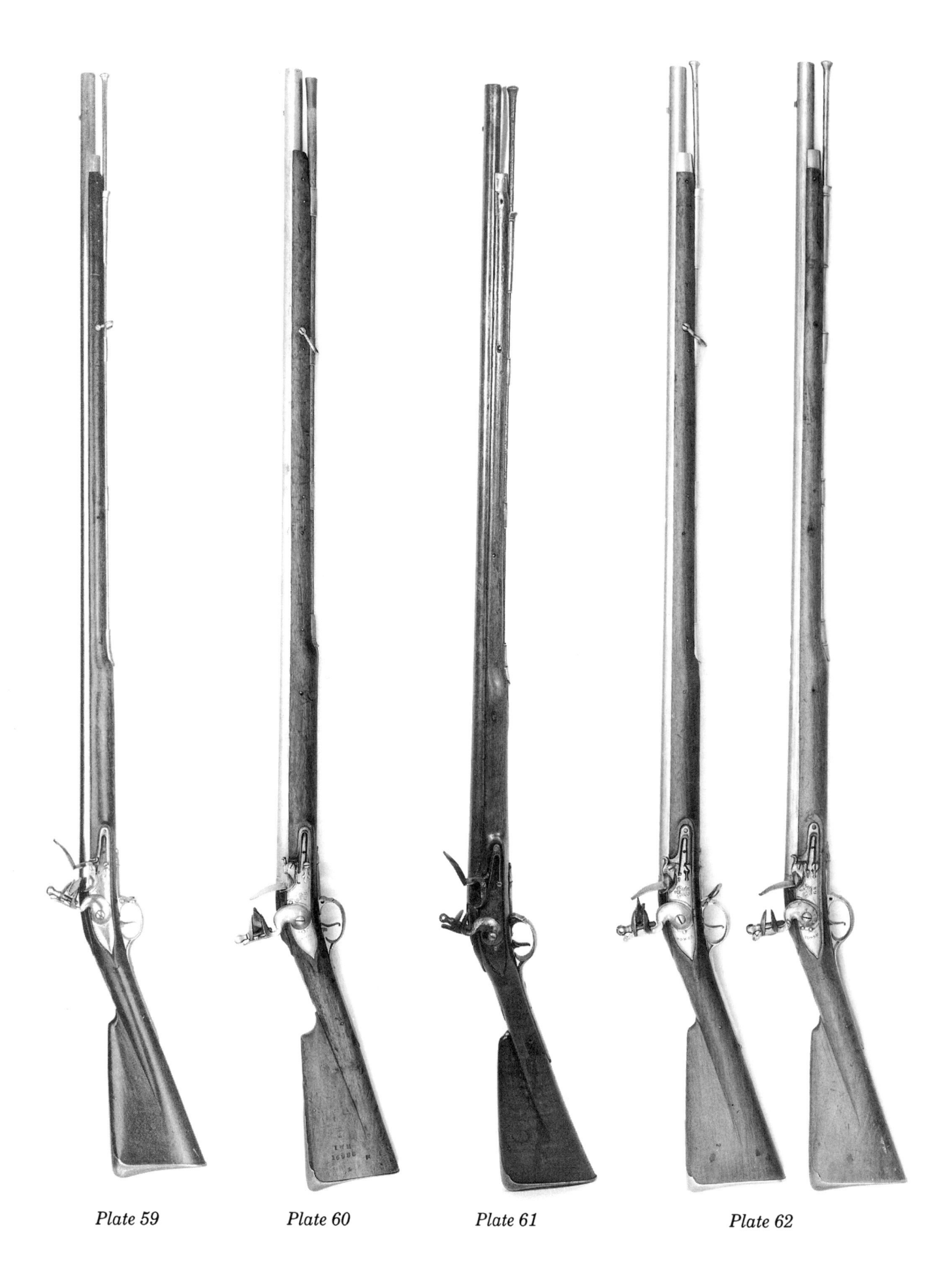

66

(Opposite page, left to right)

Plate 59. Pattern 1756 Long Land Musket.
Courtesy of the Colonial Williamsburg Foundation.

Plate 60. Pattern 1744 Short Land Musket for Dragoons. In design this is simply a Pattern 1742 Long Land produced with a 42-inch barrel, the fore-end being shortened appropriately.
Courtesy of the Board of Trustees of the Armouries.

Plate 61. Pattern 1769/75 Short Land Musket for Line Infantry.
Courtesy of Herman O. Benninghoff, II.

Plate 62. Pattern 1779 Short Land Musket for Line Infantry. Two examples, the left one being late-war production and the right a post-war of 1793-5 example. Note the Pattern 1777 lock and the Pratt pipe below the trumpet pipe.
Courtesy of the Board of Trustees of the Armouries.

Plate 63. Pattern 1779-S Short Land Musket for Line Infantry. The cock should be of the pattern shown in the close-up.
Courtesy of the Colonial Williamsburg Foundation and Clinton M. Miller.

67

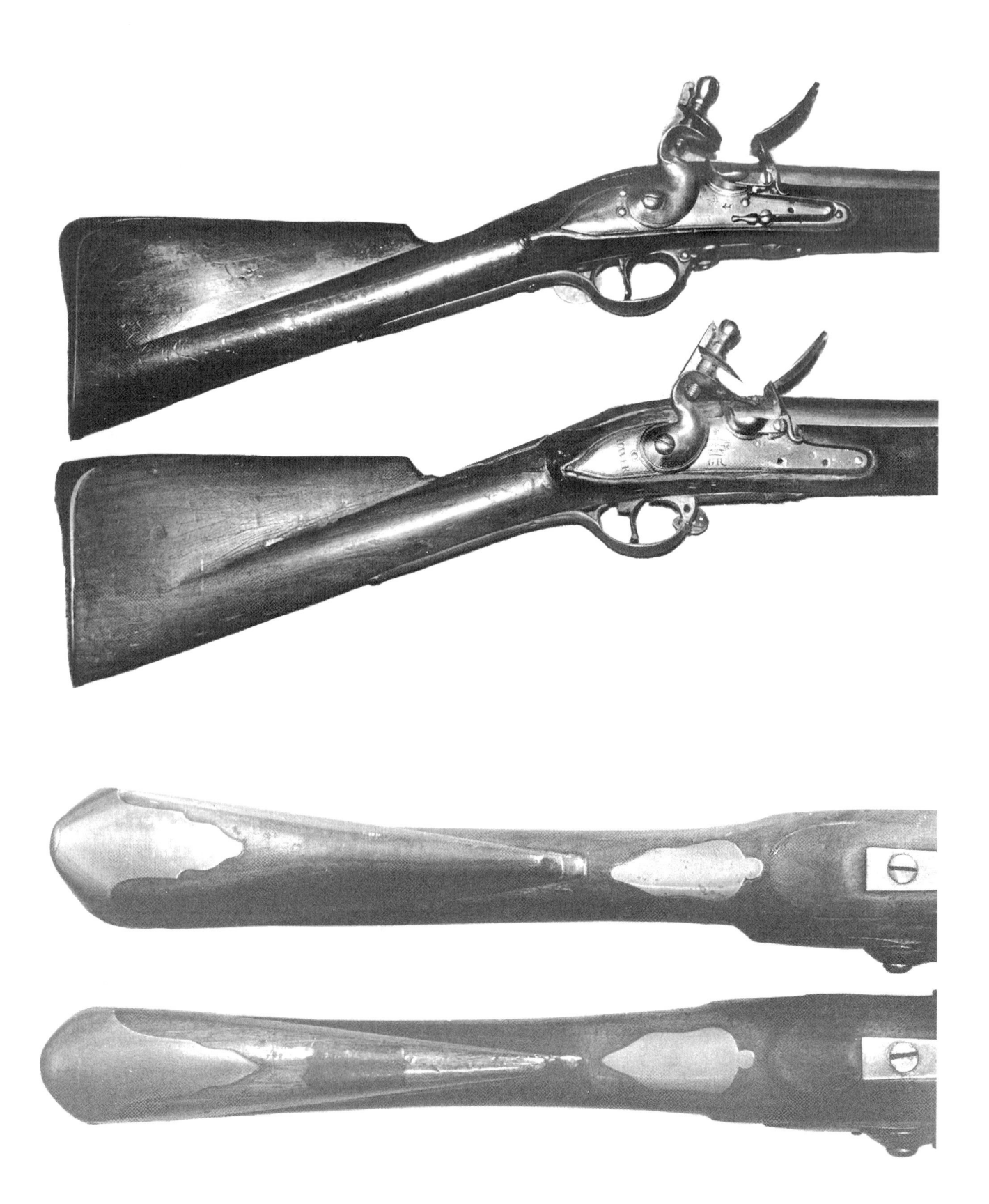

Plate 64. Comparison of Ordnance and Liège-made Short Land Pattern Muskets. (a) Upper is Pattern 1777 Ordnance example. Lower is Liège-made using Pattern 1769/75 lock with wartime cock. (b) Left example is Liège-made; note thicker comb of butt, short, broad design of buttplate tang and longer narrower thumbpiece compared with Ordnance example on right.

Courtesy of the Board of Trustees of the Armouries.

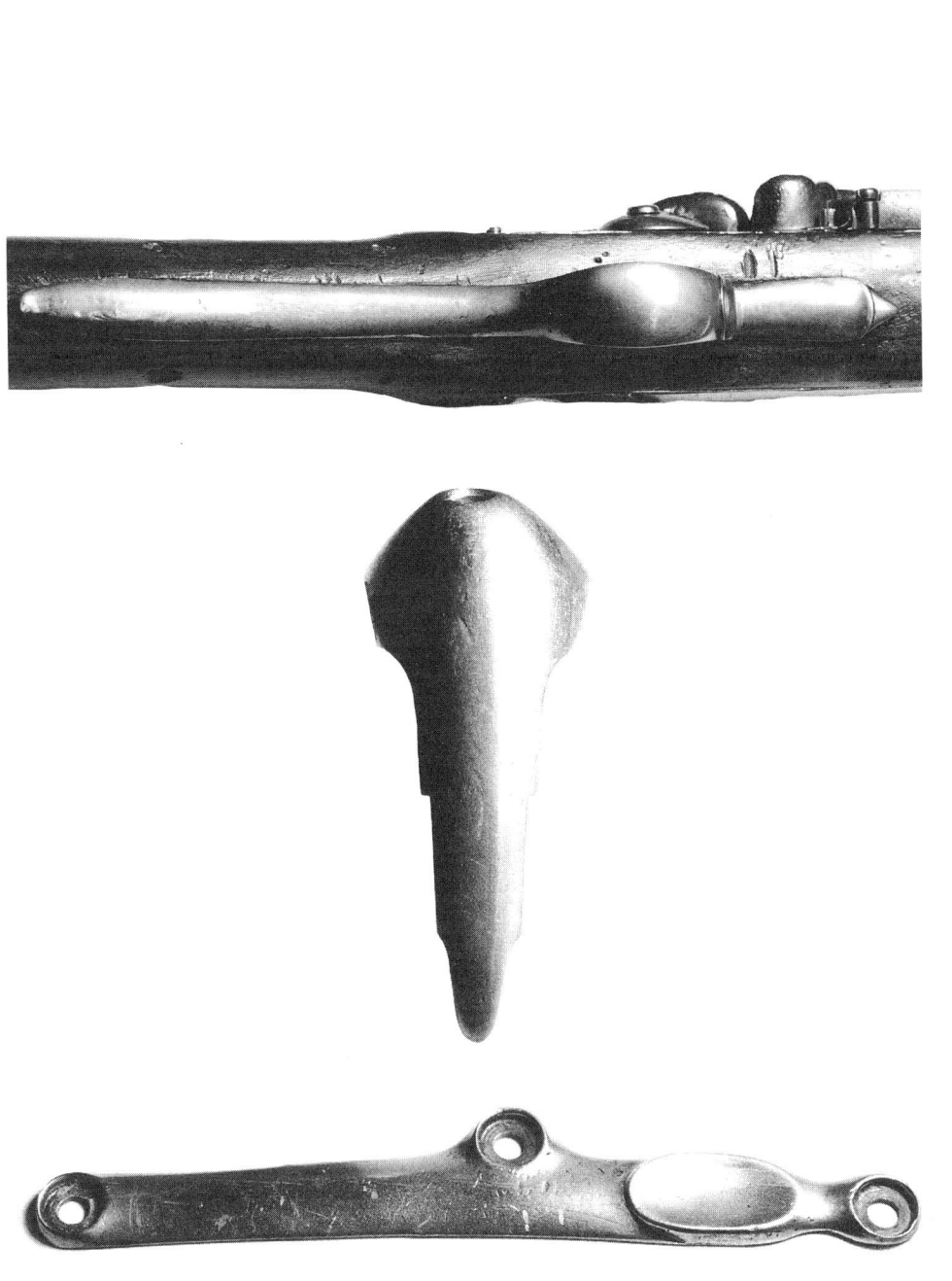

Courtesy of the Fort Ticonderoga Museum.

Plate 65. Pattern 1746 Long Land and Sea Service Musket. The middle ramrod pipe is missing. The three items of brass furniture shown represent the unique features of this pattern.

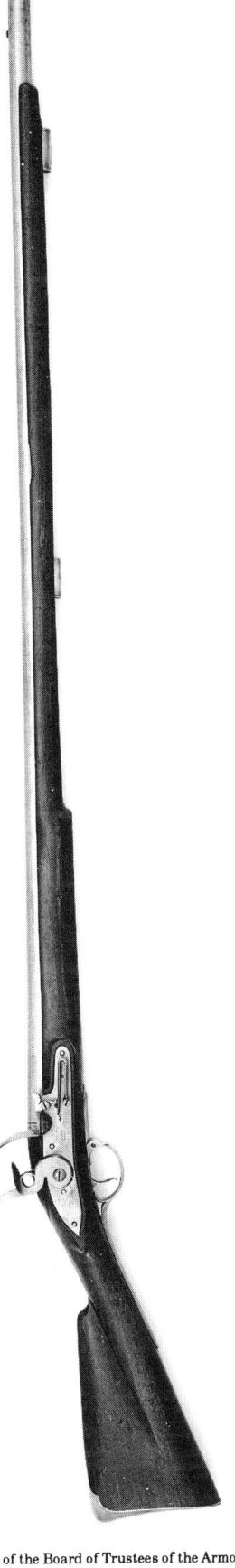

Courtesy of the Board of Trustees of the Armouries.

69

Plate 66

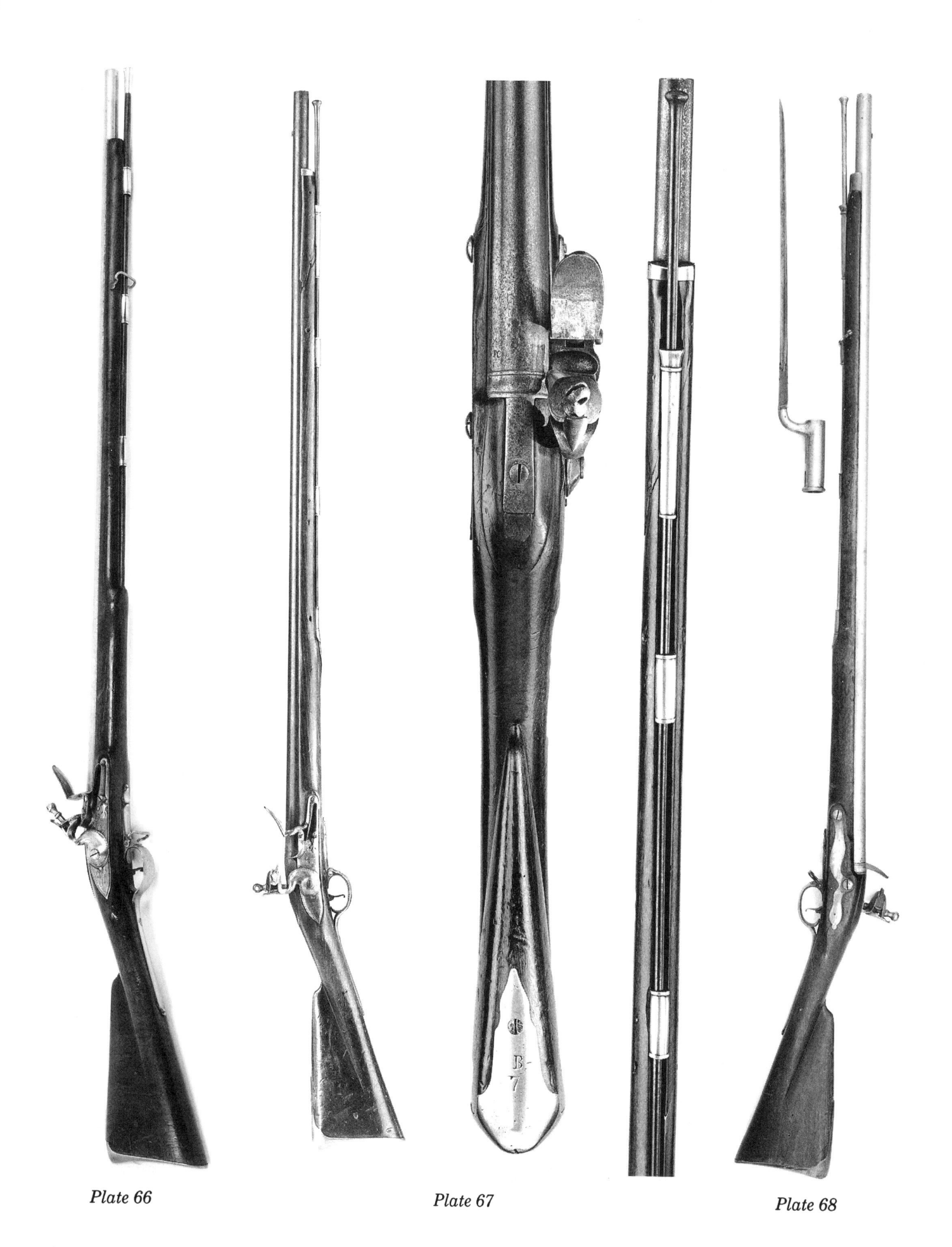

Plate 67

Plate 68

(Opposite page, left to right)

Plate 66. Pattern 1757 Marine or Militia Musket. Note wooden rammer and the absence of nosecap and tailpipe. Courtesy of the Trustees of the National Museums of Scotland.

Plate 67. Pattern 1757/59 Marine or Militia Musket. A conversion to steel rammer; note the crude nosecap and the width of the rammer channel in comparison to the diameter of the rod. Courtesy of the Colonial Williamsburg Foundation.

Plate 68. Pattern 1759 Marine or Militia Musket. Note the nosecap and tailpipe. Courtesy of the Board of Trustees of the Armouries.

Courtesy of the Board of Trustees of the Armouries.

Courtesy of the Trustees of the National Museums of Scotland.

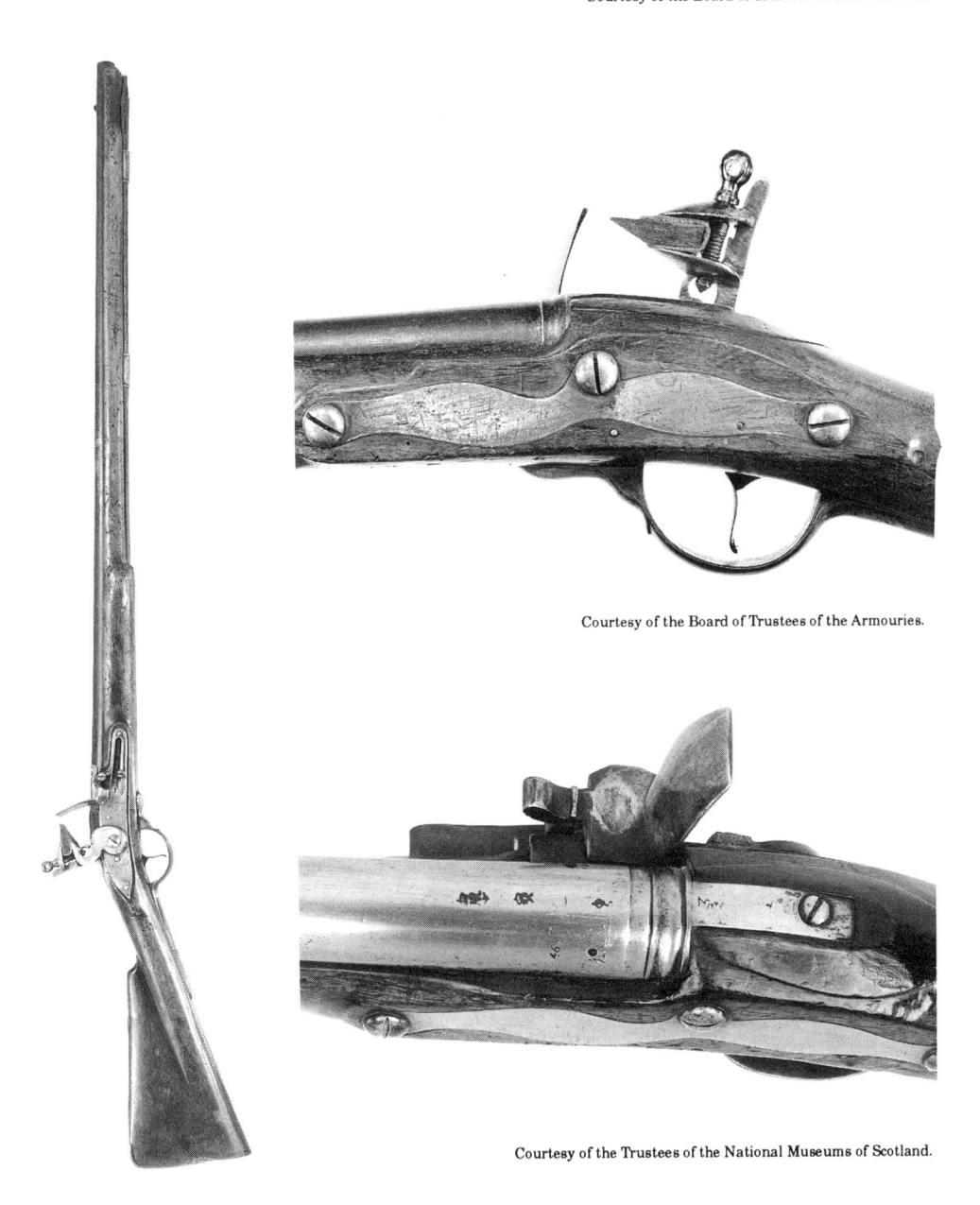

Plate 69. Pattern 1738 Black (Short) Sea Service Musket. The original design. (Left & center, top) The brass rammer cap is missing. (Right) Modified to take a grenade-launching cup. The breech closeup (center, bottom) shows the form of the steel, an excellent example of the balustre-moulding at the breech and earlier Queen Anne period proof marks. Barrels of this period often show numbers such as the 46 and 72 seen here, which have not yet been explained: they are neither dates nor of regimental origin.

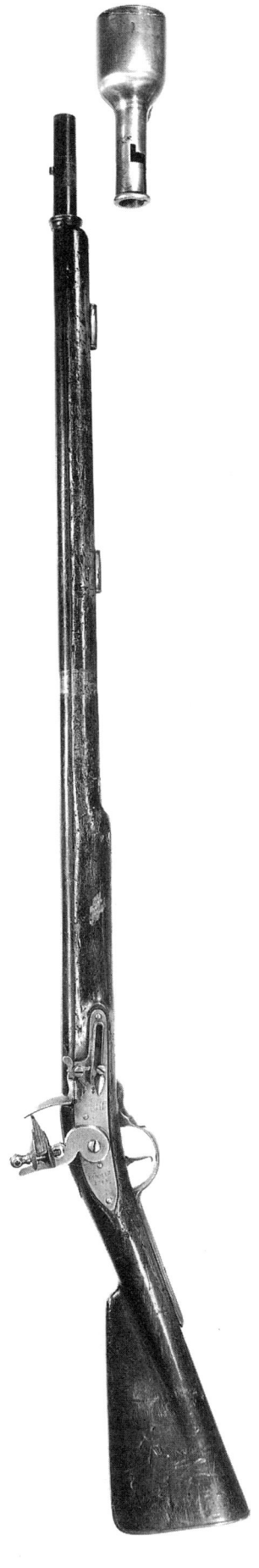

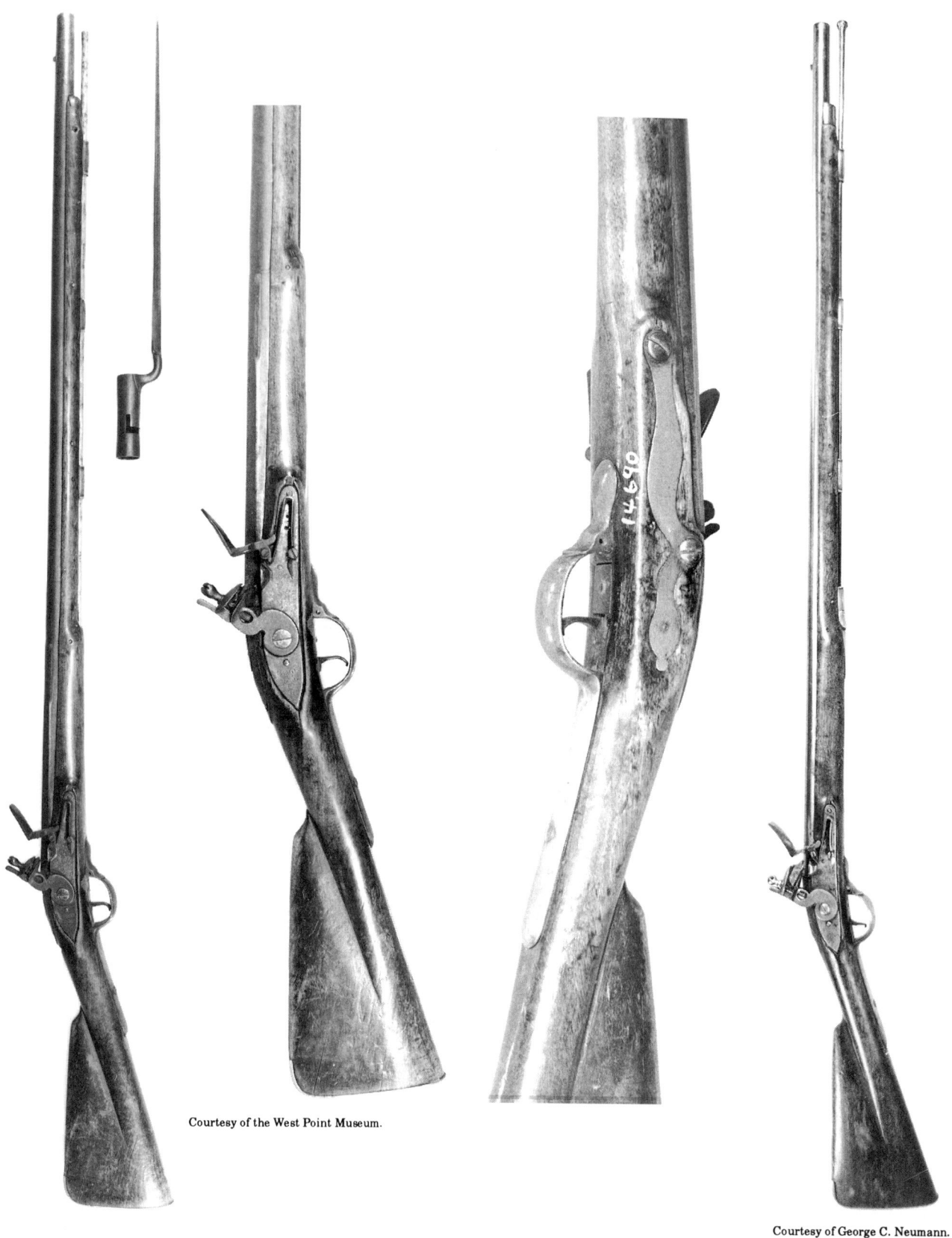

Plate 70. Pattern 1757 Bright (Long) Sea Service Musket. The original design (left & center); this example has an old "Dutch" three-stage barrel. The other specimen (right) has been converted to steel rammer, with a nosecap and a tailpipe fitted with rod-retaining spring. There is no official record of this conversion during the period of this work and the conversion probably dates to the late 1780s.

Plate 71. Pattern 1778 Black (Short) Sea Service Musket. This example is fitted with a Pattern 1777 Land Service Musket lock; others will have Pattern 1756 locks, some with updated (non-dated) markings.
Courtesy of the M. O. D. Pattern Room Collection, Nottingham.

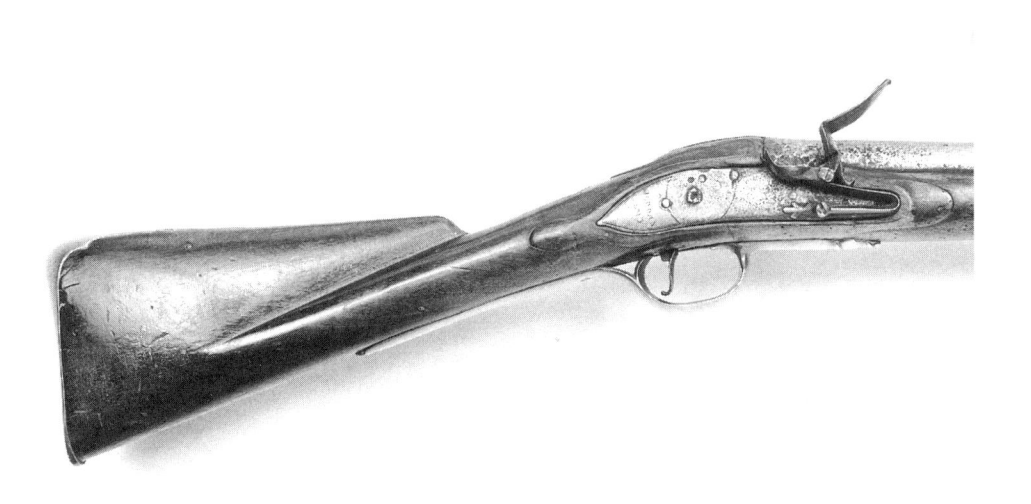

Plate 72. Pattern 1744 Cavalry Carbine.
Boughton House, courtesy of the Living Landscape Trust.

Plate 73. Pattern 1745 Lord Loudoun Light Infantry Carbine.
Courtesy of the Board of Trustees of the Armouries.

74

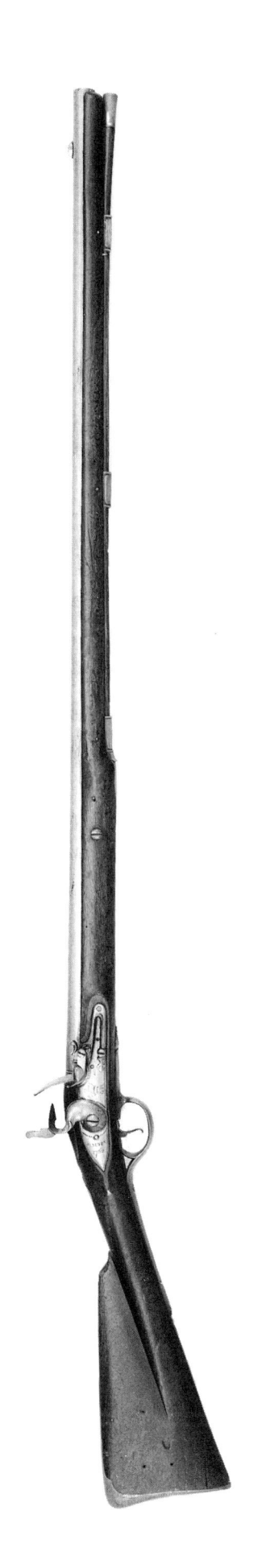

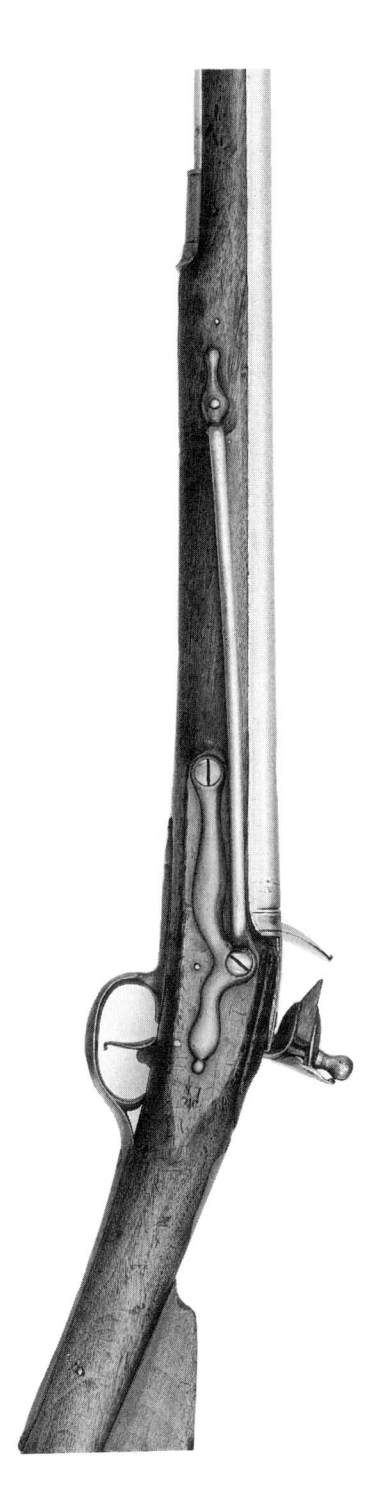

Plate 74. (Left & above) Pattern 1756 Cavalry Carbine (Carbine for Horse; "homestocked" carbine). The cock is a later replacement; it should be as shown in Plate 17.
Courtesy of the Board of Trustees of the Armouries.

Plate 75. (Right) Pattern 1779 Cavalry Carbine. Note the Pattern 1777 lock and the late use of the composite-pattern trumpet pipe and wooden rammer.
Courtesy of the Board of Trustees of the Armouries.

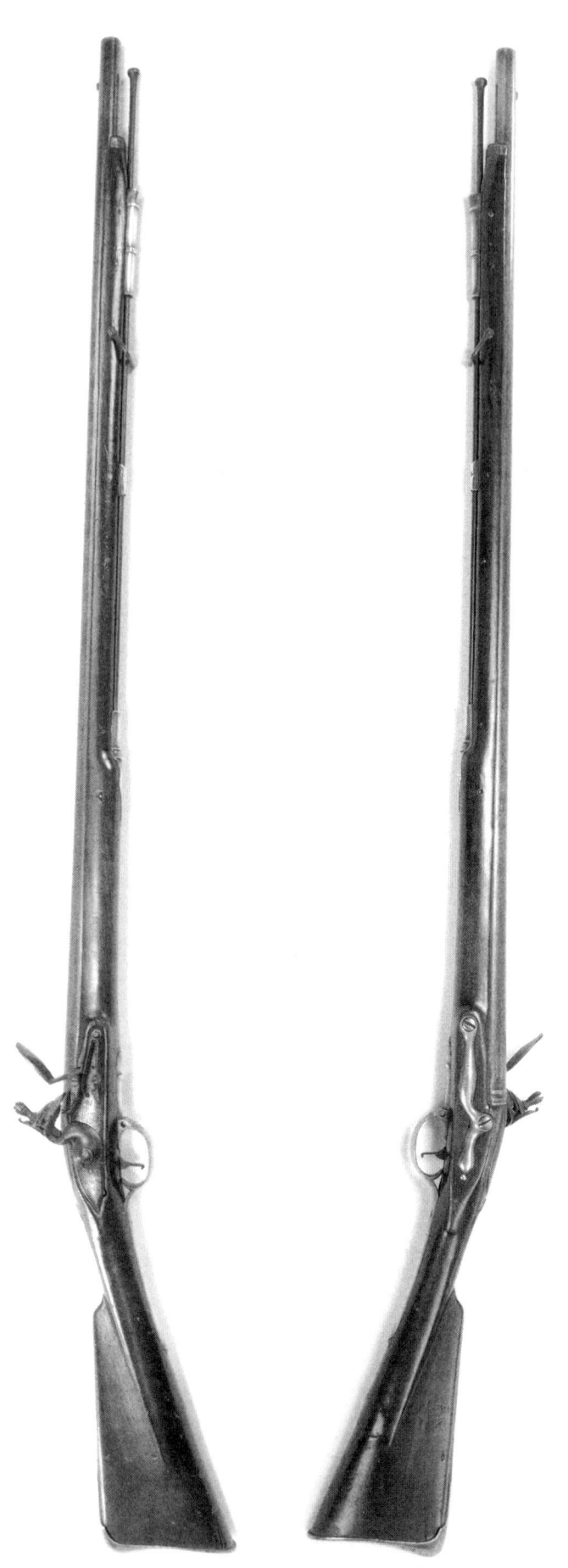

Plate 76. (Left) Pattern 1756 Royal Artillery Carbine. Note the composite-form upper pipe. Courtesy Don Troiani.

Plate 77. (Right) Pattern 1776 Royal Artillery Carbine. Fitted with the Pattern 1777 lock.
Courtesy of the Board of Trustees of the Armouries.

Plate 78 Pattern 1760 Eliott Light Dragoon Carbines. Showing three phases of production between 1760 and 1770. Upper is fitted with (missing) dog-catch; middle dated 1764 (the last year locks were dated) shows dog-catch still being fitted. These two examples originally had sling bars fitted on the left side (note cutaway to left of rear side nail). Note the undrilled lug for a slower sling swivel cast into the lower trigger-guard tang. Lower, made post-1764, has had the catch professionally removed and the lock engraving updated. Some were also fitted without catches on the locks. This example was never fitted with either a sling bar or swivels.

Courtesy of the Board of Trustees of the Armouries.

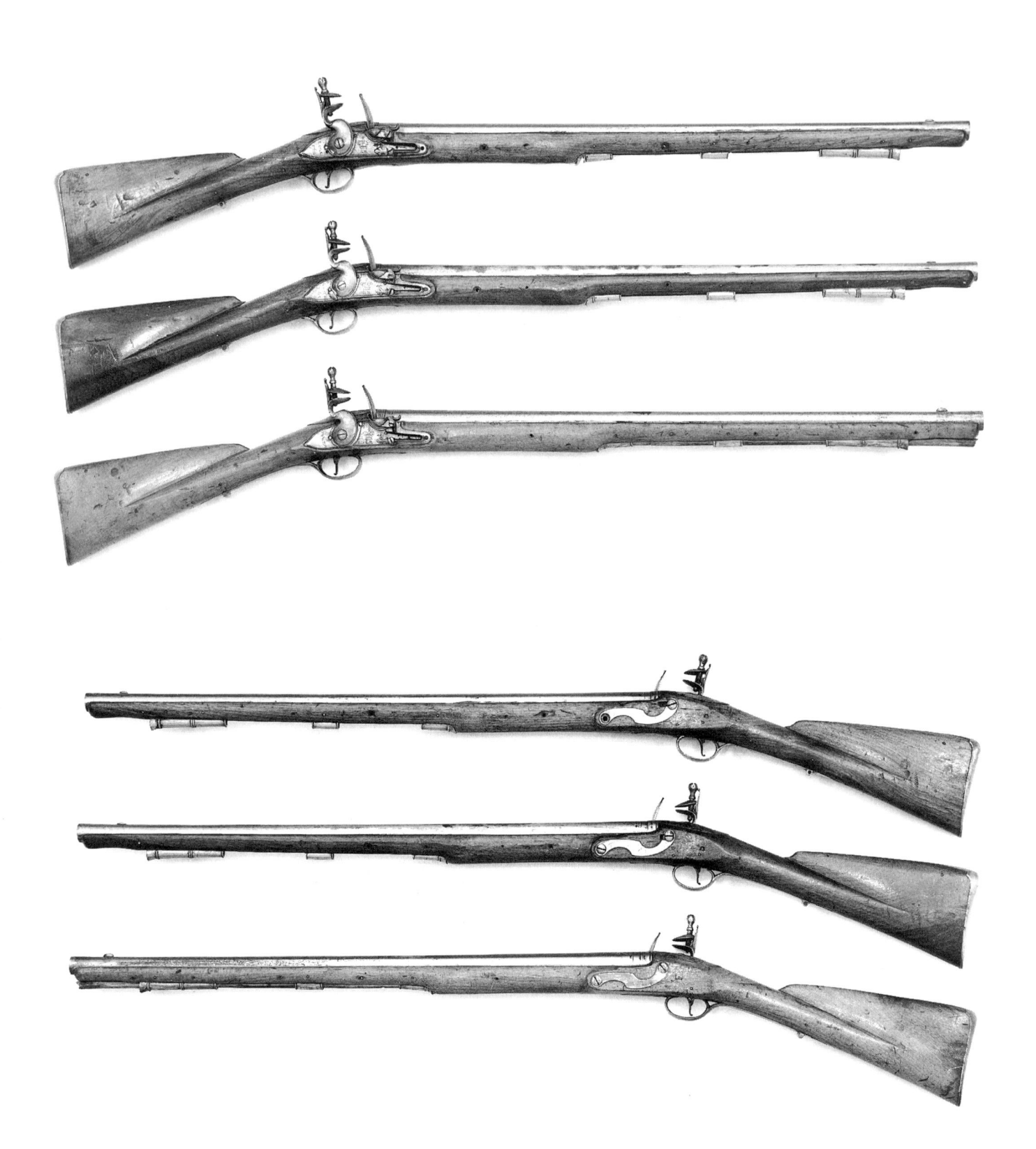

Pattern 1760 Eliott Light Dragoon Carbines. See Plate 78 for close-up views of the locks.

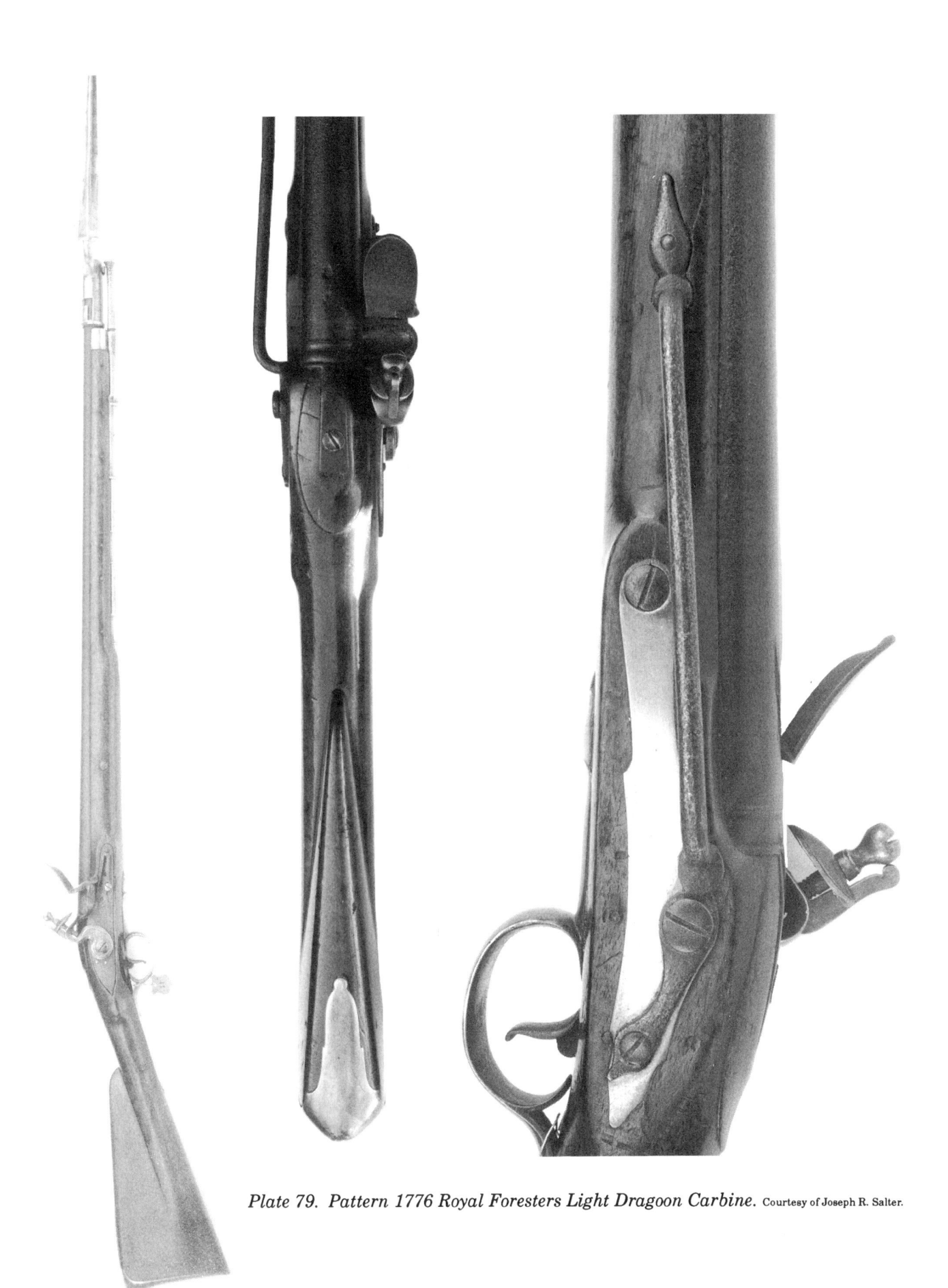

Plate 79. Pattern 1776 Royal Foresters Light Dragoon Carbine. Courtesy of Joseph R. Salter.

79

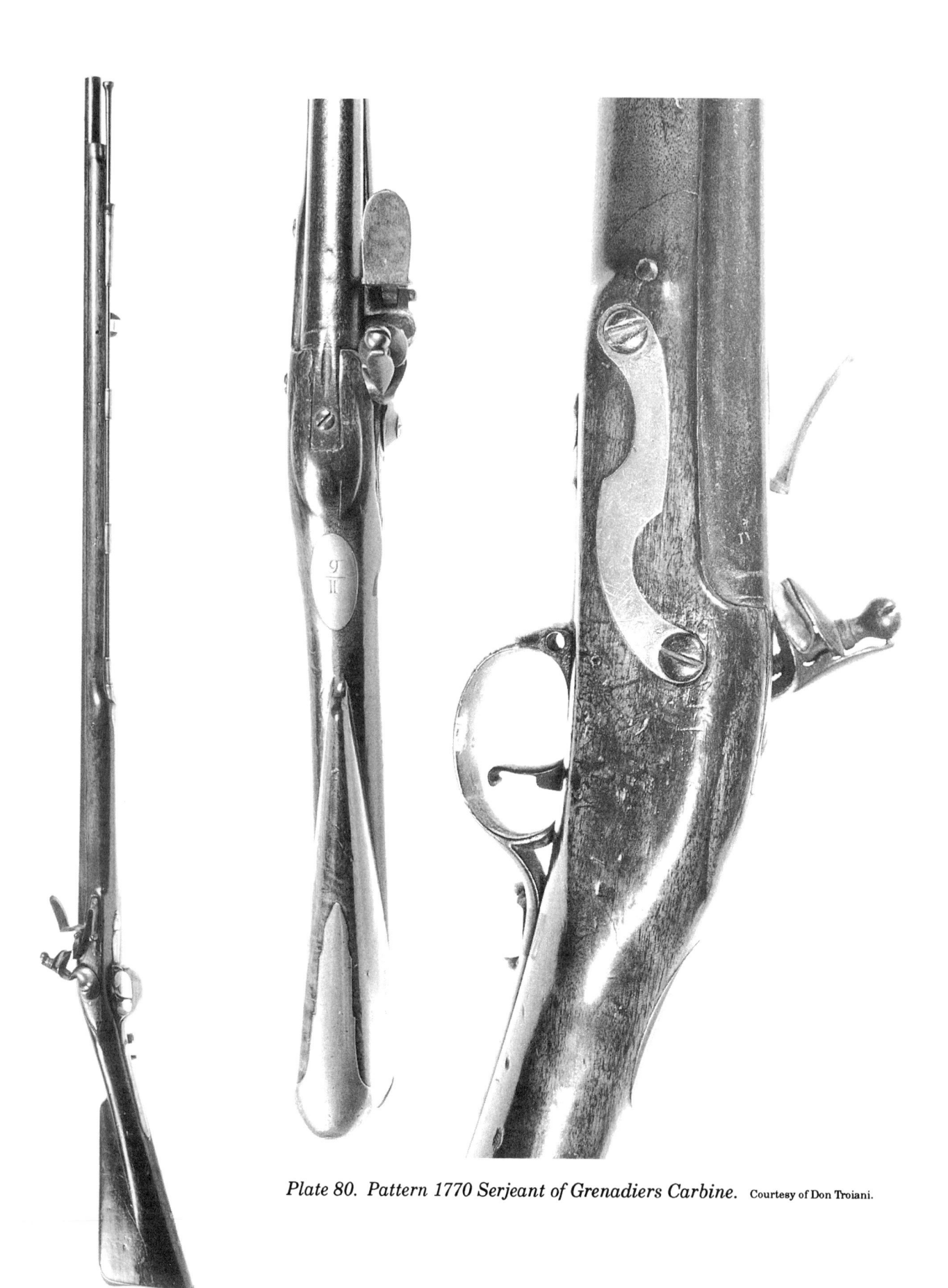

Plate 80. Pattern 1770 Serjeant of Grenadiers Carbine. Courtesy of Don Troiani.

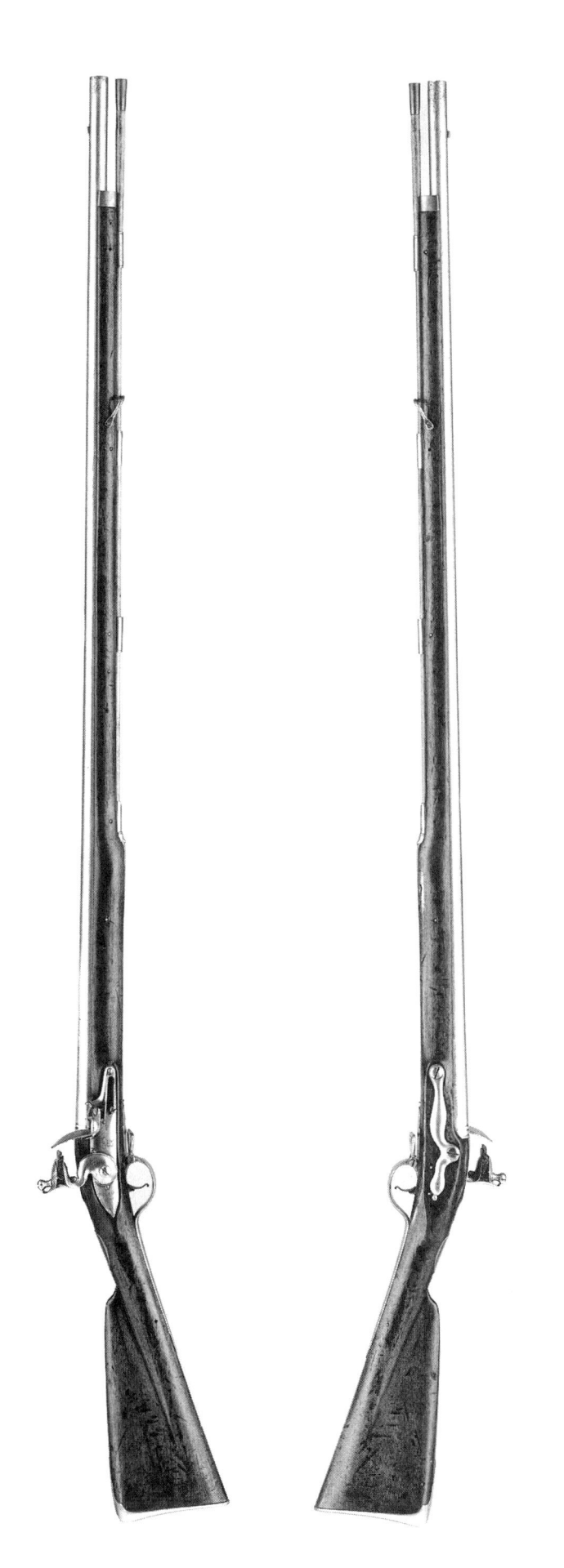

Plate 81. Pattern 1760 Light Infantry Carbine.

Courtesy of the Colonial Williamsburg Foundation
and of the Board of Trustees of the Armouries.

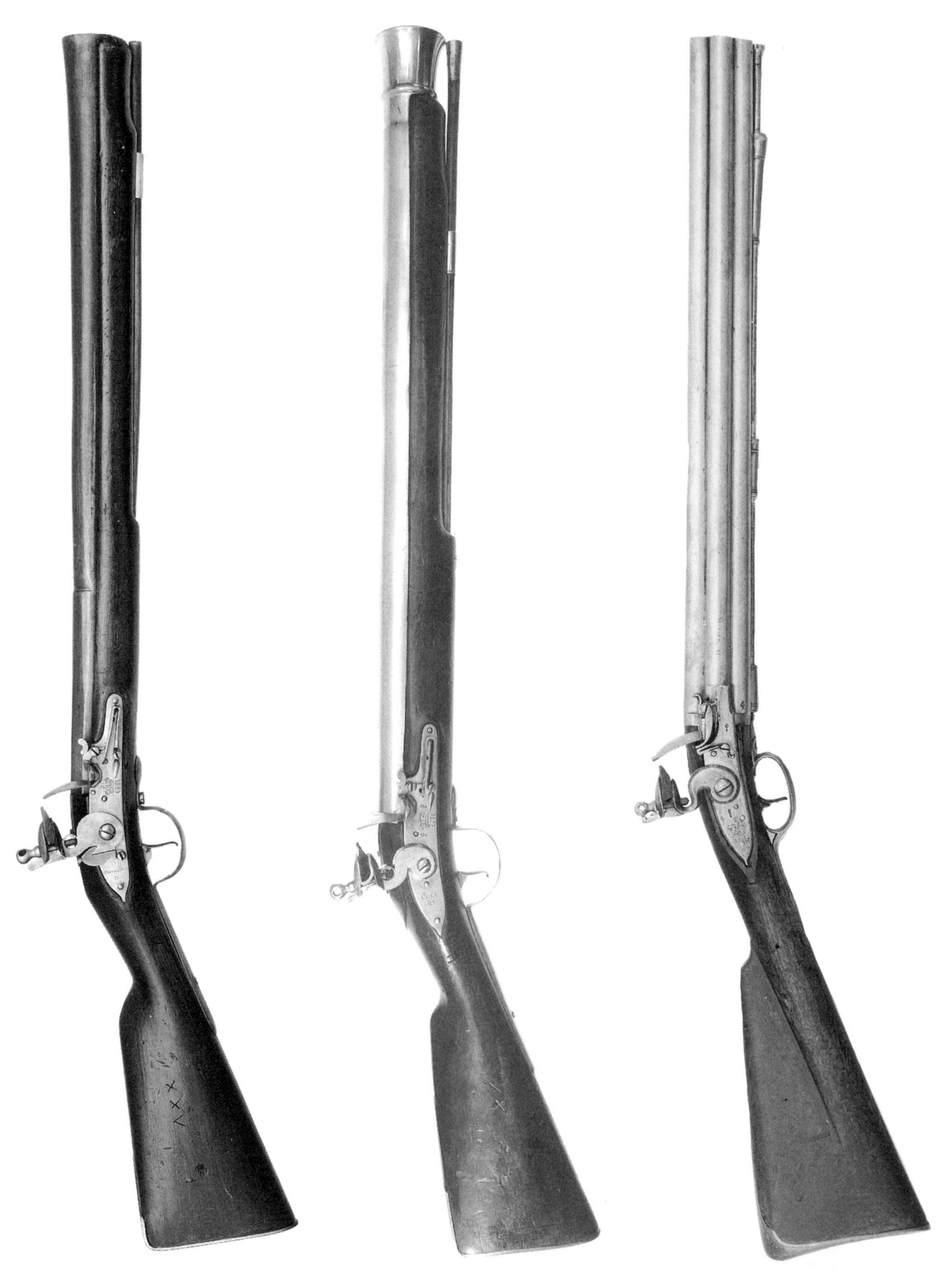

Plate 82. Pattern 1715 Sea Service Blunderbuss.
Courtesy of the Board of Trustees of the Armouries.

Plate 83. Pattern 1718 Sea Service Musketoon.
Courtesy of the Board of Trustees of the Armouries.

Plate 84. Pattern 1779 Seven-barrel Volley Gun.
Courtesy of the Board of Trustees of the Armouries.

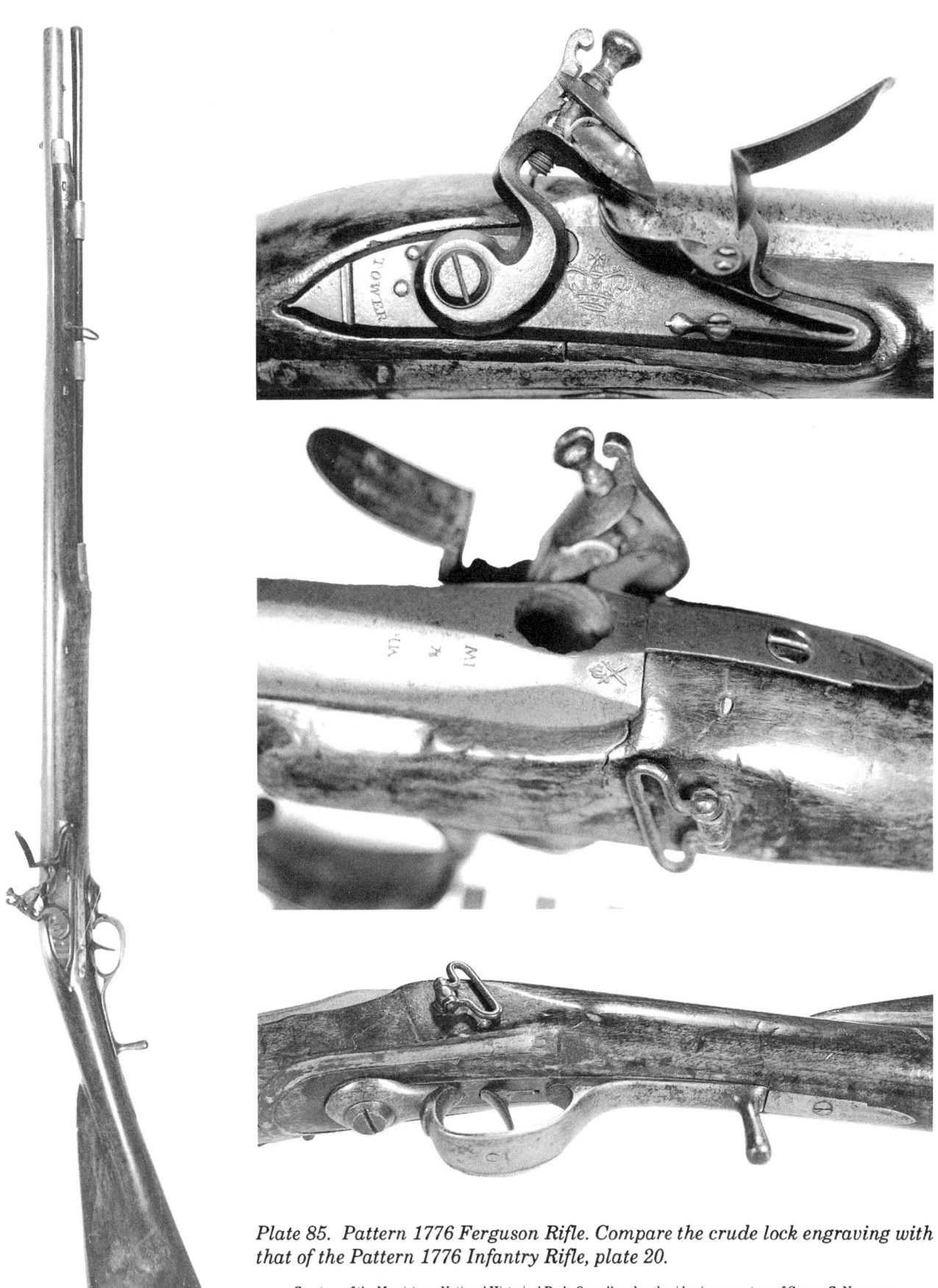

Plate 85. Pattern 1776 Ferguson Rifle. Compare the crude lock engraving with that of the Pattern 1776 Infantry Rifle, plate 20.

Courtesy of the Morristown National Historical Park. Overall and underside views courtesy of George C. Neumann.

83

Plate 87. Pattern 1730 Land Service Pistol.
Courtesy of the Director, National Army Museum, London.

(Opposite page, top to bottom)

Plate 88. Pattern 1738 Land Service Pistol.

Plate 89. Pattern 1756 Land Service Pistol.
Courtesy of the Board of Trustees of the Armouries.

Plate 90. Pattern 1756/81 Land Service Pistol. Note the plain carving around lock and sidepiece, and the barrel tang apron.
Courtesy of J. Craig Nannos.

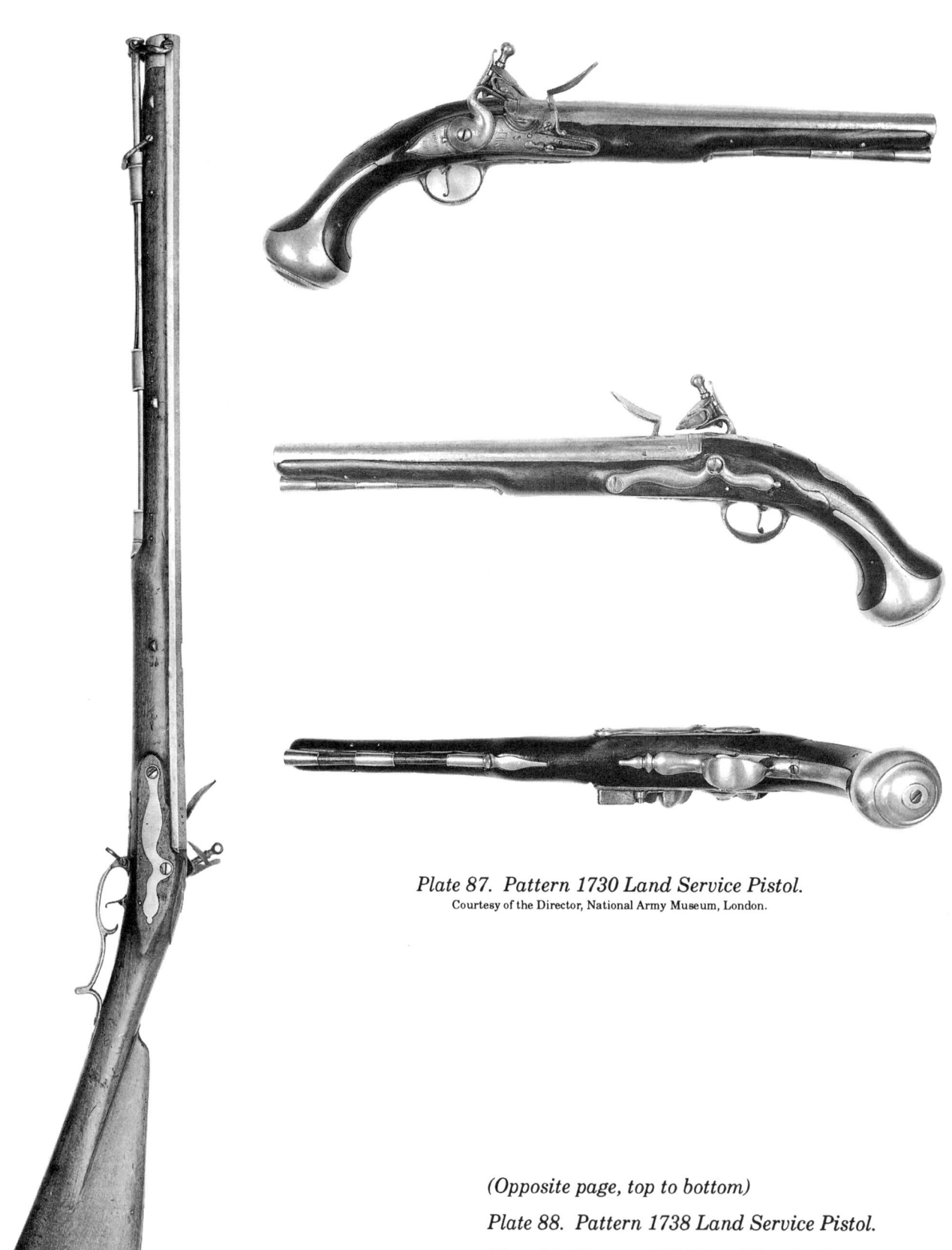

Plate 86. Pattern 1776 Infantry Rifle.
Courtesy of R.J. Whittaker.

85

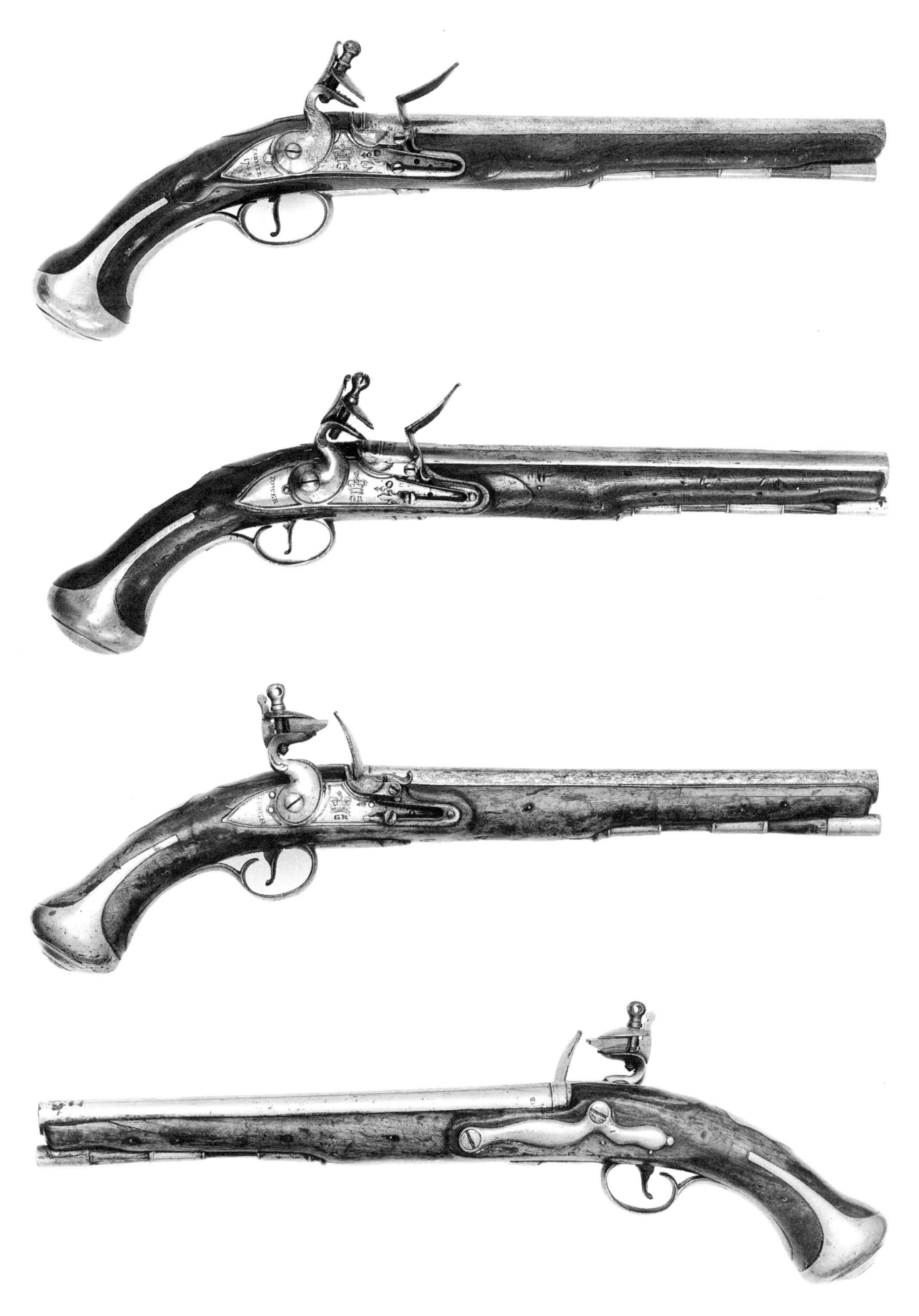

Plate 91. Pattern 1756 Light Dragoon Pistol. Courtesy of Clark R. Hoffman.

Plate 92. Pattern 1759 Eliott Light Dragoon Pistol. The chief difference between this and the Pattern 1756 Light Dragoon are the lock design and barrel length.
Courtesy of the Board of Trustees of the Armouries.

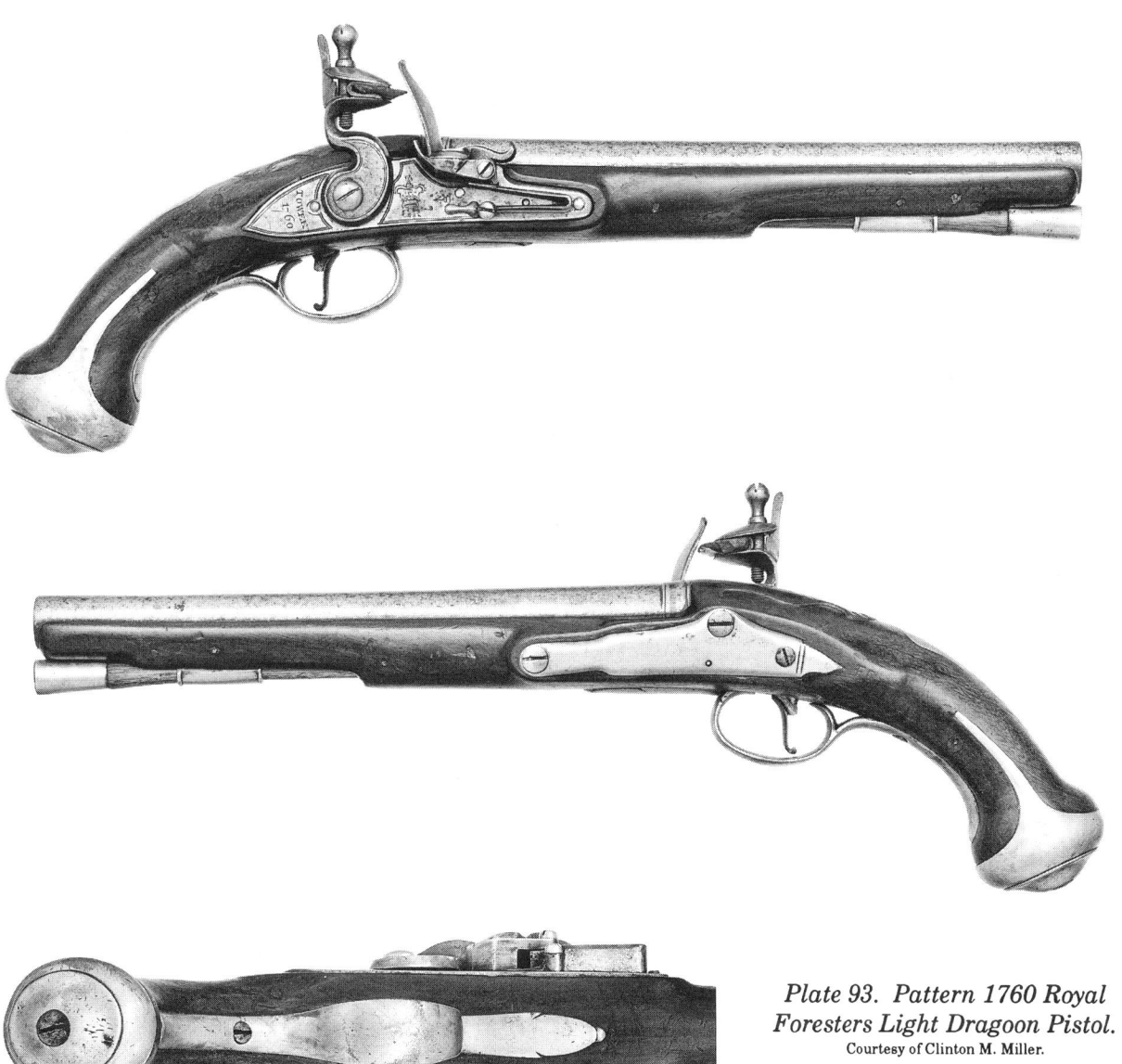

Plate 93. Pattern 1760 Royal Foresters Light Dragoon Pistol.
Courtesy of Clinton M. Miller.

87

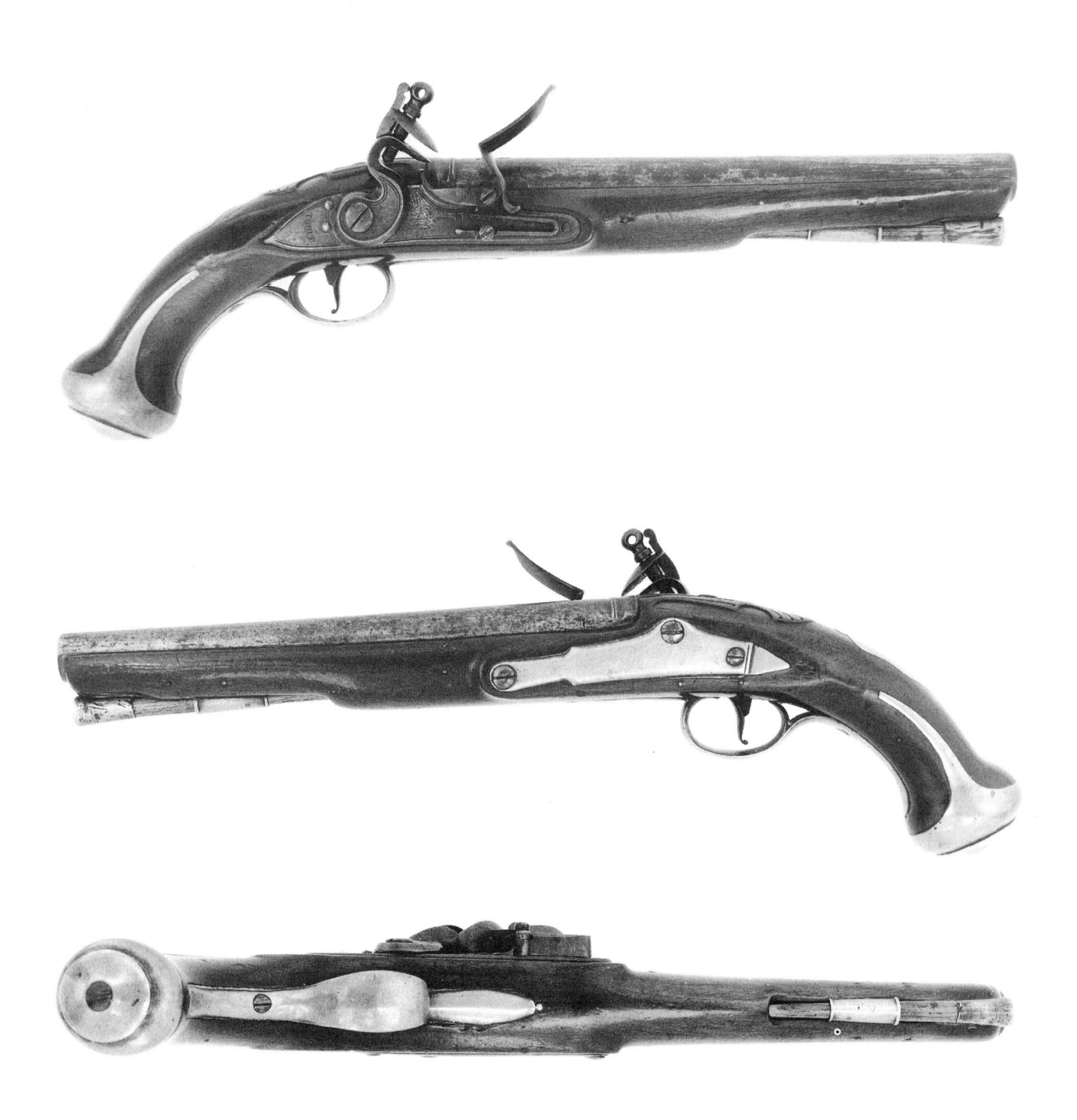

Plate 94. Pattern 1760/78 Royal Foresters Light Dragoon Pistol. Courtesy of Clark R. Hoffman.

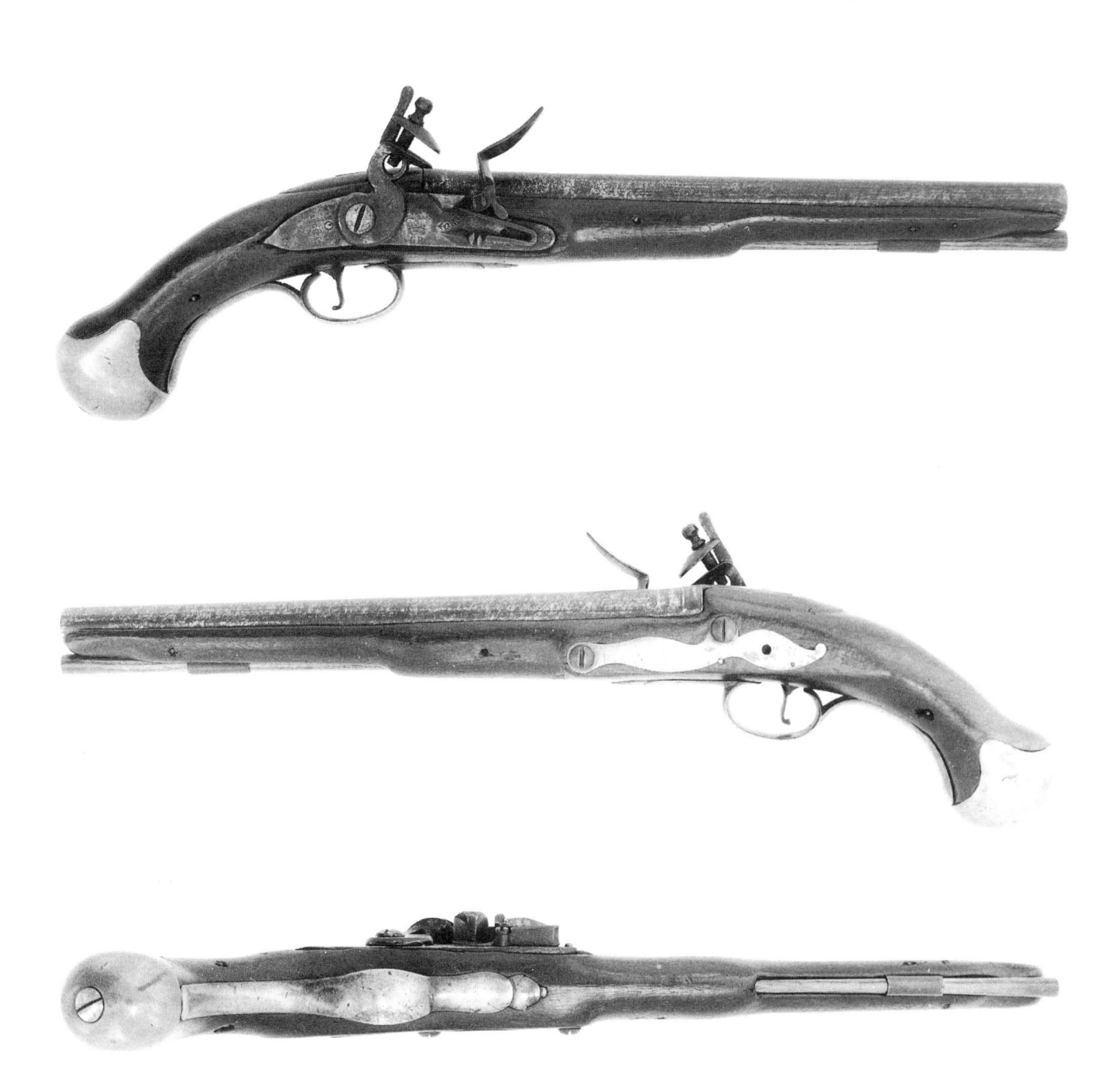

Plate 95. Pattern 1718 Sea Service Pistol. Courtesy of Clark R. Hoffman.

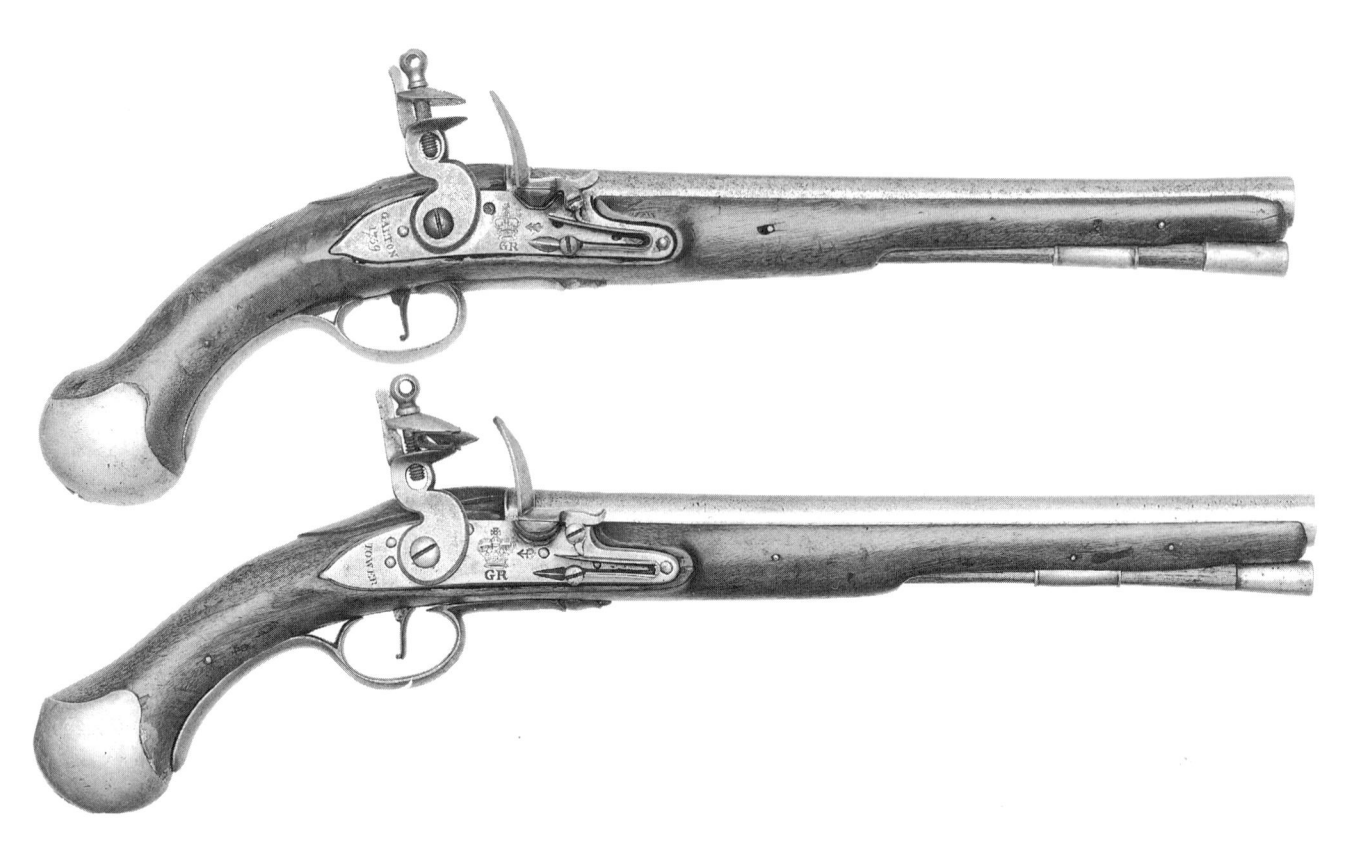

Plate 96. Sea Service Pistols, right sides. Upper: Pattern 1756. Lower: Pattern 1756/77. Courtesy of Clinton M. Miller.

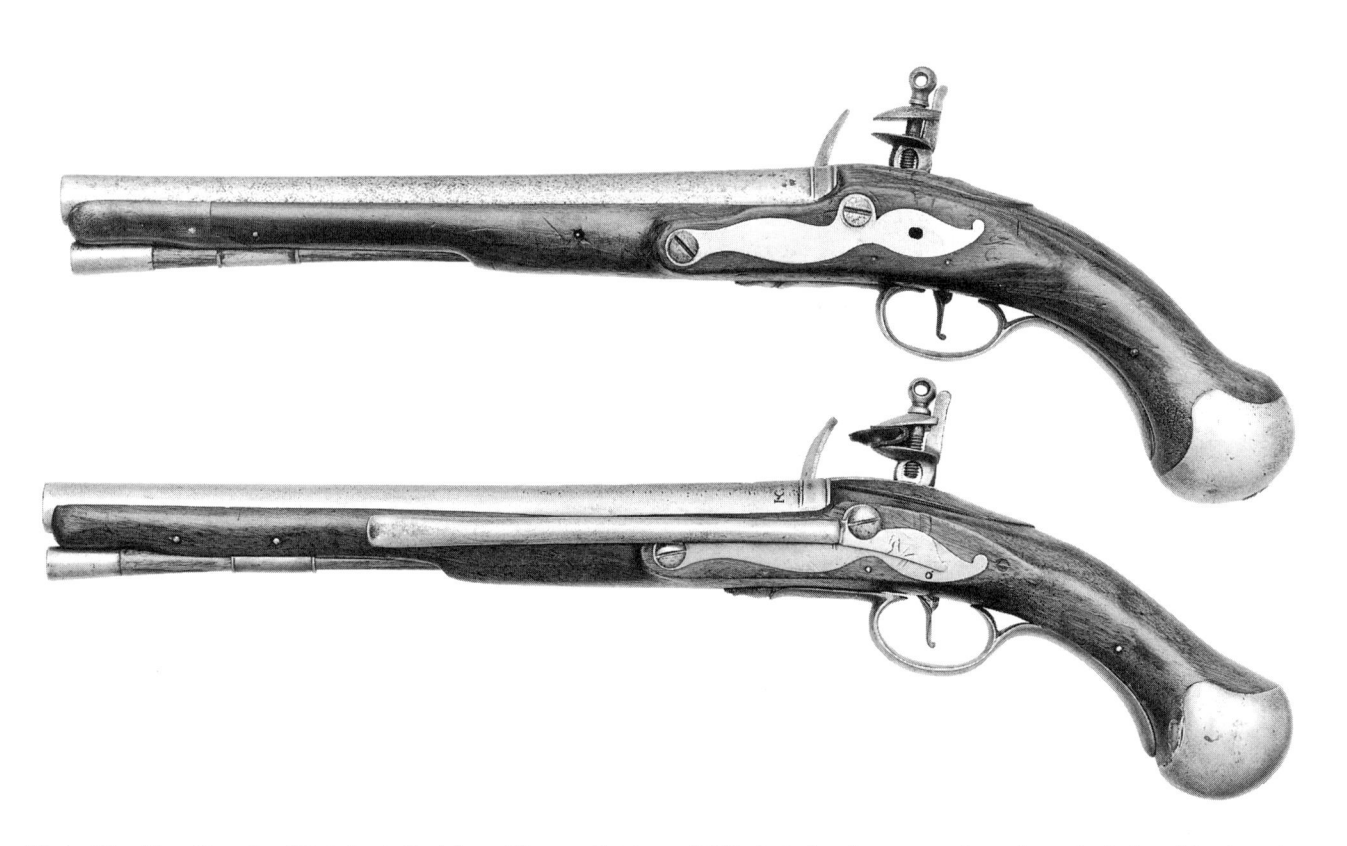

Plate 97. Sea Service Pistols, left sides. Upper: Pattern 1756, belt hook removed to show hole in sidepiece into which a stud on the inner surface of the belt-hook fits to lock it in position. Lower: Pattern 1756/77. Note the angle of the tails of the sidepieces in each pattern, and the trigger pin showing through the sidepiece on the Pattern 1756/77.

Courtesy of Clinton M. Miller.

Detailed Dimensions of Standard Patterns of British Military Small Arms used in America, 1737–1783

Note on Measurements. The use of the symbols + or - indicates a measurement equivalent to 1/32-inch, being read as "just over" or "just under" the basic unit of a sixteenth of an inch.

WALLPIECE

Pattern 1738/78 Wallpiece
RA XII-507

Overall length: 71 1/4".

Barrel: 53 5/8", balustre-moulded at breech for 15/16"; the three barrel pins located at 23 13/16", 35 11/16", 47 9/16" from the breech. The bolt for the swivel is 12" from the breech. The King's Proof Marks on top. The barrel tang is 3 1/4" long, and tapers outwards towards the rear from 13/16" to 15/16". The steel blade front sight is brazed 3 15/16" from the muzzle, and measures 1 1/16" x 1/2". Barrel diameter across breech ahead of moulding is 2 3/16+", and across muzzle 1 1/2" with a slight swamped effect.

Lock: Double-bridle, flat bevelled surface to lockplate and ring-neck cock. The plate measures 9 1/4" x 1 3/4". The comb of the cock is a pillar with slight rearward curve at the top, measuring 3/8" across at the widest point. Throw of cock is 2 5/8". The rear of the oval top-jaw is notched to fit around and move along the comb. The steel is 2 9/16" high x 1 1/2" wide. Teardrop finial to the feather-spring, short sear-spring. Plate, cock, top jaw and back of steel have fine double border lines engraved. Crowned GR engraved ahead of cock, and small crowned Broad Arrow stamped beneath faceted pan. Across the tail is engraved TOWER. The sidenail heads are 7/8" in diameter, and are not recessed into the sidepiece.

Stock: walnut, to within 5/16" of muzzle, with no cap. Lock and sidepiece flats have plain rounded front and teardrop at rear, measuring 14 1/8" overall. The raised barrel tang apron is of the earliest Land Pattern narrow wavy design in outline measuring 4 13/16" x 1 7/8".

The comb measures 9 1/2" from centre of buttplate screw to tip. The distance from the centre of the trigger to the centre of the buttplate is 15 5/8". The rod channel is 1/2" in diameter. Stamped in the rod channel: crowned 0, crowned 1, crowned 0, RE RE I. LODER. Sideplate flat has no stamps. Stamped below lower guard tang with crown and crowned number. Storekeeper's stamp in right butt.

Brass furniture: no nosecap. The upper pipe is barrel-shaped and collared, 2" long, external diameter 3/4", held by a pin 45 9/16" from the breech. The front of the pipe is 6 5/8" from the tip of the fore-end. Internal diameter 9/16". The distance between the rear of the upper pipe and the front of the second pipe is 11 11/16".

The second pipe is identical to the upper pipe, but the internal diameter is 1/2", secured by a pin 31 15/16" from the breech. The distance from the rear of the second pipe to the front of the tailpipe is 11 9/16".

The tailpipe has a 2" collared and barrel-shaped forward section and a lip and flame-shaped tang section 4 5/8" long; external diameter is 3/4" at mouth, secured by a pin 18 5/16" from the breech.

The trigger guard is a modified Land Pattern, 15 3/16" long, secured by a pin 4 5/16" from the front finial and by a woodscrew in the lower tang 2 1/4" and the thumbpiece screw 7" from the rear finial. The bow is 1 7/16" wide at its widest point. The front finial is engraved as a flame, and the rear finial is stepped and tapers in a curve to a plain point.

The sidepiece is Land Pattern with a flat flush surface, and measures 9" overall, with 5 1/4" between sidenail centres, the sidenail heads not recessed in the brass. It is engraved with double border lines and the ball-outline tail is engraved as a shell.

The thumbpiece is Land Pattern, measuring 3 3/16" x 1 3/8".

The buttplate is similar to the Long Land Pattern Musket design with a three-step tapering tang 7" long, but terminating in a plain rounded tip, and having double border lines engraved. From the first to the second shoulder is 2" from the second to the third step is 1 5/8" and from the third step to the tip is 1 3/4". The plate is 6 1/2" from heel to toe, and is 2 5/8+" at its widest point.

The tapered steel ramrod has a button-head 7/8" in diameter, and a 3/4" slot cut at the tip. It is stamped WG near the head.

LAND SERVICE MUSKETS

Pattern 1730 Long Land Musket
NAM 9002-55

Overall length: 62"

Barrel: 7/8", balustre-moulded at breech for 5/8"; the *four* barrel pins located at 13 7/8" 22 3/8", 31 1/8" and 39 1/16" from the breech; the swivel loop being 32 1/8" from the breech. The left side of the breech has a 4 stamped, and the King's Proof Marks on top. The barrel tang is 2 5/16" long, and tapers outwards towards the rear from 9/16" to 5/8". The front sight/bayonet stud is brazed 2" from the muzzle, and measures 1/4" x 1/8". Barrel diameter across breech ahead of moulding is 1 3/8", across muzzle 15/16".

The barrel is double-looped, each pair of loops also acting as the fastening point for one of the four ramrod pipes.

Lock: Pattern 1727. Single-bridle, rounded surface to lockplate and cock, the plate having the "banana" tail configuration, which drop is 1/4" below the straight lower edge of the forward part of the plate. The plate measures 6 7/8" x 1 1/4". The steel is 2" high x 1 1/4" wide. Plate, cock, round top jaw and back of steel have fine double border lines engraved. The rear surface of the top-jaw has a stud which engages in a vertical slot on the forward face of the comb. The leaf-shaped cock comb measures 15/32" across its widest point. The underside of the lower jaw has a slight but distinct reinforcing lip where the cock-screw comes through it, which is a refinement unique to this pattern. The throw of the cock is 2 1/16". Across the tail is engraved TOWER and 1727. Inside the plate is stamped crowned 30 and W I. Trefoil finial to the feather-spring, long sear-spring. The pan is deep and well rounded on its underside with a raised collar at the join with the plate, and the distance from centre of pan to centre of pivot screw is 3/4". The sidenail heads are 1/2" in diameter, and are recessed into the sidepiece, almost flush with the surface of the brass.

Stock: walnut, to within 4 1/8" of muzzle, with later noseband. Lock and sidepiece flats have full oval apron carving at front and rear, measuring 9 1/4" overall. The raised barrel tang apron is narrow with a wavy outline measuring 3 15/16" x 1 3/8", the raised portion continuing in a curve at the top to form the beginning of the lock and sideplate flat carving.

The comb measures 8 1/2" from centre of buttplate screw to tip. The distance from the centre of the trigger to the centre of the buttplate is 13 1/2". The rod channel is 3/8+" in diameter. Stamped in the rod channel with illegible marks at top, a deep 1 and more illegible initials ahead of tailpipe. Sideplate flat stamped with small H. Stamped below lower guard tang with crowned 10 over crowned 14. Storekeeper's stamp in right butt.

Brass furniture: sheet-brass closed front noseband. Four Land Pattern barrel-shaped collared ramrod pipes for wooden rammer, the upper pipe 1 3/4" long, internal diameter 3/8+"; secured by a pin 39 1/16" from the breech, with the front of the pipe 1 7/8" from the tip of the fore-end. The distance between the rear of the forepipe and the front of the second pipe is 6 5/16".

The second pipe is 1 5/8" long, internal diameter 3/8", secured by a pin 31 1/8" from the breech; the distance from the rear of the second pipe to the front of the third pipe is 7 1/8".

The third pipe is 1 11/16" long, secured by a pin 22 3/8" from the breech. Distance between the rear of the third pipe and the front of the tailpipe is 6 1/2".

Tailpipe outside diameter is 1 7/32" at mouth, the collared barrel-shaped section being 1 5/8" long and the lip and flame-shaped tail being 2 15/16" long, secured by a pin 13 7/8" from the breech. Internal diameter 3/8+".

The trigger guard is of a design peculiar to this pattern, with front and rear finials terminating in a distinct pear shape. Overall length 11 1/2", secured by pins 3 3/8" from the front finial and 2" from the rear finial, and by the thumbpiece screw 4 15/16" from the rear finial. The bow is 1 1/8" wide at its widest point, and is pinched in at the terminals and drilled for the lower sling-swivel screw at the front terminal. There is a crown stamped inside the bow.

The sidepiece is Land Pattern with rounded surface and measures 6 3/16" overall, 3 5/8+" between sidenail centres, the sidenail heads being recessed in the brass almost flush with the surface.

The thumbpiece is also Land Pattern, measuring 2 9/16" x 1 1/16". Engraved G over No. 62.

The buttplate tang is of the conventional Long Land Pattern with a three-step 6 1/16" tang: from the first step to the second measures 1 7/16"; there is then a squared step and 1 7/16" to the final step which is curved, and 1 13/16" to the tip which terminates in a disc outline. The plate is 5 1/4" from heel to toe, and is 2 3/16" at its widest point. It slightly overlaps the toe of the butt. The tang is engraved CAPt CARY.

The wooden ramrod is a replacement, but the tapered brass cap is of the correct form, 1 1/4" long.

Pattern 1742 Long Land Musket
NAM 94062

Overall length: 62".

Barrel: 46", balustre-moulded at breech for 9/16"; the three barrel pins located at 12", 20 15/16", and 39 7/8" from the breech; the swivel loop being 31 5/8" from the breech. The left side of the breech has a * over 5 stamped, and remains of maker's initials below, now illegible, as are King's Proof Marks. The barrel tang is 2 3/8" long, and tapers outwards towards the rear from 1/2 to 5/8". The front sight/bayonet stud is brazed 2" from the muzzle.

Lock: Pattern 1740. Double-bridle, rounded surface to lockplate and cock, the plate having the "banana" configuration at the tail, which drop is 1/4" below the straight lower edge of the forward part of the plate. The plate measures 6 13/16" x 1 3/16". The pan is shallow, and the distance from centre of pan to centre of pivot screw is 3/4". The swan-neck cock has a leaf-shaped comb which measures 15/32" across its widest point; the rear surface of the top-jaw has a stud which engages in a vertical slot on the forward face of the comb. The neck of the cock no longer has the reinforcing lip on the underside of the lower jaw. The steel is 2" high x 1 1/4" wide. Trefoil finial to the feather-spring, long sear-spring. Plate, cock, round top-jaw and back of steel have fine double border lines engraved. Across the tail is engraved TOWER over 1741. Inside the plate is stamped crowned V twice and crowned 49, suggesting actual manufacture by the Small Gun Office workmen. The sidenail heads are 1/2" in diameter.

Stock: walnut, to within 4 1/4" of muzzle. No nosecap. Lock and sidepiece flat carving is of the simplified form with plain rounded outline at front and teardrops at rear, measuring 7 3/4" overall. The raised barrel tang apron is plain oval, measuring 3 11/16" x 1 1/2". The comb measures 8 1/2" from centre of buttplate screw to tip. The distance from the centre of the trigger to the centre of the buttplate is 13 11/16". The rod channel is 3/8"+ in diameter. RF stamped in the rod channel. Sideplate flat stamped with small 78 at rear, and twice beneath sidepiece. Stamped below lower guard finial with crown and crowned 4.

Brass furniture: four Land Pattern barrel-shaped collared ramrod pipes for wooden rammer, the upper three 1 5/8" long, the tailpipe 4 5/8" long. The outside diameter of each pipe is 1 7/32" at mouth and rear, inside diameter 3/8"+.

The upper pipe is held by a pin 38 13/16" from the breech, and the mouth of the pipe lies 2 1/8" from the tip of the fore-end. The distance from the rear of the upper pipe to the front of the second pipe is 6 9/16".

The second pipe is secured by a pin 30 1/2" from the breech, and the distance between its rear and the front of the third pipe is 6 9/16".

The third pipe pin is 22 5/16" from the breech, and the distance from its rear to the front of the tailpipe is 6 9/16".

The front portion of the tailpipe is identical with the other pipes and is also 1 5/8" long, with the lip and flame-shaped tang being 3 1/16" long, and 3/8" internal diameter at mouth, very slightly smaller than the others. Its pin is 14 1/16" from the breech.

The sidepiece is Land Pattern with rounded surface and measures 6 1/4" overall, with 3 5/8" between sidenail centres.

The trigger guard is Land Pattern, 11 1/2" overall, secured by two pins, 3 1/8" from the front finial and 1 11/16" from the rear finial, and by the thumbpiece screw 4 13/16" from the rear finial. The bow is 1 1/8" wide at its widest point, and is reinforced at the front terminal where it is drilled for the lower sling swivel screw. Both finials terminate in a small well defined rounded ball. There is a crown stamped inside the bow.

93

The thumbpiece is Land Pattern, measuring 2 5/8"x 1 3/32".

The buttplate is Land Pattern, the tang with three steps measuring 6"; from the first step to the second measures 1 1/2"; the second, squared, step is 1 3/8" to the third step which is curved, and 1 3/4" to the tip which terminates in a flat disc outline. The plate is 5 5/16" from heel to toe, and is 2 3/16" at its widest point. It slightly overlaps the toe of the butt.

The wooden ramrod is a replacement, but the tapered brass cap is of the correct form, 1 1/4" long.

Pattern 1756 Long Land Musket
RA XII-1580

Overall length: 62".

Barrel: 46", balustre-moulded at breech for 1/2+"; the three barrel pins located at 11 15/16", 20 15/16", 39 15/16" from the breech; the swivel loop being 31 13/16" from the breech. The left side of the breech is stamped FG, and the King's Proof Marks on top. The barrel tang is 2 3/8" long, and tapers outwards towards the rear from 9/16" to 11/16". The front sight/bayonet stud is brazed 2 1/8" from the muzzle, and measures 1/4" x 3/16". Barrel diameter across breech ahead of moulding is 1 3/8", and across muzzle 15/16".

Lock: Pattern 1756. Double-bridle, rounded surface to lockplate and cock. The plate measures 6 15/16, x 1 1/4". The steel is 2+" high x 1 3/16" wide. Throw of cock 2 1/8". Plate, cock, round top-jaw and back of steel have fine double border lines engraved. The rear surface of the top-jaw has a stud which engages in a vertical slot on the forward face of the comb. The leaf-shaped cock comb measures 9/16" across its widest point. Trefoil finial to the feather-spring, long sear-spring. Crowned GR engraved ahead of cock, and small crowned Broad Arrow stamped beneath pan. Across the tail is engraved GRICE and 1756. Inside the plate is stamped crowned 2 and small coronet over WG. The sidenail heads are 9/16" in diameter, and are recessed into the plate.

Stock: walnut, to within 4 1/4" of muzzle, with cast-brass nosecap. Lock and sidepiece flats have plain rounded front and teardrop at rear, measuring 8 1/8" overall. The raised barrel tang apron is oval in outline measuring 3 11/16" x 1 1/2". The comb measures 8 5/16" from centre of buttplate screw to tip. The distance from the centre of the trigger to the centre of the buttplate is 13 7/8". The rod channel is 1/4" in diameter. Stamped in the rod channel with crowned 11, crowned 7, crowned 11, WS and VH?. Sideplate flat stamped W I. Stamped below lower guard tang with crown and crowned I. Storekeeper's stamp in right butt.

Brass furniture: cast brass nosecap, 1" long. The long trumpet forepipe is tapered with a flared mouth and collar at rear, 3 7/8" long; 11/16" diameter at mouth, 3/8+" diameter at rear; held by two pins 36 15/16" and 38 15/16" from the breech. The front of the pipe is 2" from the tip of the fore-end. Internal diameter at front 9/16", at rear 5/16". The distance between the rear of the forepipe and the front of the second pipe is 4 1/2".

The Land Pattern second pipe is barrel-shaped and collared, 1 1/2" long, internal diameter 1/4+", secured by a pin 30 13/16" from the breech; the distance from the rear of the second pipe to the front of the third pipe is 6 7/16".

The third pipe is the same pattern, 1 3/8" long, external diameter 7/16" at front and rear, secured by a pin 22 15/16" from the breech. Distance between the rear of the third pipe and the front of the tailpipe is 7 1/4".

The tailpipe has a 1 5/16" collared and barrel-shaped forward section and a lip and flame-shaped tang section 3 3/16" long; external diameter is 1/2" at mouth, secured by a pin 14 1/8" from the breech. Internal diameter 1/4+". A circular steel rod-retaining spring is riveted in the mouth of this pipe.

The trigger guard is Land Pattern, 11 1/4" overall, secured by a pin 3" from the front finial and another 1 3/4" from the rear finial, and by the thumbpiece screw 4 1/2" from the rear finial. The bow is 1 1/8+" wide at its widest point.

The sidepiece is Land Pattern and measures 6 3/16" overall, with 3 3/4" between sidenail centres, the sidenail heads recessed in the brass.

The thumbpiece is Land Pattern, 2 5/8"x 1 1/16+".

The buttplate tang is 5 7/8" long, with three steps: from the first to the second shoulder is 1 3/8+", from the second to the third is also 1 3/8+", from the third to the tip is 1 7/8". The plate is 5 1/2" from heel to toe, and is 2 1/8" at its widest point.

The steel ramrod has a button-head 5/8" in diameter.

Regimentally marked on barrel with three feathers and ICH DIEN over R 23;

on thumbpiece with 10/71, and on ramrod with 19/73.

Pattern 1779 Short Land Musket
Wartime Production.   RA XII-128

Overall Length: 58".
Barrel: 42 3/16", balustre-moulded at breech for 5/8"; retaining pins located at 10 1/8", 18 3/8", 36 1/4" from the breech, and the upper swivel screw 28 7/8". King's Proof struck on top at breech, maker's mark MB [Matthias Barker] struck on left side. Tang measures 2 5/16" x 9/16" x 11/16" at rear with no inspector's crowns. Sight/bayonet stud is brazed 2 1/4" from the muzzle and measures 1/4" x 1/4" x 1/8" high. Width across breech ahead of moulding 1 3/8", and across muzzle 15/16".
Lock: Pattern 1777. Double-bridle with rounded surfaces, the plate 7" x 1 1/4". The cock has a narrow pillar comb with notch at its front, the oval un-engraved top jaw notched to fit the comb; the comb is 1/4" thick at the front, its thickest point. Throw of cock is 2". Steel measures 2 1/8" high x 1 3/16" wide and the back is not engraved. The lockplate and cock body have double border lines engraved. Tear-drop finial to the feather-spring; short sear-spring. Engraved ahead of cock with crowned GR, and TOWER across tail. Crowned Broad Arrow struck beneath pan. Inside stamped with crowned 1, initials TH run together into monogram with crossbar of T on left vertical of H. [Thomas Hadley] with S at front of plate. Sidenail heads are 9/16" in diameter and are not recessed into the surface of the sidepiece.
Stock: walnut, fore-end to 4 1/2" of muzzle. Comb length 8 7/16" from centre of screwhole. Oval tang apron 3 13/16" x 1 7/16" with small flat extending just to the rear of the barrel tang and ending in a semi-circle. Sideflats plain rounded at front and teardrop at rear 8 1/8" overall. Diameter of rod channel 1/4". Distance from centre of trigger to centre of butt 13 3/4". Sidepiece flat stamped with small crowned IA at rear. Stamped below lower guard tang with crowned marks obliterated. In rammer channel from top, no crowns and a rectangular frame (H,F,E?) ahead of S, and Broad Arrow.
Brass Furniture: nosecap without reinforce at rear, secured by brass rivet, 7/8" long. Long forepipe 4 1/8" long, 11/16" diameter at mouth, 7/16" at rear held by two pins 32 7/8" and 34 15/16" from breech, the mouth of the pipe 1 7/8" from front of the fore-end. Internal diameter of long forepipe 9/16" at front and 5/16" at rear. Distance between rear of trumpet and front of second pipe 3 1/4".

Second pipe is Pratt design, 1 9/16" long, straight tapered with collars, 1/2" wide at mouth, 7/16" at rear, secured by a pin 27 11/16" from breech. Internal diameter of Pratt 5/16". Distance between rear of Pratt pipe and front of third pipe 5 7/8".

Third pipe is barrel-shaped and collared, 1 3/8" long, 3/8" wide at front and rear, secured by a pin 20 5/16" from breech. Distance between rear of third pipe and front of tailpipe is 5 3/4".

Tailpipe is Land Pattern with 1 5/16" barrel-shaped and collared section and 3 3/16" lip and tang section, 1/2" diameter at mouth, secured by a pin 13 1/8" from the breech. A rod-retaining spring is riveted inside the mouth of the pipe.

Sidepiece is Land Pattern, flat and flush with the surface of the wood, 6 7/16" long, 3 13/16" between sidenail centres.

Trigger guard is Land Pattern, 11 5/16" overall, secured by a pin 3 1/4" from the front finial and another 1 1/4" from the rear finial, and the thumbpiece screw 4 1/2" from the rear finial. The bow is 1 1/4" at its widest point.

Thumbpiece is Land Pattern, 2 5/8" x 1 1/16+".

Buttplate is of the Short Land Pattern, the two-step tapering tang measuring 3 3/4" from the centre of the screwhole. Distance from first step to second 1 1/2"; from second to the tip 1 3/16". The plate measures 5 5/16" from top to bottom x 2 1/16" at its widest point. It slightly overlaps the toe of the stock.

Steel ramrod has button-head 9/16" diameter, rounded front. Threaded at tip and engraved in line G 10 near head.

Pattern 1779 S Sidepiece Short Land Musket
HOB 167B18

Overall Length: 58".
Barrel: 42 1/8", balustre-moulded at breech 9/16"; retaining pins located at 10 1/8", 18 5/16", 36 1/8" from the breech, and the upper swivel screw 28 7/8". King's Proof struck on top at breech. Tang measures 2 5/16" long, tapering from 9/16" to 11/16" at rear with inspector's crown at tip. Sight/bayonet stud is brazed 2 1/8" from the muzzle and measures 1/4" x 1/8". Width across breech ahead of moulding 1 3/8", and across muzzle 15/16".

95

Lock: Pattern 1777: Double-bridle with rounded surfaces, the plate 7 1/16" x 1 1/4". The cock has a narrow pillar comb with notch at its front, the oval un-engraved top jaw notched to fit the comb; the comb is 3/16" thick at the front, its thickest point. Throw of cock is 1 15/16". Steel measures 2" high x 1" wide and the back is not engraved. The lockplate and cock body have double border lines engraved. Tear-drop finial to the featherspring; short sear-spring.

Engraved ahead of cock with crowned GR, and TOWER across tail. Crowned Broad Arrow struck beneath pan. Inside stamped with crowned 1 and Galton. Sidenail heads are just over 9/16" diameter and are not recessed into the surface of the sidepiece.

Stock: walnut, fore-end to 4 1/2" of muzzle. Comb length 8 1/2" from centre of screwhole. Drop at comb 1 3/4", and at heel 1 7/8". Oval tang apron 3 15/16" x 1 1/2" with small flat extending just to the rear of the barrel tang and ending in a semi-circle. Sideflats plain rounded at front and teardrop at rear 8 1/4" overall. Diameter of rod channel just over 1/4". Distance from centre of trigger to centre of butt 13 1/2". Sidepiece flat stamped with small crowned C at rear. Stamped below lower guard tang with crown and crowned A. Stamped in rammer channel from top, crown?, crown A twice, crowned P, two crowns with illegible numbers, PRATT. Undated Storekeeper's stamp in right butt.

Brass Furniture: nosecap without reinforce at rear, secured by brass rivet, 7/8" long. Long forepipe 4 1/8" long, 11/16" diameter at mouth, 7/16" at rear, held by two pins 32 7/8" and 34 7/8" from breech, the mouth of the pipe 1 7/8" from front of the nosecap. Internal diameter of forepipe 3/8". Distance between rear of trumpet and front of second pipe 3 1/4".

Second pipe is Pratt design, 1 5/8" long, straight tapered with collars, 1/2" wide at mouth, 7/16" at rear, secured by a pin 27 5/8" from breech. Distance between rear of Pratt pipe and front of third pipe 5 15/16".

Third pipe is barrel-shaped and collared, 1 3/8" long, 7/16" wide at front and rear, secured by a pin 20 1/4" from breech. Distance between rear of third pipe and front of tailpipe is 5 3/4".

Tailpipe is Land Pattern with 1 3/8" barrel-shaped and collared section and 3 1/4" lip and tang section, 1/2" diameter at mouth, secured by a pin 13 1/16" from the breech. A rod-retaining spring is riveted inside the mouth of the pipe.

Sidepiece is the salient feature of this variant wartime product. It is S-shaped (sometimes spelled "ess" in the records) with a rounded surface, 4 1/2" long, with 3 15/16" between sidenail centres.

Trigger guard is Land Pattern, 11 1/4" overall, secured by a pin 3 1/16" from the front finial and another 1 3/4" from the rear finial, and by the thumbpiece screw 4 7/16" from the rear finial. The bow is 1 3/16" at its widest point.

Thumbpiece is Land Pattern, 2 11/16" x 1 1/16+".

Buttplate is of the Short Land Pattern, the two-step tapering tang measuring 3 7/8" from the centre of the screwhole. Distance from first step to second 1 9/16"; from second to the tip 1 1/4". The plate measures 5 1/16" from top to bottom x 2 1/16" at its widest point. It slightly overlaps the toe of the stock.

Steel ramrod has button-head 9/16" in diameter, rounded front.

Pattern 1779 post-war example
Private Collection

Overall length: 58".

Barrel: 42", balustre-moulded at breech for 5/8"; retaining pins located at 10 1/16", 18 3/8", and 36 3/8" from the breech, and the upper swivel screw 28 7/8". King's Proof struck on top at breech. Tang measures 2 1/4" x 5/8" x 21/32" at rear with inspector's crowns at join and rear edge. Width across breech 1 3/8", and across muzzle 15/16". Vent diameter (unfired condition): 3/32".

Sight/bayonet stud is brazed 2 1/8" from the muzzle and measures 5/16" x 1/4" x 1/8" high.

Lock: Pattern 1777. Double-bridle with rounded surfaces, the plate 7" x 1 1/4". The cock has the pillar comb with pronounced rounded top and clearly defined notch at its front, the oval un-engraved top jaw notched to fit the comb, measures 1 9/16" x 1 1/8"; the comb is 5/32" thick at the back, and is thicker at the front, with the jaw notch filed accordingly. Throw of cock is 1 15/16". Steel measures 2 1/8" high x 1 3/16" wide and the back is not engraved. The lockplate and cock body have double border lines engraved. Tear-drop finial to the feather-spring; short sear-spring. Inside stamped with crowned 8, small BW [Benjamin Willetts] and small 6, and at front IH [Jonathan Hennem?].

Deeply engraved ahead of cock with crowned GR, and TOWER across tail. Crowned Broad Arrow struck beneath pan. Distance from centre of pan to centre of pivot screw 3/4". Sidenail heads are 19/32" diameter and are not recessed into the surface of the sidepiece.

Stock: light walnut, to 4 1/4" of muzzle. Comb length 8 1/2" from centre of screwhole. Oval tang apron 4" x 1 5/8" with small flat extending just to the rear of the barrel tang and ending in a semi-circle. Side flats plain rounded at front and teardrop at rear 8 3/8" overall. Stamped IA twice (and once under sidepiece) on sidepiece flat at rear, Crown and crowned 8 to rear of rear guard finial, Storekeeper's stamp with date 1786 on right butt; in rammer channel from top, crowned 13, crowned 8 and crowned 10 between first two pipes, TC and assembly cuts ahead of tailpipe. Diameter of ramrod channel 5/16".

Brass Furniture: nosecap without reinforce at rear, secured by brass rivet, 15/16" long.

Long forepipe 4 1/16" long, 11/16" diameter at mouth, 7/16" at rear, held by two pins 33 1/4" and 35 1/4" from breech, the mouth of the pipe 1 3/4" from front of fore-end. Internal diameter 5/16".

Second pipe is Pratt design, 1 9/16" long, straight tapered with collars, 1/2" wide at mouth, 13/32" at rear, secured by a pin 27 13/16" from breech. Internal diameter at mouth 7/16", at rear 5/16". Distance between rear of trumpet and front of Pratt 3 5/16".

Third pipe is conventional barrel-shaped and collared, 1 3/8" long, 13/32" wide at front and rear, secured by a pin 20 1/2" from breech. Internal diameter 5/16". Distance between rear of Pratt pipe and front of third pipe 5 7/8".

Tailpipe is Land Pattern with 1 5/16" barrel-shaped and collared section and 3 1/16" lip and tang section, 4 7/16" overall, 15/32" diameter at mouth, secured by a pin 13" from the breech. Internal diameter 5/16+". Distance between rear of third pipe and front of tailpipe is 5 7/8".

Sidepiece is Land Pattern, flat and flush with the surface of the wood, 6 3/8" long, 3 3/4" between sidenail centres.

Trigger guard is Land Pattern, 11 1/4" overall, secured by a pin 3 1/4" from the front finial and another 1 5/8" from the rear finial, and the thumbpiece screw 4 3/8" from the rear finial. The bow is reinforced at its front for the lower sling-swivel screw, and the bow is 1 1/8" at its widest point. Both finials terminate in a small ball atop an outward curling lip.

Thumbpiece is Land Pattern, 2 11/16" x 1 1/8", inlaid flush and secured by a screw through the trigger guard.

Buttplate is of the Short Land Pattern, the two-step tapering tang measuring 3 7/8" from the centre of the screwhole. The plate measures 5 1/8" from top to bottom x 2 1/8" at its widest point. It slightly overlaps the toe of the stock.

Steel ramrod has button-head 19/32" diameter, rounded front. Not threaded at tip.

Pattern 1757 Marine or Militia Musket
Wood Rammer NAM-7507-54

Overall length: 58".

Barrel: 42 1/8", balustre-moulded at breech for 5/8"; the three barrel pins located at 10 1/8", 18 1/4", and 36 3/16" from the breech; the upper swivel loop screw being 28 13/16" from the breech. The King's Proof Marks stamped on top. The barrel tang is 2 3/8" long, and tapers outwards towards the rear from 5/8" to 11/16". The front sight/bayonet stud is brazed 2 1/8" from the muzzle, and measures 1/4" x 3/16". Barrel diameter across breech ahead of moulding is 1 3/8", and across muzzle 7/8+".

Lock: Pattern 1756. Double-bridle, rounded surface to lockplate and cock. The plate measures 7" x 1 1/4". The steel is 2" high x 1 3/16" wide. Throw of cock 1 15/16". Plate, cock, round top jaw and back of steel have fine double border lines engraved. The rear surface of the top-jaw has a stud which engages in a vertical slot on the forward face of the comb. The leaf-shaped cock comb measures 7/16" across its widest point. Trefoil finial to the feather-spring, long sear-spring. Crowned GR engraved ahead of cock, and small crowned Broad Arrow stamped beneath pan. Across the tail is engraved JORDAN and 1759. Inside the plate are stamped crowned numerals. The sidenail heads are 9/16" in diameter, and are not recessed into the plate.

Stock: walnut, to within 4 5/16" of muzzle, with no cap. Lock and sidepiece flats have plain rounded front and teardrop at rear, measuring 8 1/8" overall. The raised barrel tang apron is oval in outline measuring 3 3/4" x 1 9/16". The comb measures 8 1/2" from the centre of the heel screw to the tip. The distance from the centre of the trigger to the centre of the buttplate is 13 5/8". The rod channel is 3/8" in diameter. Stamped in the rod channel from the top crowned 11, crowned 7, crowned 11, WP, Broad Arrow. Sideplate flat stamped at rear T. Stamped below lower guard tang with crown and crowned I. Storekeeper's stamp in right butt.

Brass furniture: no nosecap. The upper pipe is barrel-shaped and collared, 1 5/8" long; 1/2+" diameter at mouth, and rear; held by a pin 35" from the breech. The front of the pipe is 2" from the tip of the fore-end. Internal diameter 7/16". The distance between the rear of the upper pipe and the front of the second pipe is 5 11/16".

The second pipe is barrel-shaped and collared, 1 9/16" long, internal diameter 3/8", secured by a pin 27 3/4" from the breech; the distance from the rear of the second pipe to the front of the third pipe is 6 5/8".

The third pipe is the same pattern as the second, 1 5/8" long, external diameter 1/2" at front and rear, secured by a pin 19 1/2" from the breech. Distance between the rear of the third pipe and the entry point is 6 5/8".

There is no tailpipe.

The trigger guard is Land Pattern, 11 1/4" overall, secured by a pin 3 3/16" from the front finial and another 1 9/16" from the rear finial. A woodscrew replaces the thumbpiece screw 4 3/4" from the rear finial. The bow is 1 1/4" wide at its widest point.

The sidepiece is the same as the current Sea Service, Land Pattern outline with a flat surface inlaid flush with the surface of the wood, and measures 6 3/8" overall, with 3 3/4" between sidenail centres, the sidenail heads 9/16" diameter and not recessed in the brass.

There is no thumbpiece.

The buttplate tang is peculiar to this pattern with a 3/8" diameter woodscrew located 2 5/8" from the heel-screw hole. The tang is 3 3/4" long, with two steps: from the first to the second shoulder is 1 1/2", and from the second to the tip is 1 1/4". The plate is 5 3/8+" from heel to toe, and is 2 1/16+" at its widest point.

The wood ramrod has a tapered closed brass cap.

The bayonet which is numbered to the gun, has a 17" blade and a 4" socket of 15/16" internal diameter. The blade is 1 3/8" at the shoulder and the shank just beneath is 7/16" diameter. The round shoulder is just even with the apex of the two edges of the blade. Crown over 6 stamped at the base of the blade, and engraved on socket is 1/50 which agrees with the ABD over 1/50 on the buttplate tang.

Pattern 1759 Militia Musket
Steel Rammer   RA XII-85

Overall length: 58".

Barrel: 42", balustre-moulded at breech for 9/16"; the three barrel pins located at 10 1/4", 18 3/8" and 36 5/16" from the breech; the swivel loop being 28 15/16" from the breech. The left side of the breech has * over R I? stamped, and the King's Proof Marks on top. The barrel tang is 2 3/8" long, and tapers outwards towards the rear from 5/8" to 5/8+". The front sight/bayonet stud is brazed 2 1/8" from the muzzle, and measures 1/4" x 3/16". Barrel diameter across breech ahead of moulding is 1 3/8", and across muzzle 15/16".

Top of barrel engraved Militia New Pattern referring to the new-production steel rammer with nosecap, trumpet forepipe and tailpipe.

Lock: Double-bridle, rounded surface to lockplate and cock. The plate measures 7 1/16" x 1 1/4+". The steel is 2 1/16" high x 1 1/8" wide. Throw of cock 2 1/16". Plate, cock, round top jaw and back of steel have fine double border lines engraved. The rear surface of the top-jaw has a stud which engages in a vertical slot on the forward face of the comb. The leaf-shaped cock comb measures 9/16" across its widest point. Trefoil finial to the feather-spring, long sear-spring. Crowned GR engraved ahead of cock, and small crowned Broad Arrow stamped beneath pan. Across the tail is engraved FARMER over 1762. Inside the plate is stamped crowned 3 and FG, and a very small P in a poinçon. The sidenail heads are 9/16" in diameter, and are not recessed into the sidepiece.

Stock: walnut, to within 4 3/8" of muzzle, with brass cap. Lock and sidepiece flats have plain rounded front and teardrop at rear, measuring 7 15/16" overall. The raised barrel tang apron is oval in outline measuring 3 11/16" x 1 1/2". The comb measures 8 3/8" from centre of buttplate screw to tip. The distance from the centre of the trigger to the centre of the buttplate is 13 3/4". The rod channel is 1/4+" in diameter. Stamped in the rod channel with three crowned illegible marks at top, FC L and Waller in a rectangular frame ahead of the tailpipe. Sideplate flat stamped with crude 9, with reversed 99 stamped under sidepiece. Stamped below lower guard tang with crown and crowned I. Storekeeper's stamp in right butt.

Brass furniture: cast brass nosecap, 1" long. The Land Pattern long trumpet forepipe is tapered with a flared mouth and collar at rear, 4 1/16" long; 5/8+" diameter at mouth, 7/16" diameter at rear; held by two pins 33 1/8" and 35 1/8" from the breech. The front of the pipe is 1 3/4" from the tip of the fore-end. Internal diameter at front 9/16", at rear 1/4+". The space between the rear of the forepipe and the front of the second pipe is 3 5/16".

The second pipe is barrel-shaped and collared, 1 7/16" long, internal diameter 1/4+", secured by a pin 27 15/16" from the breech; the distance from the rear of the second pipe to the front of the third pipe is 5 15/16".

The third pipe is same pattern and length as second, external diameter 3/8" at front and rear, secured by a pin 20 9/16" from the breech. Distance between the rear of the third pipe and the front of the tailpipe is 6".

The tailpipe has a 1 3/8" collared and barrel-shaped forward section and a lip and flame-shaped tang section 3 3/16" long; outside diameter is 1/2" at mouth, secured by a pin 13 3/16" from the breech. Internal diameter 1/4". A circular steel rod-retaining spring is riveted in the mouth of this pipe.

The trigger guard is Land Pattern, 11 1/4" overall, secured by a pin 3 1/8" from the front finial and another 1 3/4" from the rear finial. A woodscrew replaces the usual thumbpiece screw 4 3/4" from the rear finial. The bow is 1 1/8" wide at its widest point.

The sidepiece is the same as the current Sea Service, with a flat surface inlaid flush with the surface of the wood, and measures 6 3/8" overall, with 3 11/16" between sidenail centres, the sidenail heads not recessed in the brass.

There is no thumbpiece.

The buttplate tang is peculiar to this pattern with a 3/8" diameter wood-screw located 2 5/8" from the heel-screw hole. The tang is 4" long, with two steps: from the first to the second shoulder is 1 9/16", and from the second to the tip is 1 3/8". The plate is 5 1/8+" from heel to toe, and is 2" at its widest point.

The steel ramrod has a button-head 9/16" in diameter.

SEA SERVICE MUSKETS

Pattern 1757 Bright (Long) Sea Service Musket
West Point 14,690

This example uses an old, probably Liège-purchase, four-stage barrel.

Overall length: 57 3/4".

Barrel: 41 3/4", octagonal for 8" from breech, then 16-sided for 3", two pairs of grooves turned to form a 1/4" collar between them, and a second collar 3" up the barrel, then full round to muzzle. The three barrel pins located at 11 1/8", 20 3/4" and 36" from the breech; the upper sling swivel loop 28 3/8" from the breech. The top of the breech is stamped with a single indecipherable mark, and a second single mark is stamped on the left flat. The barrel tang is 2 1/16" long, and tapers outwards towards the rear from 9/16" to 5/8". The front sight is brazed 2" from the muzzle, and measures 1/4" x 1/8". Barrel diameter across breech is 1 3/8" and across the muzzle 15/16".

Lock: Pattern 1757. Plain, flat surface to lockplate and ring-neck cock. The plate measures 7 5/16" x 1 5/16". Faceted pan. Throw of cock 1 15/16". The rear surface of the oval top-jaw is notched to fit around the straight pillar comb which is 1/4" thick. The steel is round-topped, 1 7/8" high x 1 3/16" wide, leaf-shaped finial to the feather-spring, long sear-spring. Crowned GR engraved ahead of cock, and small crowned Broad Arrow stamped beneath pan. Across the tail is engraved EDGE over 1759. Inside the plate is stamped crowned(?) 2, RE. The two domed sidenail heads are 9/16" and 5/8" in diameter, and are not recessed into the plate.

Stock: walnut, to 4" of muzzle, with no cap. Lock and sidepiece flats have plain rounded front and long teardrop at rear, measuring 8 1/2" overall. The raised barrel tang apron is oval in outline measuring 4" x 1 9/16". The comb measures 8 3/4" from the vertical line of the buttplate. The distance from the centre of the trigger to the centre of the buttplate is 14 1/4". The rod channel is 3/8"-7/16+" in diameter. Distance from tip of fore-end to entry point of rod 26". No markings in the rod channel. Sideplate flat not marked. Stamped below rear guard tang with crowned number and crown. Storekeeper's stamp in right butt.

Brass furniture: no nosecap. The upper pipe is barrel-shaped and collared, 1 11/16" long, 9/16" diameter at mouth and rear; held

99

by a pin 34 3/4" from the breech. The front of the pipe is 2 3/16" from the tip of the fore-end. Internal diameter of pipe is 7/16". The distance between the rear of the upper pipe and the front of the second pipe is 6 1/16".

The second pipe is barrel-shaped and collared, 1 11/16" long, widest external diameter 1/2", internal diameter 3/8", secured by a pin 27 1/8" from the breech; the distance from the rear of the second pipe to the front of the third pipe is 6 9/16".

The third pipe is identical to the second in design and dimensions, and secured by a pin 19" from the breech. The distance between the rear of the third pipe and the entry point is 6 3/8".

The trigger guard is Sea Service Pattern, 9 3/4" overall, the circular rounded surface front finial being 1" in diameter, and the rear tang 13/16" in width; secured by a pin 1 1/4" from the front finial and a wood screw 2 1/4" from the rear finial. The bow is 1 1/16" wide at its widest point. There is no triggerplate, an iron nut 7/8" x 1/2" inlaid ahead of the trigger serving to anchor the barrel tang screw.

The sidepiece is the two-screw Sea Service Pattern, which is Land Pattern in outline but with a flat surface inlaid flush with the surface of the wood, and measures 6 3/4" overall, with 4 1/8" between the sidenail centres, the domed sidenail heads not recessed in the brass.

There is no thumbpiece.

The buttplate tang is Sea Service, being flat brass, curved at the heel and secured by a tang screw 5/8" from the tip as well as a heel screw 1 1/16" below the flat plane of the tang and the usual screw near the toe. The short parallel-sided tang is 3 1/4" long by 3/4" wide, with a plain rounded finial. From the deeply curved step to the tip is 2 1/8". The plate is 5 1/4" from heel to toe, and is 1 7/8" at its widest point.

The wooden ramrod has been replaced with a button-head steel rod, possibly a working-life replacement.

Pattern 1738 Black (Short) Sea Service Musket
RA XII-82

Overall length: 51 3/4".
Barrel: 36 3/16", balustre-moulded at breech for 7/16+"; the three barrel pins located at 14 1/8", 22 1/2", and 32 3/16" from the breech; no provision for swivel loops. The top of the breech is stamped with a single King's Proof Mark. The barrel tang is 2 1/4" long, and tapers outwards towards the rear from 9/16" to 5/8". The front sight is brazed 2 1/8" from the muzzle, and measures 1/4" x 1/8". This particular barrel has double pin-loops, but they are not associated with the fastening of the rammer pipes. Barrel diameter across breech ahead of moulding is 1 3/8" and across the muzzle 15/16+".
Lock: Pattern 1718. Plain, flat surface to lockplate and ring-neck cock. The plate measures 7 11/16" x 1 1/4". Faceted pan. Throw of cock 2 1/16". The rear surface of the oval top-jaw is notched to fit around the straight comb which is 1/4" thick. The steel is hexagonal, 2" high x 1 3/8" wide. Spearpoint finial to the feather-spring, long sear-spring. Crowned GR engraved ahead of cock, and small crowned Broad Arrow stamped beneath pan. Across the tail is engraved FARMER over 1745. Inside the plate is stamped crowned 2 F, A, and a very small W in a poincon.

The three domed sidenail heads are 9/16" in diameter, and are not recessed into the plate.
Stock: walnut, to 1/4" of muzzle, with no cap. Lock and sidepiece flats have plain rounded front and long teardrop at rear, measuring 8 9/16" overall. The raised barrel tang apron is oval in outline measuring 3 1/4" x 1 1/2". The comb measures 8 1/2" from the vertical line of the buttplate. The distance from the centre of the trigger to the centre of the buttplate is 13 7/16". The rod channel is 5/16" in diameter. Distance from tip of fore-end to entry point of rod 24 11/16". No markings in the rod channel. Sideplate flat not marked. Stamped below lower guard tang with crowned 4. Storekeeper's stamp in right butt.
Brass furniture: no nosecap. The upper pipe is barrel-shaped and collared, 1 5/8" long, 9/16" diameter at mouth and rear; held by a pin 30 7/8" from the breech. The front of the pipe is 4 9/16" from the tip of the fore-end. Internal diameter is 3/8". The distance between the rear of the upper pipe and the front of the second pipe is 8 9/16".

The second pipe is barrel-shaped and collared, 1 5/8" long, internal diameter 3/8", secured by a pin 20 5/8" from the breech; the distance from the rear of the second pipe to the entry point of the rod is 8 1/2".

The trigger guard is Sea Service Pattern, 9 3/4" overall, the circular rounded surface front finial being 15/16" in diameter, and the lower tang 1 3/16" in width; secured by a pin 1 1/2" from the front finial and a wood screw 2 1/4" from the rear finial. The bow is 1 3/16" wide at its widest point.

The sidepiece is of the early three-screw Sea Service Pattern, with a flat surface inlaid flush with the surface of the wood, and measures 7 5/16" overall, with 3 11/16" between the front and centre sidenail centres, and 3 3/16" between the centre and rear sidenail centres, the domed sidenail heads not recessed in the brass.

There is no thumbpiece.

The buttplate tang is Sea Service, being flat brass, curved at the heel and secured by a tang screw 5/8" from the tip as well as an upper screw 1 1/16" below the flat plain of the tang and the usual screw near the toe. The short parallel-sided tang is 3 1/4" long, with a plain rounded finial. The plate is 5 7/16" from heel to toe, and is 2 1/8" at its widest point.

The wooden ramrod has a closed tapered brass cap.

Pattern 1778 Black Sea Service Musket
HOB 14B2

The salient feature of this variant is the use of a round Land Service lock.

Overall Length: 52 7/8".

Barrel: 37", balustre-moulded at breech 9/16"; retaining pins located at 7 3/4", 18 1/4", 30 9/16" from the breech, and the upper swivel screw 25 7/8". King's Proof struck on top at breech; maker's mark of crowned D M [Daniel Moore] and crowned 6 also struck on top at breech. Tang measures 2 5/16" long, tapering from 9/16" to 5/8" at rear with inspector's crown at tang joint. Sight/bayonet stud is brazed 2 1/8" from the muzzle and measures 1/4" x 3/16". Width across breech ahead of moulding 1 3/8", and across muzzle 15/16". The surface of the barrel is draw-filed and blacked.

Lock: Pattern 1756 Land Service: Double-bridle with rounded surfaces, the plate 7" x 1 1/4". The cock has a leaf-shaped comb which is 1/2" across the back. Throw of cock is 1 7/8". Steel measures 7/8" high x 1 1/16" wide and the back is engraved. The lockplate and cock body, top-jaw and back of the steel have double border lines engraved. Trefoil finial to the featherspring; long sear-spring. Engraved ahead of cock with crowned GR, and IORDAN over 1762 across tail. Crowned Broad Arrow struck beneath pan. Sidenail heads are just over 9/16" diameter and are not recessed into the surface of the sidepiece. This is an "Old Pattern" lock; "New Pattern" or Pattern 1777 locks are also found on this variant.

Stock: walnut, fore-end to 4 3/8" of muzzle. Comb length 8 1/2" from centre of screwhole. Drop at comb 1 11/16" and at heel 1 13/16". Oval tang apron 3 7/8" x 1 11/16". Sideflats plain rounded at front and teardrop at rear 8 1/2" overall. Diameter of rod channel 1/4". Distance from fore-end tip to entry point of rod 21". Distance from centre of trigger to centre of butt 13 3/4". Sidepiece flat stamped with script F at rear. Stamped below rear guard tang with crown and crowned 1. Stamped in rammer channel from top, WE or D, RR. Undated Storekeeper's stamp in right butt.

Brass Furniture: no nosecap. Forepipe is barrel-shaped and collared, 1 11/16" long, with a steel rod-retaining spring riveted inside it. External diameter 9/16", internal diameter is 3/8". Secured by a pin 28 15/16" from breech. The mouth of the pipe is 3" from the tip of the fore-end. Distance between rear of the upper pipe and front of second pipe is 7 3/16".

Second pipe is of the same pattern as the upper pipe 1 11/16" long, and otherwise identical to it, secured by a pin 20 1/16" from breech. Distance between rear of second pipe and entry point 7 9/16".

There is no tailpipe.

The sidepiece is Sea Service with flat surface flush with the wood, 6 1/4" long, with 3 3/4" between sidenail centres.

The trigger guard is Sea Service, 9 5/8" overall, hollow cast, the circular domed finial being 1" wide. Secured by a pin 1 9/16" from the front finial and a screw 2 3/16" from the rear finial. The bow is 1 1/8" at its widest point.

There is no thumbpiece.

Buttplate is Sea Service, the plain parallel-sided tang measuring 3 1/2" from the centre of the screwhole. Distance from the shoulder to the tip 2 1/8". The plate measures 5 1/8" from heel to toe and is 2 3/16" at its widest point.

Steel ramrod has a button-head 9/16" in diameter with rounded front.

CARBINES—LAND SERVICE

Pattern 1745 Lord Loudoun Light Infantry Carbine
RA XII-5256

Overall length: 57 1/2".

Barrel: 41 15/16", balustre-moulded at breech for 7/16"; the three barrel pins located at 9", 18 11/16", and 36 1/2" from the breech; the swivel loop being 28 9/16" from the breech. The left side of the breech has a stamped coronet over I and an oval poinçon with crown over I and ?O, and King's Proof Marks on top. The barrel tang is 2 1/4" long, and tapers outwards towards the rear from 1/2" to 5/8" with inspector's crown at end. The front sight/bayonet stud is brazed 1 7/8" from the muzzle and measures 1/2" x 1/8". Diameter of barrel at breech ahead of turning 1 1/4", at muzzle 3/4".

Lock: Round carbine lock slightly different in outline from the Land Pattern. Double-bridle. The plate measures 6 1/8" x 1 1/8". Outer edge of pan filed flat in line with bridle. The steel is 1 7/8" high x 1" wide. There is no border-line engraving on the lock. The throw of the swan-neck cock is 1 3/4". The notched pillar cock comb measures 1/4" across its widest point. The lockplate is engraved BARBAR ahead of the cock, and stamped with a crowned 2 beneath the pan. Inside the plate is stamped in small letters WG. Fine-tapered spearpoint finial to the feather-spring, long sear-spring. The sidenail heads are 1/2" in diameter and recessed into the sidepiece.

Stock: walnut, to within 3 15/16" of the muzzle. Lock and sidepiece flat carving is of the simplified Pattern 1742 form with no aprons at the front and teardrops at rear, measuring 7" overall. The raised barrel tang apron is of the earlier narrow wavy outline (Pattern 1730), measuring 3 3/8" x 1 1/8". The comb measures 9" from centre of buttplate screw to end of flat section. The distance from the centre of the trigger to the centre of the buttplate is 13 1/2". The rod channel is 5/16" in diameter. Illegible initials in block letters stamped in lower rod channel, with two illegible crowned number stamps at top. Stamped to rear of rear trigger guard finial with crown, crowned 8. Drop of butt at comb 1 5/8", and at heel 2 5/8". Storekeeper's stamp on right side of butt.

Brass furniture: Sheet brass nosecap with closed front, measuring 15/16" long, secured by one rivet (missing). Four cylindrical collared ramrod pipes for wooden rammer, the upper pipe 1 7/16" long, 1/2" external diameter at front and rear, internal diameter 7/16", secured by a pin 35 9/16" from the breech. The front of the pipe is 1 13/16" from the front of the nose cap. Distance from rear of upper pipe to front of second pipe 6 1/2".

The second pipe is 1 3/8" long, held by a pin 27 5/8" from the breech. Distance from rear of second pipe to front of third pipe is 6 1/16".

The third pipe is identical to the second, secured by a pin 20 1/4" from the breech. Distance from rear of third pipe to front of tailpipe is 6 1/16".

The tailpipe has a 1 3/8" collared cylindrical forepart and the flame-shaped tail and lip section are 1 13/16" long. Secured by a pin 12 3/4" from the breech.

The trigger guard is of a design first used on this pattern and subsequently on the Pattern 1760 Light Infantry Carbine, with a curved tapered front finial terminating in a ball; the flaring section measures 11/16" wide at its base against the bow, 1 1/4" long to a step, and 1" across at the step; overall the front finial is 2 3/16" long. The rear finial is stepped from the tang and is a plain curved taper to a point. Guard is 10 5/8" overall, secured by two pins 2 1/2" from the front finial and 1 5/8" from the rear finial, and by the thumbpiece screw 5 3/16" from the rear finial. The bow is 1 1/8" wide at its widest point.

There is no trigger plate, a rectangular iron nut ahead of the trigger serves to anchor the barrel tang screw.

The sidepiece is unique to this pattern, being roughly triangular in outline with a slightly convex surface, and measures 5 3/4" overall with 3 1/16" between sidenail centres. The sidenails are recessed almost flush with the brass and the sidenail bases have a narrow raised rim standing up from the surface of the plate. There is a small 5/16" head-diameter woodscrew to the rear of the rear sidenail, and the trigger pivot pin protrudes through the plate just to the rear of this woodscrew.

The thumbpiece is an oval with a trefoil blossom outline at the bottom, held in position by a screw from the trigger guard just in rear of the bow. It measures 2 1/8" x 1 1/16".

The buttplate tang is short with one step from the basic plate 3/4" long and then 1 1/16" in a curved arc to a point. The tang measures 2 3/4" from the centre of the screwhole. The plate is 5" from heel to toe, and is 2 1/8" at its widest point. There is no pin for the short tang, with the lower butt screw 1 1/2" from the toe and 3 1/4" between centres of the two screws.

The wooden ramrod is a replacement and may have had a flat iron face disc rather than the conventional Ordnance tapered brass cap.

Pattern 1744/56 Carbine For Horse
RA XII-162

Overall length: 52 1/2".

Barrel: 37", balustre-moulded at breech for 1/2"; the three barrel pins located at 10 1/2", 23 1/16", and 33 1/16" from the breech; the sling-bar screw being 9 1/4" from the breech. The left side of the breech has * over IO [Joseph Oughton] stamped, and the King's Proof Marks on top. The barrel tang is 1 15/16" long, and tapers outwards towards the rear from 1/2" to 9/16". The steel blade front sight is brazed 1 15/16" from the muzzle, and measures 5/8" long x 3/16+". Barrel diameter across breech ahead of moulding is 1 1/4", and across muzzle 7/8".

Lock: Pattern 1756 Carbine. Double-bridle, rounded surface to lockplate and cock. The plate measures 6 1/8" x 1 1/16+". The steel is 1 3/4" high x 1 1/16" wide. Throw of cock 1 3/4". Plate, cock, round top jaw and back of steel have fine double border lines engraved. The rear surface of the top-jaw has a stud which engages in a vertical slot on the forward face of the comb. The leaf-shaped cock comb measures 7/16" across its widest point. Trefoil finial to the feather-spring, long sear-spring. Crowned GR engraved ahead of cock, and small crowned Broad Arrow stamped beneath pan. Across the tail is engraved GALTON over 1762. Inside the plate is stamped crowned 2 and FG, and WS.

The sidenail heads are 1/2" in diameter, and the front one only is recessed into the sidepiece.

Stock: walnut, to the muzzle, without cap. Lock and sidepiece flats have plain rounded front and teardrop at rear, measuring 7 1/4" overall. The raised barrel tang apron is oval in outline measuring 3 1/4" x 1 3/8". The comb measures 8 1/2" from centre of buttplate screw to tip. The distance from the centre of the trigger to the centre of the buttplate is 13 1/2". The rod channel is 1/4+" in diameter. Stamped in the rod channel from the top with crowned 6, crowned 8, crowned 5; TC or G, PW. Sidepiece flat stamped with crude JC. Stamped below lower guard tang with crown and crowned 3. Storekeeper's stamp in right butt.

Brass furniture: no nosecap. Two barrel-shaped and collared pipes, each 1 5/16" long, widest external diameters of 1/2", with internal diameters of 5/16". The upper pipe is secured by a pin 31 5/8" from the breech, and its front is 4 5/8" from the stock tip. The space between the rear of the upper pipe and the front of the second pipe is 8 1/4".

The second pipe is secured by a pin 22" from the breech; the distance from the rear of the second pipe to the front of the tailpipe is 7 13/16".

The tailpipe has a 1 3/8" collared and barrel-shaped forward section and a lip and flame-shaped tang section 2 9/16" long; outside diameter is 7/16" at mouth, secured by a pin 12 3/4" from the breech.

The trigger guard is Land Pattern, 11" overall, secured by a pin 2 5/8" from the front finial and another 1 5/8" from the rear finial, and by the thumbpiece screw 4 15/16" from the rear finial. The bow is 1 1/16" wide at its widest point, and is pinched-in at the front.

The sidepiece is Land Pattern with a rounded surface, 5 1/2" long, with 3 5/16" between sidenail centres. The rear of the sling-bar is shaped like a flat washer and fastened beneath the rear sidenail, fully recessed into the sidenail recess of the sidepiece, which is cut away at the front (left) for the bar. The longer rear sidenail lies against the upper surface of the inlet bar and is part of the sidepiece. The front of the sling-bar, which is 8 15/16" long, terminates in a rounded teardrop shaped finial and is held by a screw from the right side of the fore-end 9 1/4" from the breech.

The thumbpiece is Land Pattern and measures 2 3/8" x 15/16".

The buttplate tang is Land Pattern Carbine. The three-step tang is 4 3/4" long; from the first shoulder to the second is 1 3/8", and from the second step to the third is 1 1/16+"; from the third step to the tip is 1 1/8-". The plate is 4 7/8" from heel to toe, and is 2" at its widest point.

The tapered wooden ramrod has a closed brass cap.

Pattern 1760 Eliott Light Dragoon Carbine
RA XII-3512

Overall length: 43 1/4".

Barrel: 28 3/8", balustre-moulded at breech for 9/16"; the three barrel pins located at 7 5/8", 14 3/16" and 25 1/4" from the breech, the lug for the upper sling swivel 18" from breech. King's Proof marks struck on top of barrel at breech, maker's stamp WG [William Grice] on left breech. Barrel tang is 1 15/16" long, filed with a sighting groove, and tapering towards the rear from 1/2" to 9/16". The steel blade foresight is brazed 1 1/2" from the muzzle and is 1/2" long by 3/16" thick at the base. Barrel diameter across breech ahead of moulding is 1 1/4", and across muzzle 7/8".

Lock: Pattern 1756 Carbine, rounded lockplate measures 6 1/16" x 1 1/8"; this example never fitted with dog-catch used on early production and subsequently removed. Throw of cock 1 1/16", steel measures 1 3/4" x 15/16". Trefoil feather-spring finial. Long sear-spring. Standard double border lines engraved on lockplate, cock and top-jaw, back of steel. Crowned GR engraved ahead of cock, crowned Broad Arrow stamped beneath pan. Across tail is engraved TOWER indicating manufacture post-1764. Inside of plate stamped crowned 2 and WG. The sidenail heads are just over 7/16" in diameter and are recessed into the sidepiece.

Stock: walnut, to 3/16" of the muzzle, without cap. Lock and sidepiece flats have plain rounded front and teardrop at rear, measuring 7" overall. Barrel tang apron is oval, measuring 3 3/8" x 1 3/8". The comb measures 8 3/4" from centre of buttplate screw to tip. The distance from the centre of the trigger to centre of the buttplate is 13 7/16". The ramrod channel is 5/16" in diameter. Stamped in the rod channel with crowned 8 and RT. Sidepiece flat stamped with large F at rear. Below trigger guard tang is stamped crown and crowned I. Right side of butt stamped with variant form of Storekeeper's mark, crown over GR over Broad Arrow, resembling the King's Proof mark.

Brass furniture: no nosecap. Composite-pattern trumpet forepipe 3 11/16" long, held by two pins 22 3/8" and 24 1/14" from the breech; the flared mouth of the pipe is 2 3/16" from the fore-end tip. Internal diameter of the pipe tapers from 9/16" to 5/16". The space between the rear of the trumpet-pipe and the front of the second pipe is 3 7/8".

The second pipe is Land Pattern, 1 3/8" long, held by a pin 16 3/4" from the breech. Internal diameter is just over 5/16". Distance from rear of second pipe to front of tailpipe is 3 3/4".

The tailpipe is Land Pattern for wood rammer, the front section 1 3/8" long and the lip and tang 2 5/16" held by a pin 11 5/8" from the breech.

The trigger guard is of a design introduced on this pattern with a slightly flared and then tapering front finial with a ball tip, 10 1/4" overall, held by a pin 3 3/8" from the front finial and a second pin 1 5/16" from the rear finial. The rear finial is stepped and tapers to a point. The bow is 1" at its widest point.

The sidepiece is flat and flush with the surface of the wood, 3 3/4" long with 3 1/4" between sidenail centres. This example is not cut for mounting a sling-bar. The design of the sidepiece is taken from a pattern popular on arms by Lewis and James Barbar earlier in the century, introduced on the Pattern 1756 Light Dragoon Pistol and continued in use on several patterns of Ordnance arms including the Serjeant of Grenadiers Carbine and the Baker Rifle.

There is no thumbpiece.

The buttplate tang is unique to this pattern, and measures 2 7/8" from buttplate screw to tip, with two steps, 1 1/4" from first to second and 7/8" from the second to the tip. The plate measures 4 9/16" from heel to toe, and is 1 7/8" at its widest point.

The tapered wooden ramrod has a closed tapered brass cap. In March 1770, a set of steel rammers and springs for the carbine tailpipes of Eliott's Light Dragoons were made available by the Ordnance, and they had been converted by Jan. 1772. If any Eliott carbines went to America with light dragoons in 1776, they would have been these converted Pattern 1760 examples.

Pattern 1760 Light Infantry Carbine
RA XII-9469

Overall length: 57".

Barrel: 42", balustre-moulded at breech for 7/16"; the three barrel pins located at 8 13/16", 18 1/2", and 36 1/2" from the breech; the upper swivel loop being 28 1/2" from the breech. The left side of the breech has a coronet over IG [Joseph Grice] stamped and King's Proof Marks. The barrel tang is 2 1/8" long, and tapers outwards towards the rear from 1/2" to 9/16" with inspector's crown at end. The front sight/bayonet stud is brazed 1 7/8" from the muzzle and measures 1/4+" x 1/8+". Diameter of barrel at breech ahead of moulding 1 3/16", at muzzle 13/16".

Lock: Pattern 1756 Carbine. Double-bridle, rounded surface to lockplate and cock. The plate measures 6 1/8" x 1 1/16+". The steel is 1 3/4" high x 1" wide. Plate, cock, round top jaw and back of steel have fine double border lines engraved. The rear surface of the top-jaw has a stud which engages in a vertical slot on the forward face of the comb. The throw of the cock is 1 3/4". The leaf-shaped cock comb measures 7/16" across its widest point. Across the tail is engraved VERNON over 1757. Inside the plate is stamped small GV and crowned 2. Trefoil finial to the feather-spring, long sear-spring. The sidenail heads are 1/2" in diameter.

Stock: walnut, to within 4 3/8" of muzzle, with noseband. Lock and sidepiece flat carving is of the modernised simplified form with no aprons forward and teardrops at rear, measuring 6 7/8" overall. The raised barrel tang apron is of the old-fashioned narrow wavy outline, measuring 3 3/16" x 1 1/8". The comb measures 8 3/4" from centre of buttplate screw to tip. The distance from the centre of the trigger to the centre of the buttplate is 13 1/16". The rod channel is 5/16" in diameter. RH stamped in lower rod channel, with crowned 11 and illegible similar stamps at top. Sideplate flat stamped with elongated JC. Stamped below rear guard tang with illegible crowned numbers.

Brass furniture: noseband of sheet-brass with closed front, 5/8" long, secured by an iron rivet. Four Land Pattern barrel-shaped collared ramrod pipes for wooden rammer, the upper pipe 1 7/16" long, 7/16" external diameter at front and rear, internal diameter 5/16", secured by a pin 35 5/8" from the breech. The front of the pipe is 1 1/4" from the front of the noseband. Distance from rear of upper pipe to front of second pipe 6 5/8".

The second pipe is identical in measurements to the upper pipe, held by a pin 27 1/2" from the breech. Distance from rear of second pipe to front of third pipe is 6 1/4".

The third pipe is identical with the other two, secured by a pin 20 1/16" from the breech. Distance from rear of third pipe to front of tailpipe is 5 9/16".

The tailpipe has a 1 5/16" collared barrel-shaped forepart and the flame-shaped tail and lip section are 3 11/16" long. Secured by a pin 12 7/8" from the breech.

The trigger guard is of the same general pattern as the Pattern 1745 Lord Loudoun Carbine with a curved tapered front finial terminating in a ball; this section measures 1 1/16" to an outward step, which is 13/16" wide, tapering slightly to the guard bow. The rear finial is a curved taper to a point. 10 1/2" overall, secured by two pins 2 7/16" from the front finial and 1 1/2" from the rear finial, and by the thumbpiece screw 4 3/4" from the rear finial. The bow is 1 1/8" wide at its widest point.

The sidepiece is conventional Land Pattern with rounded surface and measures 5 1/2" overall, 3 3/16" between sidenail centres. The sidenails are recessed almost flush with the brass.

The thumbpiece is also of the same pattern as on the Lord Loudoun Carbine, being an oval with a trefoil outline at the bottom. It measures 2 1/8" x 1".

The buttplate tang is also of the Lord Loudoun design with two steps from the basic plate 7/8" long and 1" then a curved taper to a point. The tang measures 2 3/4" from the centre of the screwhole. The plate is 5 13/16" from heel to toe, and is 2 1/16" at its widest point.

The wooden ramrod is tapered, with a tapered closed brass cap.

Pattern 1770 Serjeant Of Grenadiers Carbine
Valley Forge Nat. Pk. 18/160

Overall length: 54".

Barrel: 39 1/4", baluster-moulded at breech for 3/8"; the three barrel pins located at 12 9/16", 20 9/16", and 34" from the breech, the upper sling loop being 29 5/16" from the breech. The left side of the breech has * over IW stamped, and the King's Proof Marks on top. The barrel tang is 1 15/16" long, and measures 9/16" at front and rear. The front sight/bayonet stud is brazed 1 9/16" from the muzzle, and measures 3/16" long x 1/8". Barrel diameter across breech ahead of moulding is 1 1/4", and across muzzle 3/4+".

Lock: Pattern 1756 Carbine. The rounded plate measures 6 1/16" x 1 1/16". The steel is 1 3/4" high x 15/16" wide. Throw of cock 1 3/4". Plate and cock have fine double border lines engraved. The comb of the cock is leaf-shaped, and measures 1/2" across widest part (at front). Trefoil finial to the feather-spring, long sear-spring. Crowned GR engraved ahead of cock, and small crowned

Broad Arrow stamped beneath pan. Across the tail is engraved GALTON over 1762. The sidenail heads are 7/16" in diameter, and are not recessed into the sidepiece.

Stock: walnut, to 2 15/16" of the muzzle, with cap. Lock and sidepiece flats have plain rounded front and teardrop at rear, measuring 7" overall. The raised barrel tang apron is oval in outline measuring 3 1/4" x 1 7/16". Drop at comb 1 3/16", and at heel 1 3/8". The comb measures 8 5/8" from centre of buttplate screw to tip. The distance from the centre of the trigger to the centre of the buttplate is 13 1/4". The rod channel is 1/4" in diameter.

Brass furniture: sheet brass noseband 5/8" long. Long tapered trumpet forepipe measures 3 9/16", diameter at mouth 5/8", at rear 3/8", the mouth of the pipe 2 5/8" from stock tip. Secured by two pins 30 7/16" and 32 1/2" from breech. Distance from rear of forepipe to front of second pipe is 4 1/2".

The second pipe is barrel-shaped and collared, 1 3/8" long, secured by a pin 24 1/2" from the breech. The distance from the rear of the second pipe to the front of the third pipe is 4 1/2".

The third pipe is identical to the second, secured by a pin 18 7/8" from the breech. Distance between rear of third pipe and front of tailpipe is 4 9/16".

The tailpipe has a 1 5/16" collared and barrel-shaped forward section and a lip and flame-shaped tang section 2 11/16" long; secured by a pin 12 5/8" from the breech. A rod-retaining spring is riveted in the mouth.

The trigger guard is Land Pattern, 10 1/2" overall, secured by a pin 2 3/4" from the front finial and another 1 1/2" from the rear finial, and by the thumbpiece screw 4 7/16" from the rear finial. The bow is 1" wide at its widest point, and is reinforced and drilled for the lower sling loop screw at the front.

The sidepiece is Light Dragoon with a flat flush surface 3 11/16" long, with 3 3/16" between sidenail centres.

The thumbpiece is a plain oval measuring 1 7/8" x 15/16".

The buttplate is Land Pattern Carbine. The three-step tang is 4 11/16" long; from the first shoulder to the second is 1 7/16", from the second step to the third is 1 1/8", and from the third to the tip is 1". The plate is 4 3/4" from heel to toe, and is 2" at its widest point.

The tapered steel ramrod has a buttonhead.

Pattern 1776 Artillery Carbine
RA XII-109

Overall length: 52 1/2".

Barrel: 37 1/4", balustre-moulded at breech for 7/16"; the three barrel pins located at 10 11/16", 18 7/16", and 32 1/8" from the breech, the upper sling loop being 26 3/8" from the breech. The left side of the breech has * over IO [Joseph Oughton] stamped, and the King's Proof Marks on top, crowned 6 ahead over vent. The barrel tang is 1 7/8+" long, and tapers outwards towards the rear from 1/2+" to 9/16+". The front sight/bayonet stud is brazed 1 5/8+" from the muzzle, and measures 3/16" long x 1/8". Barrel diameter across breech ahead of moulding is 1 1/4", and across muzzle 3/4+".

Lock: Pattern 1777 Carbine. Double-bridle, rounded surface to lockplate and cock. The plate measures 6 1/8" x 1 1/16+". The steel is 1 13/16" high x 1" wide. Throw of cock 1 3/4". Plate and cock have fine double border lines engraved. The comb of the cock is a pillar with well developed notch at front, and the rear surface of the oval top jaw is notched to fit the comb. The comb measures 3/16" across thickest part (at front). Teardrop finial to the feather-spring, short sear-spring.

Crowned GR engraved ahead of cock, and small crowned Broad Arrow stamped beneath pan. Across the tail is engraved TOWER. Inside the plate is stamped crowned 3 and HN, and badly struck TG across front. There is also a tiny circle with six rays.

The sidenail heads are 1/2" in diameter, and are recessed into the sidepiece.

Stock: walnut, to 3 5/8" of the muzzle, with cap. Lock and sidepiece flats have plain rounded front and teardrop at rear, measuring 7 1/4" overall. The raised barrel tang apron is oval in outline measuring 3 3/8" x 1 3/8+". The comb measures 8 3/8" from centre of buttplate screw to tip. The distance from the centre of the trigger to the centre of the buttplate is 13 1/4". The rod channel is 1/4" in diameter. Stamped in the rod channel from the top with crowned 7, crowned 1, crowned ?; crowned V and I. LODER. Sidepiece flat stamped with * over DG. Stamped below lower guard tang with crown and crowned 6. Storekeeper's stamp in right butt.

Brass furniture: cast brass nosecap 3/4" long. Long tapered trumpet forepipe measures 3 9/16", diameter at mouth 5/8", at rear 3/8+", the

106

mouth of the pipe 1 15/16" from stock tip. Secured by two 28 7/8" and 30 13/16" from breech. Internal diameter of pipe is 1/2" at front and 1/4" at rear. Distance from rear of forepipe to front of second pipe is 2 3/16".

The second pipe is barrel-shaped and collared, 1 3/8" long, secured by a pin 25 3/8" from the breech; internal diameter 1/4", maximum external width 7/16". The distance from the rear of the second pipe to the front of the third pipe is 4 1/4".

The third pipe is identical to the second, secured by a pin 19 13/16" from the breech. Distance between rear of third pipe and front of tailpipe is 5 1/4".

The tailpipe has a 1 3/8" collared and barrel-shaped forward section and a lip and flame-shaped tang section 2 3/4" long; external diameter is 3/8+" at mouth, secured by a pin 13 1/16" from the breech. A rod-retaining spring is riveted in the mouth.

The trigger guard is Land Pattern, 10 1/2" overall, secured by a pin 2 3/4" from the front finial and another 1 1/2" from the rear finial, and by the thumbpiece screw 4 9/16" from the rear finial. The bow is 1 1/16" wide at its widest point, and is reinforced and drilled for the lower sling loop screw at the front.

The sidepiece is Land Pattern with a rounded surface, 5 1/2" long, with 3 5/16" between sidenail centres.

The thumbpiece is Land Pattern and measures 2 3/8" x 15/16".

The buttplate tang is the standard pattern for Land Pattern carbines. The three-step tang is 4 3/4" long; from the first shoulder to the second is 1 3/8", and from the second step to the third is 1 1/16", and from the third step to the tip is 1 1/8". The plate is 4 3/4" from heel to toe, and is 1 7/8" at its widest point.

The tapered steel ramrod has a button-head 5/8" in diameter.

Regimentally engraved on top of barrel Royl Artillery 1st Bn.

Pattern 1779 Carbine for Horse
RA XII-161

Overall length: 52".

Barrel: 37 3/16", balustre-moulded at breech for 1/2"; the three barrel pins located at 10 7/16", 23", and 32 15/16" from the breech. The left side of the breech has * over IW stamped on the left side, and the King's Proof Marks on top. The barrel tang is 1 15/16" long, and tapers outwards toward the rear from 1/2" to 9/16". The steel blade front sight is brazed 2 3/16" from the muzzle, and measures 1/2" long x 1/4". Barrel diameter across breech ahead of moulding is 1 1/4", and across the muzzle 7/8".

Lock: Pattern 1777 Carbine. Double-bridle, rounded surface to lockplate and cock. The plate measures 6 1/8" x 1 1/16". The swan-neck cock has a narrow pillar comb with a notch at the front of the top, and measures 1/4" across its widest point. Throw of cock is 1 3/4". The steel is 1 11/16" high x 15/16" wide. Plate, cock, and oval top-jaw have fine double border lines engraved. The rear surface of the top-jaw is notched to fit around and move along the comb. Teardrop finial to the feather-spring, short sear-spring. Crowned GR engraved ahead of cock, and small crowned Broad Arrow stamped beneath pan. Across the tail is engraved TOWER. Inside the plate is stamped crowned 1 and WH, and H at right angles, and 3.

The front sidenail head is 7/16" diameter and is recessed into the sidepiece, while the rear sidenail is 1/2" in diameter and is proud of the sidepiece, the rear of the sling-bar being recessed into the brass beneath the nail.

Stock: walnut, to 1/8" of the muzzle, without cap. The raised barrel tang apron is oval in outline measuring 3 5/16" x 1 5/16". Lock and sidepiece flats have plain rounded front and teardrop at rear, measuring 7 1/8" overall. The comb measures 8 1/2" from centre of buttplate screw to tip. The distance from the centre of the trigger to the centre of the buttplate is 13 1/8". The rod channel is 5/16" in diameter. Stamped in the rod channel from the top with four crowned numbers, two letters illegible and TUCKER and Broad Arrow. Sidepiece flat not marked. Stamped below lower guard tang with crown and crowned number. Storekeeper's stamp in right butt.

Brass furniture: no nosecap. Composite-pattern trumpet forepipe 3 3/4" overall, the upper section 2 1/16", the lower part 1 5/8" long; diameter at mouth 11/16", and at rear 1/2". Secured by two pins 30" and 31 11/16" from the breech. Internal diameter of the pipe is 9/16" at the mouth and 3/8" at the rear. The mouth of the pipe is 4 1/2" from the tip of the stock. From the rear of the forepipe to the front of the second pipe measures 7 1/2".

The second pipe is barrel-shaped and collared, and measures 1 5/16" long, widest external diameter of 1/2", with internal diameter of 3/8". Secured by a pin 20 5/8" from the breech; the distance from the rear of the second pipe to the front of the tailpipe is 6".

The tailpipe has a 1 3/8" collared and barrel-shaped forward section and a lip and flame-shaped tang section 2 7/16" long; outside diameter is 7/16" at mouth, secured by a pin 12 5/8" from the breech.

The trigger guard is Land Pattern, 11" overall, secured by a pin 3 3/4" from the front finial and another 1 9/16+" from the rear finial, and by the thumbpiece screw 5 1/16" from the rear finial. The bow is 1 1/16" wide at its widest point, and is pinched-in at the front to a diameter of 3/8".

The sidepiece is Land Pattern with a rounded surface, 5 1/2" long, with 3 3/8" between sidenail centres. The rear of the sling-bar is fastened beneath the rear sidenail, shaped like a flat washer and fully recessed into the sidenail recess of the sidepiece, which is cut away at the front (left) for the bar. The longer rear sidenail lies against the upper surface of the inlet bar and is proud of the sidepiece. The front of the sling-bar, which is 8 5/8" long, terminates in a rounded-surface elongated teardrop shaped finial and is held by a screw from the right side of the fore-end 9" from the breech.

The thumbpiece is Land Pattern and measures 2 3/8" x 15/16".

The buttplate tang is Land Pattern Carbine. The three-step tang is 4 3/4" long; from the first shoulder to the second is 1 7/16", and from the second step to the third is 1 1/8", and from the third step to the tip is 1 1/8". The plate is 4 11/16" from heel to toe, and is 1 7/8" at its widest point.

The tapered wooden ramrod has a closed brass cap.

CARBINES—SEA SERVICE

Pattern 1715 Iron-Barrelled Blunderbuss
RA XII-279

Overall length: 42 9/16".
Barrel: 26 1/2", heavy-walled iron, three stage: 3 7/16" octagonal, 3 11/16" sixteen-sided and filed with a narrow groove and ring; then 19 1/4" round to a slightly flared muzzle, with a draw-filed and blacked surface. Two barrel pins located at 9 9/16" and 22 5/8" from the breech. The barrel tang is 2 5/8" long, and tapers outwards toward the rear from 9/16" to 5/8+". Barrel diameter across the octagonal breech is 1 1/2", and across the flared muzzle 2 15/16". Bore diameter is 1.9". The breech is struck with a Queen Anne proofmark of AR over the Broad Arrow.

Lock: Pattern 1703 Musket, with back-catch. Plain (without tumbler- or pan-bridle), flat surface to lockplate and ring-neck cock. The plate measures 7 5/16" x 1 1/4". The separate pan is faceted on its underside. The ring-neck cock has a narrow pillar comb which is straight at the top, and measures 1/4" across its widest point. The rear face of the oval top-jaw is notched to fit around and move along the comb. The throat-hole is shaped like a tear-drop. Throw of cock is 2". The steel is hexagonal in form, 1 3/4" x 1 5/16" wide. There is no border engraving. Spearpoint finial to the feather-spring, short sear-spring.

Crowned GR engraved ahead of cock, but lacking the usual crowned Broad Arrow stamped beneath pan. Across the tail is engraved WOLLDRIDGE over 15. Inside the plate is stamped crowned 6, an H within a sunken heart, J O and the name of the engraver CASLON.

The three sidenail heads are 5/8+" in diameter and are not recessed into the wood.

Stock: walnut, to 1/4" of the muzzle, without cap. There is a narrow parallel raised barrel tang apron, the lock- and sidepiece flats being plain narrow outlines of the lockplate, measuring 8" overall. The comb measures 8" from centre of vertical plane to end of flat surface at front. The distance from the centre of the trigger to the centre of the buttplate is 14". The rod channel is 3/8" in diameter, and the entry point is 16 3/4" from the tip of the fore-end. Storekeeper's stamp in right butt.

Furniture: no fore-end cap. There is a slightly tapered plain brass ramrod pipe 1 5/8" long; external diameter at widest point 9/16", for wooden ramrod. Secured by a pin 22 5/8" from the breech. The front of the pipe is 3 7/8" from the tip of the stock. From the rear of the pipe to the entry point is 11 5/16".

There is no tailpipe, no sidepiece and no thumbpiece.

The trigger guard is very similar to the standard Sea Service Pattern with convex surface, but hammered sheet iron, beaten hollow at the typical domed circular finial and along the rear strap. 10 5/8" overall, secured by large screw just ahead of the flat guard bow and another 2 1/8" from the rear finial. The bow is 1 1/4" wide at its widest point, and the rear finial is a plain rounded form.

There is no trigger-plate and the barrel tang screw enters from the underside of the stock ahead of the trigger, with the head inlet flush with the surface of the wood.

The brass buttplate is the standard Sea Service pattern. The tang is 3 3/8" long; from the base of the tang to the first step is 1 1/4", and 2 1/16" to the tip. The plate measures 5 5/8" from heel to toe, and is 2 3/8" at its widest point.

The tapered wooden ramrod has a plain iron face-plate.

This blunderbuss weighs 13 lbs. 4 ozs.

Pattern 1718 Brass-Barrelled Musketoon
RA XII-9259

Overall length: 44".
Barrel: 28 9/16", heavy-walled brass. Cast into the barrel breech at the join with the iron tang is a raised rounded collar 3/16" high and 5/16" thick. Two barrel pins located at 11" and 22 1/2" from the breech. The left side of the breech has 52 and 41 stamped on the left side, and the King's (Charles II) Proof Marks on top. The barrel tang is 2 15/16" long, and tapers outwards towards the rear from 5/8" to 3/4". Barrel diameter across breech ahead of collar is 1 15/16", and across the flared muzzle 2 3/4". Bore diameter is 2 1/8".
Lock: Pattern 1718 Musket. Plain (without tumbler- or pan-bridle), flat surface to lockplate and ring-neck cock. The plate measures 7 11/16" x 1 1/4". The ring-neck cock has a narrow pillar comb which is straight at the top, and measures 1/4" across its widest point. The rear face of the top-jaw is notched to fit around and move along the comb. The throat-hole is shaped like a teardrop. Throw of cock is 2". The steel is hexagonal in form, 1 13/16" x 1 1/4" wide. There is no border engraving. Spearpoint finial to the feather-spring, short searspring. Crowned GR engraved ahead of cock, and small crowned Broad Arrow stamped beneath pan. Across the tail is engraved COLE over 21. Inside the plate is stamped crowned 20 and E. The sidenail heads are 5/8" in diameter and are not recessed into the sidepiece.
Stock: walnut, to 2 9/16" of the muzzle, without cap. The raised barrel tang apron is oval in outline measuring 4 3/8" x 1 15/16". Lock and sidepiece flats have plain rounded front and teardrop at rear, measuring 8 1/4" overall. The comb measures 8" from centre of buttplate screw to tip. The distance from the centre of the trigger to the centre of the buttplate is 13 5/8". The rod channel is 7/16" in diameter, and the entry point is 16" from the tip of the foreend. Stamped in the rod channel RIR. Sidepiece flat not marked. Stamped below rear guard tang with crowned 10.

Storekeeper's stamp in right butt.
Brass furniture: no nosecap. There is a single cylindrical and collared ramrod pipe 1 5/8" long; diameter at widest point 9/16", for wooden ramrod. Secured by a pin 20 3/4" from the breech. Internal diameter of the pipe at the mouth is 7/16". The front of the pipe is 4 1/2" from the tip of the stock. From the rear of the pipe to the entry point is 9 7/8".

There is no tailpipe, no sidepiece and no thumbpiece.

The trigger guard is very similar to the standard Sea Service Pattern with convex surface, but the front finial has flats filed along each side before the typical domed circular termination. It is hollow-cast and is 11 1/2" overall, secured by a screw 1 1/4" from the front finial and another 2 3/4" from the rear finial. The bow is 13/16" wide at its widest point, and the rear finial is a plain rounded form.

There is no trigger-plate and the barrel tang screw enters from the underside of the stock ahead of the trigger, with the head inlet flush with the surface of the wood.

The buttplate tang is a slight variant of the standard Sea Service pattern. The tang is 5 1/8" long; from the base of the tang to the first step is 2", and tapers for 3 1/4" to the tip. The plate measures 5 15/16" from heel to toe, and is 2 3/4" at its widest point.

The tapered wooden ramrod has a closed brass cap.

Pattern 1779 Seven-Barrelled Volley Gun
RA XII-1187

Overall length: 37".
Barrels: 20", seven .52 calibre plain tapered tubes fastened to a 5/16" thick breechplate by their individual breechplugs. There is an upper and a lower tang to this plate, the lower tang acting as a trigger-plate. The barrel tang is 2 15/16" long, and is stepped with a

109

tapered rounded end. Barrel diameter across breech is .770" and across the muzzle 11/16".

Lock: Back-action, flat surface to lockplate and swan-neck cock both with bevelled edges. The plate measures 5 7/16" x 11/16". The swan-neck cock has a narrow pillar comb with a typical war-period slight curl with notch at the front, and measures 1/4" across its widest point. The rear face of the top-jaw is notched to fit around and move along the comb. Throw of cock is 1 11/16". The steel measures 1 3/4" x 15/16". Curled pointed finial to the feather-spring, which is L-shaped with the long leaf extending beneath the pan and the short leaf vertically behind the pan.

Small crowned Broad Arrow stamped horizontally below pan; TOWER engraved horizontally along top of plate in rear of the cock and crowned GR engraved across tail of lockplate. Inside the plate is stamped HN.

The two sidenail heads are 1/2" in diameter and are recessed into the sidepiece.

Stock: walnut, butt-stock only, of conventional handrail design as used on the Short Land series. Drop at comb is 1 7/8" and at heel 2 1/2". There is no apron carving at the barrel tang. Lock and sidepiece flats have plain short teardrop at rear, the left side flat being roughly oval in outline, right flat measuring 4 3/4" overall. The comb measures 9 1/4". The distance from the centre of the trigger to the centre of the buttplate is 14". Stamped twice below lower guard tang with crowned numbers. Undated Storekeeper's stamp in right butt.

Brass furniture: no nosecap. All three ramrod pipes differ from the current Land Pattern designs although similar in overall design. Long trumpet forepipe measures 3 5/16" and has a flat tapering 2" rod-retaining spring inlet into its outer surface. The mouth is 5/8" in diameter, internal diameter is 5/16" and the mouth of the pipe is 3" from the muzzles.

The second pipe is 1 3/4" long with a distinctive pattern of flared mouth, with two collars and a cylindrical central section. It is 1 13/16" long, 1/2" in diameter at the mouth and just over 1/4" internal diameter; the front of the pipe is 5 3/16" behind the rear of the trumpet pipe.

The lower pipe is basically cylindrical with two fine collars having a broader band between them at each end. It is 1 7/16" long, with an external diameter of 7/16". It is 5 3/16" behind the rear of the second pipe and butts against the breechplate of the barrels. All three pipes are brazed into the groove between the two lower barrels.

The sidepiece has a rounded surface and is 3 5/8" in length, with 3" between sidenail centres.

There is no thumbpiece.

The trigger guard is very similar to the standard Land Service pattern with convex surface, but the front finial is much shorter; it is 6 3/4" overall, secured by a screw 7/8" from the front finial and a screw 1 1/8" from the rounded ball-terminal rear finial. The bow is 11/16" at its widest point.

The buttplate is the standard Short Land Pattern. The tang is 3 3/4" long; from the shoulder of the tang to the first step is 1 3/8", and from the first step to the tip is 1 1/2". The plate measures 5 5/16" from heel to toe, and is 2 1/8" at its widest point.

The tapered steel ramrod has a conventional button-head 7/16" in diameter, and the tip is threaded.

RIFLES

Pattern 1776 Ferguson Breech-Loading Rifle
Morristown National Historical Park

Overall Length: 49".

Barrel: 34" to tang, 30" to face of breechplug; .65 calibre, rifled with eight rectangluar grooves making one turn in 60 inches. The bore is badly worn and shows signs of having been used as a muzzle-loader; three barrel slides although the barrel is not fitted with a false-breech, located at 1 3/4", 9 3/4" and 24" from the nose-cap. King's Proof struck on left in rear of breech opening, and King's View similarly on right. Maker's mark, MB & IW [Matthias Barker and John Whately] stamped on left flat of the breech. Ferguson's inspection/approval mark of a small crowned PF is stamped just behind the breech opening. The issue-number is engraved at the rear of the barrel tang. The two-leaf block backsight is dovetailed 4 3/4" from the tang; brass blade front sight is brazed to the barrel 4 3/8" from the muzzle to allow fitting the socket bayonet, whose stud is on the underside of the barrel.

Lock: Double-bridle with flat lockplate and swan-neck cock having beveled edges, the plate measuring 5 3/16 x 1". The cock has a narrow pillar comb with notch at its front, the oval un-engraved top-jaw notched to fit the

110

comb. Tear-drop finial to the feather-spring; short sear-spring. Crudely and lightly engraved ahead of cock with crowned GR and TOWER across tail, probably by the same hand that engraved the P/1776 rifle locks. There is no crowned Broad Arrow on the external surface nor any maker's or inspector's marks stamped internally. There is one short sidenail entering from the right into the side of the breech.

Stock: walnut, fore-end to 4 3/8" of muzzle. Comb length 9" from centre of screwhole. Drop at comb 1 1/2" and at heel 2 1/2". No tang apron. Sideflats plain rounded at front and teardrop at rear. Distance from centre of trigger to centre of butt 13 3/4". Undated Storekeeper's stamp in right butt.

Brass Furniture: nosecap without reinforce at rear, secured by brass rivet. Forepipe is barrel-shaped and collared, 1 1/2" long, held by a pin 2 7/16" from the nose-cap.

Second pipe is identical in design and measurement to the upper pipe, secured by a pin 8" from the nosecap.

Tailpipe is similar to the Land Pattern with a barrel-shaped and collared section and a lip and tang section, secured by a pin 15 3/4" from the nose-cap. All pipes and channel are for a wooden rammer.

There is no sidepiece, but there is a screw-held sling-swivel let into the sidepiece flat.

The front of the trigger guard is fixed by a large screw to the underside of the breechplug, and by rotating the guard counter-clockwise one full turn the 7/8" diameter breechplug drops down to expose the opening in the top of the breech for loading. The rear of the guard has a downward turn forming a short handle for turning.

There is no thumbpiece.

Buttplate is similar to the Land Pattern Carbine.

Pattern 1776 Infantry Rifle
R.J. Whittaker

Overall Length: 44 3/4".

Barrel: 28 13/16", .65 calibre, rifled with eight rectangular grooves .020" deep x .150" wide, making one turn in 56 1/2"; octagonal, slightly swamped. Barrel slides located at 7 1/16", 15 11/16", and 26 3/8" from the breech, and the upper swivel screw 25" from the breech. King's Proof struck on top at breech; maker's mark of MB & IW [Matthias Barker and John Whately] in three lines on the upper left flat. Fitted with a hook-breech. Tang measures 2 5/16" long, tapering. Block backsight with two hinged leaves and a two-stage tapering ornamental finial (now missing) dovetailed 6 5/16" from breech; brass blade foresight (now missing) dovetailed 11/16" from muzzle. Width across breech 13/16", and across muzzle 13/16", tapering to .860" at 9 5/8" from the muzzle. There are two 1/8"-long circular ramrod-stops, threaded into the side-flats of the barrel about 1/16" behind the muzzle.

Lock: Carbine Extra Flat pattern, flat lockplate and swan-neck cock with beveled edges and a faceted pan. Double-bridle, the plate measuring 6" x 1+". The cock has a narrow pillar comb with notch at its front, the oval engraved top-jaw notched to fit the comb; the comb is 1/4" thick at the front, its thickest point. Throw of cock is 1 11/16". Steel measures 1 3/4" high x 1+" wide and the back is engraved. The lockplate and cock body, top-jaw and back of steel have fine double border lines engraved. Tear-drop finial to the feather-spring; long sear-spring. Crudely and lightly engraved ahead of cock with crowned GR, and TOWER across tail. Crowned Broad Arrow struck beneath pan. Sidenail heads are 7/16" diameter and are recessed into the surface of the sidepiece.

Stock: walnut, fore-end to muzzle. Comb length 8 3/4" from centre of screwhole. Oval tang apron 3 7/16" x 1 3/8". Sideflats plain rounded at front and teardrop at rear 6 15/16" overall. Diameter of rod channel 7/16". Distance from centre of trigger to centre of butt 13 1/2". Sidepiece flat stamped with small IC at rear. Stamped below rear guard tang with crown and crowned 6. Undated Storekeeper's stamp in right butt.

Brass Furniture: iron nosecap with internal screw fastening; sides measure 1 3/16"; the upper edges of the cap have 1/2" semi-circular cut-away sections 3/16" from the front to allow for the swivel-rammer screws into the sides of the barrel. The front of the cap has three facets each about 1/8" wide.

Forepipe is 1 3/4" long, with a flared mouth, and a cylindrical section between two collars, secured by a pin 23 1/8" from the breech and an internal screw through a plate inlet into the barrel-bed. The mouth is 11/16" in diameter, internal diameter 1/2". The mouth of the pipe is 4 1/2" from front of nosecap. The distance between rear of the forepipe and front of second pipe is 5 1/2". Between the two pipes, riveted at each end, is a rounded rod-retaining spring.

Second pipe is cylindrical and collared, 1 7/16" long, 1/2" external diameter 5/8", internal diameter, secured by two pins 16 3/8" and 17 3/8" from breech. Distance between rear of pipe and front of tailpipe 4 1/2".

Tailpipe is very similar to the Land Pattern with 1 1/8" cylindrical and collared section, 1 13/16" lip and tang section, 5/8" diameter at mouth, secured by two pins 10 3/4" and 11 5/8" from the breech.

Sidepiece is flat Land Pattern, flush with the wood, 5 1/2" long, with 3 5/16" between sidenail centres.

Trigger guard is fitted with a slightly curving grip-guard 2 1/16" long from guard bow to curl, 9 1/4" overall, secured by a pin 2 7/16" from the front finial and a screw 1 1/16" from the rear finial which terminates in an acorn. The bow is 1" at its widest point. The trigger plate is iron.

There is no thumbpiece.

Buttplate is similar to the Land Pattern Carbine, with a three-step tapering tang measuring 4 3/8" from the centre of the screwhole. Distance from first step to second 1 1/4"; from second to third 1 1/8+"; from third to the tip 1". The plate measures 5" from top to bottom x 2" at its widest point.

Heavy steel ramrod about 5/16" diameter, with swivels attached through the sides of the barrel. The flattened buttonhead is 3/4" in diameter, rounded front. The tip of the rod has a brass collar with a female thread for cleaning tools.

PISTOLS—LAND SERVICE

Pattern 1730 Land Service Pistol
NAM 7506-68

Overall length 18 3/4".
Barrel 12", .66 cal. (carbine-bore), secured by two pins 3 1/2" and 10" from the breech. No sights. Balustre-moulded at breech. King's Proof struck on top. Tang 2" x 1/2".
Lock: Pattern 1729 Pistol. Rounded surfaces, single-bridle, lockplate 5 7/16" x 1", the tail with "banana" configuration. No pan bridle. Distance from centre of pan to centre of pivot-screw 11/16". Crowned GR engraved ahead of cock, small crowned Broad Arrow stamped below pan. Underside of cock lower jaw has slight reinforce lip same as on musket cock. Narrow leaf-shaped comb, 3/8" wide. Edges of plate, cock, top-jaw and back of steel have double lines engraved. Stamped inside WH and crowned 30. Feather-spring finial is like an unsplit trefoil.

Stock: full length, with raised elliptical aprons at front and rear of lock and sidepiece flats, 6 1/2" overall, and a narrow wavy-outline tang apron 3" x 15/16" at barrel tang. Inspector's crowned numerals in rammer channel; Storekeeper's stamp on upper right wrist.
Brass furniture: no nosecap. One barrel-shaped collared ramrod pipe 1 3/16" in length, with pin 9" from breech. Tailpipe with barrel-shaped and collared section 1 1/16" in length, lip and tail 2" long, with pin 6 1/4" from breech; front of tailpipe 5 1/16" from muzzle.

Rounded Land Pattern sidepiece 4 3/4" long, but narrower in outline than subsequent patterns.

Land Pattern thumbpiece 2 1/8" x 7/8".

Pattern 1730 rounded trigger guard 7 3/8" long, secured by crosspin at front and rear and thumbpiece screw in centre.

Buttcap measuring 2 9/16" x 2 1/8" with *two* masks: the usual outer one measuring 1 7/8" by 1 9/16", and a smaller inner one surrounding the central screw, measuring 3/4" x 5/8". This is the only Ordnance pistol with this pattern of undecorated double-masks. The long tapering sidespurs extend 4" up the sides of the grip.

Tapered wooden rammer with tapered closed brass cap.

Pattern 1738 Land Service Pistol
RA XII-5053

Overall length: 19 1/4".
Barrel: 12 1/16", .56 calibre, balustre-moulded at breech for 7/16". Two barrel pins 4" and 9 7/8" from breech. No sights. King's Proof stamped on top at breech, maker's mark of coronet over E I [Edward Jordan] on left side. Tang measures 1 11/16" long, tapering outwards from 7/16" at join to 1/2" at rear. Inspector's crown at join with crossed sceptres at rear. Diameter of barrel across breech ahead of moulding 1", and at muzzle 3/4".
Lock: Pattern 1738 Pistol. Double-bridle, rounded surface to plate and cock, plate measures 5 7/16" x 1". Swan-neck cock with leaf-shaped comb 3/8" across at widest point; the circular jaw has a stud at its back which moves in a groove along the comb. Throw of cock is 1 5/8". Steel measures 1 9/16" high x 1" wide. Trefoil finial to feather-spring. The plate, cock body, top-jaw, and back of steel are engraved with double border lines. Plate engraved ahead of cock with crowned GR, and struck beneath pan with small crowned Broad Arrow. Across tail engraved TOWER over 1738. Internal stamps are

crowned 49 and initials EI. The sidenail heads are 7/16" diameter and are recessed in the sidepiece.

Stock: Walnut, full length, ramrod enters 6 5/8" from muzzle. Lock and sidepiece flats have full, oval aprons front and rear, measuring 7 13/16" overall. Barrel tang apron has narrow wavy outline and measures 3 1/16" x 15/16". Diameter of rod channel is 1/4+". Storekeeper's stamp on upper right wrist. Sidepiece flat stamped at rear: 8. Stamped alongside lower guard tang crowned 5 and crowned 6. Rammer channel stamped from top with three crowned illegible numbers.

Brass Furniture: One 1 1/8" barrel-shaped collared rammer pipe, 7/16" diameter at front and rear, internal diameter 5/16+", secured by a pin 9 3/16" from the breech.

Tailpipe is Land Pattern with 1 3/16" barrel-shaped and collared section and a lip and tang section 2 1/4" long, 3/8" diameter at mouth, 5/16" internal diameter; secured by a pin 6 1/4" from the breech.

Typical Land Pattern thumbpiece 2 1/8" x 7/8".

Sidepiece also Land Pattern, rounded surface, 4 3/4" long, with 2 5/8+" between sidenail centres.

Trigger guard is Land Pattern, 8" overall, secured by a pin 2 1/4" from the front finial, and another 1 7/16" from the rear finial, and by the thumbpiece screw 2 3/8" from the rear finial. The bow is 1" at its widest point.

Buttcap, measuring 2 5/16" x 1 15/16" with a single mask measuring 1 3/4" x 1 1/2", the long tapering sidespurs extending 3 5/8" up the grip.

Wooden ramrod is tapered and has a closed brass cap 1 3/16" long.

Pattern 1756 Light Dragoon Pistol
(Clark R. Hoffman)

Overall length: 16 3/16".
Barrel: 10 1/16", .66 calibre, balustre-moulded at breech for 1/2". Two barrel pins 3 7/16" and 8 1/8" from breech. No sights. King's Proof stamped on top at breech. Tang measures 1 5/8" long, tapering outwards from 7/16" at join to 1/2" at rear. Inspector's crown with crossed sceptres at rear. Diameter of barrel across breech ahead of moulding 1 1/16", and at muzzle 7/8".
Lock: Pattern 1756 Extra Flat. Double-bridle, flat bevelled surface to plate and cock, plate measures 5 3/16" x 1". Flat swan-neck cock with straight comb; the top-jaw is slotted and fits around the comb. Steel measures 1 1/2" high x 7/8" wide. Teardrop finial to feather-spring. The plate, cock body, top-jaw, and back of steel are engraved with double border lines. Plate engraved ahead of cock with crowned GR, and struck beneath pan with small crowned Broad Arrow. Across tail engraved TOWER over 1760. Stamped internally with initials GV. The sidenails heads are 3/8" diameter and are not recessed in the sidepiece.

Stock: Walnut, full length, ramrod enters 4 5/8" from muzzle. Lock and sidepiece flats have teardrop at rear, measuring 6 1/8" overall. Barrel tang apron is oval and measures 3" x 1 1/4". Diameter of rod channel is 5/16". Storekeeper's stamp on upper right wrist. Sidepiece flat stamped at rear: M. Stamped alongside lower guard tang crowned 8. Rammer channel stamped from top with crowned 13, crowned 8, crowned 13, and crowned illegible number.

Brass Furniture: No nosecap. One 1 1/4" tapered collared rammer pipe, secured by a pin 7 3/16" from the breech. The mouth of the pipe is 2 3/16" from the stock tip. No tailpipe.

Sidepiece is flat and flush, of Light Dragoon pattern resembling addorsed "Cs" attached, 3 1/16" long, with 2 15/16" between sidenail centres.

Trigger guard is Light Dragoon Pattern, 6 1/4" overall, secured by a pin 1 3/4" from the front finial, and another 1 3/4" from the rear finial. The bow is 7/8" at its widest point.

Buttcap measuring 2 1/16" x 1 5/8" with a single plain mask measuring 1 9/16" x 15/16"; the short blunt or rounded terminal sidespurs extend 1 1/2" up the sides of the grip.

Wooden ramrod is tapered and has a closed brass cap 1 1/8" long.

Pattern 1759 Eliott's Light Dragoon Pistol
RA XII-5054

Overall length: 15".
Barrel: 9", .66 calibre, balustre-moulded at breech for 7/16". Two barrel pins 3 1/4" and 7 5/16" from breech. No sights. King's Proof on top at breech. Maker's mark IW struck on left breech. Tang measures 1 9/16" long, 1/2" at front and rear, crowned crossed sceptres at front and crown at tail. Diameter of barrel across breech ahead of moulding 1 1/16", across muzzle 7/8".

Lock: Pattern 1759 Eliott. Round cock and plate, plate measures 5 5/16" x 15/16". The comb of the cock is a narrow notched pillar, 1/4" thick, tapered from front to back. Oval top-jaw notched to fit pillar. Throw of the cock 1 1/2". Steel measures 1 1/2" x 7/8+". Steel pivot-screw enters from inside the lockplate. HASKINS over 1759 across tail, crowned GR engraved ahead of cock. Plate, cock, top-jaw and back of steel with double border lines engraved. Trefoil feather-spring finial. Struck inside plate with crowned 2, and small GH.

Stock: Walnut, full length. Plain rounded front and teardrop carving at flats, 5 3/4" overall. Oval tang apron measures 3" x 1 1/4". Storekeeper's stamp on upper right wrist. Illegible crowned numbers in rod channel and assembly number. Sidepiece flat stamped at rear IP 36.

Brass furniture: of a design unique to this pattern except the rammer pipe; no nosecap, tailpipe or thumbpiece.

One 1 1/4" barrel shaped collared rammer pipe, 7/16" diameter at front and rear, internal diameter 3/8", the securing pin 3 3/16" from the breech; mouth of pipe is 2" from tip of fore-end. Distance from rear of pipe to entry point 15/16".

Sidepiece is flat and flush with wood, 3 1/8" long, the sidenail holes 2 3/4" between centres. Sidenails are dome-headed and are not recessed in brass.

Trigger guard is 6 1/2" long, held by a pin 1 9/16" from the front finial, and a lower pin 1 1/8" from the lower finial. The front finial tapers to a point and terminates with a ball, tapering back from a flare to the bow. The bow is 3/4" at its widest point.

Buttcap is the same as that used on the Pattern 1756 Light Dragoon Pistol, measuring 2 1/16" x 1 5/8" with a single plain mask measuring 1 5/8" x 1 3/8"; the short blunt or rounded terminal sidespurs extending 1 7/16" up the sides of the grip.

**Pattern 1760 Royal Foresters
Light Dragoon Pistol.**
(Clinton L. Miller)

Overall Length: 16 1/4".
Barrel: 10", .66 calibre. Two barrel pins 3 1/2" and 8" from breech. No sights. King's Proof on top at breech.
Lock: Pattern 1756 Extra Flat. Flat, cock and plate with narrow bevelled edges, 5 1/4 x 15/16". Swan-neck cock with notched top-jaw and un-notched straight pillar comb. Faceted pan. Crowned GR engraved ahead of cock and small crowned Broad Arrow stamped beneath pan; TOWER over 1760 engraved across tail. Plate, cock, top-jaw and back of steel engraved with double border lines. GH and crowned 2 stamped inside.

Stock: Walnut, full length, ramrod enters 4 7/8" from muzzle. Storekeeper's stamp on upper right wrist. Two crowned numbers in rod channel and assembly number. Teardrop carving at rear of lock and sidepiece flats, crude imitation shell carved apron at tang.

Brass furniture: One 1 1/4" barrel shaped collared rammer pipe, the pin 2 3/4" from muzzle; no tailpipe.

Typical Land Pattern thumbpiece 2" x 3/4".

Special pattern sidepiece with flat, bevelled edge, forward section proud of wood; stepped tail which is flat and flush with wood. Two sidenails and small woodscrew at rear. The crosspin of the trigger shows through the brass.

Special pattern front trigger guard finial, guard is 7" long held by pin at front and screw at rear.

Buttcap measuring 2 1/16" x 1 3/4" with a single plain mask measuring 1 9/16" x 1 3/8"; the long tapering sidespurs extending 3 1/4" up the side of the grip.

PISTOLS—SEA SERVICE

Pattern 1718
(Clark R. Hoffman)

Overall length: 18 15/16".
Barrel: 12 1/8", .56 calibre, balustre-moulded at breech for 1 3/8". Two barrel pins 4 7/8" and 15/16" from breech. No sights. King's Proof on top at breech. Maker's mark EI struck on left breech. Tang measures 1 5/8+" long, 7/16" at front and 1/2" at rear, crowned crossed sceptres on tang at join with barrel. Diameter of barrel across breech ahead of turning 15/16+", and across muzzle 11/16+".
Lock: Pattern 1718. Flat plate and ring-neck cock with narrow bevelled edges, plate measures 5 1/4" x 15/16". Faceted pan without bridle. The comb of the cock is a straight pillar, 3/16" thick. Oval top-jaw slotted to fit pillar. Throw of the cock 1 5/8-". Flat-topped (hexagonal) steel has a faceted back and measures 1 7/16" x 15/16+". Spearpoint finial to the feather-spring. Crowned GR engraved ahead of cock, VAUGHAN over 1744 across tail. No border engraving on any

Stock: lock parts. Struck inside plate with crowned 2, and coronet over EI. Sidenail heads are 1/2-" and 7/16-" diameter and are not recessed in sidepiece.

Stock: walnut, full length, ramrod enters 6 1/8" from muzzle. Plain rounded front and teardrop carving at side flats, 6 1/4" overall. Oval tang apron measures 2 3/4" x 1 1/8". Storekeeper's stamp on upper right wrist. Illegible crowned numbers in rod channel and assembly number. Sidepiece flat stamped at rear crown over addorsed Rs. No trigger plate. Barrel tang screw is threaded into square iron washer (nut) inlet ahead of trigger and beneath front base of trigger guard bow.

Brass Furniture: no nosecap, tailpipe or thumbpiece.
One 1 1/8+" cylindrical rammer pipe, 3/8+" diameter at front and rear, internal diameter 5/16+", the securing pin 9 1/8" from the breech; mouth of pipe is 2 3/8" from tip of the fore-end. Distance from rear of pipe to entry point is 2 1/2+".
Sidepiece is Sea Service pattern flat and flush with wood, 4 3/4" long, the sidenail holes 2 5/8+" between centres. Sidenails are not recessed in brass.
Trigger guard is Land Service 6 7/8" long, held by a pin 2" from the front finial, and a lower pin 1 3/4" from the lower finial. The bow is 1" at its widest point.
Iron belt-hook 8 7/8" overall (hook section 7 1/4") on left side, held by the rear sidenail and a small flush woodscrew through its tail.
Buttcap measures 2 1/4" x 1 11/16" and is smooth overall without a mask, the short blunt sidespurs extending 1 7/8" up the sides of the grip.
Ramrod is tapered wood with standard pattern tapered brass cap.

Pattern 1756
(Clinton M. Miller)

Overall length: 18 13/16".
Barrel: 11 7/8", .56 calibre, balustre-moulded for 7/16" at breech. Crosspins 4" and 10 1/16" from breech. No sights. King's Proof stamped on top, * over -W (probably John Whately) on left. Tang measures 1 11/16" long by 7/16" at front tapering outward to 9/16" at rear. Diameter of barrel 1" across breech, 13/16" across muzzle.
Lock: Pattern 1756. Flat lockplate and ring-necked cock with narrow bevelled edges, 5 1/8" x 15/16". Faceted pan without bridle, flat-topped (hexagonal) steel 1 1/2" high with faceted back. Cock has thin pillar comb with rounded tip very slightly curved back, oval top-jaw slotted to fit comb. Oval throat-hole. Cock-screw is pierced and slotted. Leaf-shaped feather-spring finial with central spine. Stamped beneath pan with crowned Broad Arrow, engraved crowned GR ahead of cock; GALTON over 1759 engraved across tail. No double border-lines engraved on any parts. Inside stamped FG and crowned 2. Two sidenails 2 5/8" centre to centre.

Stock: walnut, stocked to 1/16" of muzzle. Ramrod enters stock 6 1/4" from tip. Raised oval apron at barrel tang 3 1/8" x 1 3/16". Terminals of side flats rounded at fronts and plain points at rear. Stamped with crowned numerals in rammer channel and assembler's cuts. Storekeeper's stamp struck in upper right wrist, crowned I struck alongside lower finial of trigger guard just to rear of bow; JC struck on rear of sidepiece flat. No trigger plate. Barrel tang screw is threaded into square iron nut inlet ahead of trigger and beneath front base of trigger guard bow.

Brass Furniture: no nosecap, tailpipe or thumbpiece.
One barrel-shaped and thin-collared ramrod pipe 1 1/4" in length, its crosspin located 9 7/8" from the breech.
Flat flush sidepiece 4 7/8" long with tail curled upwards at rear, stamped inside with Broad Arrow and assembler's file-cuts.
Land Pattern trigger guard 7 1/2" long.
Iron belt-hook 8 7/8" overall (hook section 7 1/4") on left side, held by the rear sidenail and a small flush woodscrew through its tail.
Buttcap measures 2 3/16" x 1 13/16" and is smooth overall without a mask, the short blunt sidespurs extending 1 3/4" up the sides of the grip.
Tapered wood rammer with 1 1/4" closed tapered brass cap.

Pattern 1756/77
(Clinton M. Miller)

The significant change in this variant is the lock design.
Overall length: 18 13/16".
Barrel: 12", .56 calibre, balustre-moulded for 1/2" at breech, tapered from 1" across breech to 13/16" across muzzle. No sights. Crosspins located 4" and 10" from breech. King's Proof and small crown struck on top, I.G [Joseph Grice] on left side. Tang measures 1 5/8" x 1/2".
Lock: Pattern 1777 Sea Service. Flat lockplate and ring-necked cock with narrow bevelled edges, 5 5/16" x 15/16". Short sear-spring

115

with two screws showing behind the cock. Under-surface of pan smooth rounded without bridle. Rounded-top steel 1 1/2" high with vertical-spine back. Cock has thin pillar comb with rounded tip very slightly curved back, and oval, slotted, top-jaw. Oval throat-hole. Cock-screw is pierced and slotted. Spearpoint feather-spring finial. No tumbler bridle. Stamped beneath pan with crowned Broad Arrow, crowned GR engraved ahead of cock; TOWER engraved across tail. No double border lines engraved on any parts. Inside stamped TB [Thomas Blakemore], H on reinforce, and crowned 1. Two sidenails 2 7/8" centre to centre.

Stock: walnut, stocked to 1/8" of muzzle. Ramrod enters stock 5 5/16" from tip. Oval tang apron measures 3 1/4" x 1 1/4". Terminals of narrow flats are rounded at fronts with plain points at rear. Stamped in rammer channel with crowned 7, crown and crowned G and assembler's cuts. Storekeeper's stamp with date 1786? struck in upper right wrist, crowned 4 struck alongside lower finial of trigger guard just to rear of bow; indecipherable mark struck on rear of sidepiece flat. No trigger plate. Barrel tang screw is threaded into square iron nut inlet ahead of trigger and beneath front base of trigger guard bow.

Brass Furniture: no nosecap, tailpipe or thumbpiece. One barrel-shaped and thin-collared ramrod pipe 1 1/4" long, the crosspin located 3 1/2" from the muzzle.

Flat flush sidepiece 5 1/16" long with tail curled upwards at rear, stamped inside with Broad Arrow and assembler's file-cuts. The trigger crosspin runs through the plate and is visible externally.

Land Pattern trigger guard 7 1/2" long secured by two crosspins with inspector's crown struck twice on inside of bow.

Iron belt-hook 8 7/8" overall (hook section 7 1/4") on left side, held by rear sidenail and a small stud on the back of its tail which fits into a corresponding hole in the tail of the sidepiece.

Buttcap is identical in design and dimensions to that on the basic Pattern 1756.

Tapered wood rammer with 1 1/8" closed tapered brass cap.